D0769333

PRAYERS IN STONE

PRAYERS IN STONE

CHRISTIAN SCIENCE ARCHITECTURE

IN THE UNITED STATES

1894–1930

Paul Eli Ivey

UNIVERSITY OF ILLINOIS PRESS : URBANA AND CHICAGO

Publication of this book was supported by a grant from
the Provost's Author Support Fund, University of Arizona, Tucson.

© 1999 by the Board of Trustees of the University of Illinois
Manufactured in the United States of America
C 5 4 3 2 1
♾ This book is printed on acid-free paper.

For permission to reprint copyrighted material, acknowledgment is
made to the following: Church History Department, The First
Church of Christ, Scientist, in Boston, Massachusetts, for
quotations from published and unpublished works; The Christian
Science Publishing Society for quotations from works owned by it.

Library of Congress Cataloging-in-Publication Data
Ivey, Paul Eli, 1959–
Prayers in stone : Christian Science architecture in the United States,
1894–1930 / Paul Eli Ivey.
p.   cm.
Includes bibliographical references (p.   ) and index.
ISBN 0-252-02445-1 (cloth : acid-free paper)
1. Christian Science church buildings—United States. 2. Architecture,
Modern—19th century—United States. 3. Architecture, Modern—
20th century—United States. I. Title.
NA5210.I83   1999
726.5'895—ddc21
98-25358
CIP

CAL
NA
5210
I83
1999

For, and because of, Mack and Mahla Ivey,

Ned Garnhart, Betty Ann Ridley, Bill Farmer

From architrave to royal dome,
Love framed this beauteous Christian home.
Here Truth shines forth with fadeless beam;
Here peace and joy are all supreme.

—William Bradford Dickinson,
Christian Science Journal, 1897

One thing is certain: for a religion which has
been organized only thirty years, and which
erected its first church only twelve years ago,
Christian Science has more fine church
edifices to its credit in the same time than
any other denomination in the world, and
they are all paid for.

—*Boston Globe,* 1906

CONTENTS

ILLUSTRATIONS

PREFACE

I recall as a youngster driving by what I thought of then as an intimidating and rather mysterious classical building in downtown Oklahoma City and asking my mother what "Christ, Scientist" meant, imagining a congregation of bow-tied, white-coated, and bespectacled scientists like my father. I was told that, contrary to my idea, Christian Scientists were "people who did not go to doctors." Years later I was introduced to the teachings of Christian Science by a Christian Science chaplain at a Boy Scout Jamboree and found that the religion's direct and logical approach and promise of practical results fed my own inner need for security and stability as I entered those troubling adolescent years.

When I was an enthusiastic Sunday school student at First Church of Christ, Scientist, Nichols Hills, Oklahoma, and then at the Mother Church in Boston, I could have scarcely reckoned that my journey through Christian Science would be completed by this book. I left the church in my undergraduate years, but after I studied with the distinguished church historian Martin Marty at a Scholarship/Leadership Enrichment Program while a Letters student at the University of Oklahoma, an approach to Christian Science history with my perspective began to seem plausible. Several years later, as I was completing my requirements for a Ph.D. in the history and theory of art and architecture at the State University of New York at Binghamton, I was suddenly compelled to consider the complex relationship between Christian Science and classical architecture. It occurred to me that I should revisit my youth armed with the academic cross-disciplinary social history tools gaining popularity in my field. With the critical support of my advisers, Charles Burroughs and Anthony King, I embarked on a dissertation project designed to make sense of the early triumphant vision of Christian Science as solidified by its numerous classical churches, which seemed to be losing members rapidly. The dissertation contained the seeds of the current project. With three more years of research, and fortified with the many suggestions and criticisms of mentors and colleagues, I conceived a much broader view of Christian Science in the built environment. An early version of my findings appeared in *Chicago History* (Spring 1994).

I have benefited greatly from the groundbreaking studies of the Christian Science movement by Robert Peel, Stephen Gottschalk, and Thomas Johnsen, all of them church members. Though the church has a long-standing reputation for being difficult to approach and guarded in its policy toward outside scholars, I found my contacts at the Church Center in Boston to be very supportive. Frank L. Smith was often on the lookout for material for me from the church's large archive of branch church history. In particular, I have enjoyed immensely the support of Yvonne C. von Fettweis and the staff members in the Church History Division in Boston. Over the past decade they have allowed me access to every source I have requested—well over five hundred historical files. Smith and Fettweis advised me to contact official Committee on Publication representatives in various states on my research trips, and these representatives were always helpful in introducing me to church members who shared their knowledge of and zeal for Christian Science church architecture. Margaret Pinkham provided many insights on the Mother Church.

I have had numerous contacts with persons in the architectural history and preservation professions during the course of my research. In particular I would like to thank Timothy Wittman, Raymond Terry Tatum, and Tim Samuelson for sharing their parallel research interests and encouraging the project. Also in Chicago I was aided by knowledgeable librarians at Northwestern University, the Newberry Library, and Garrett Theological Institute. Thanks go to Luigi Mumford at the Art Institute of Chicago and to Claudia Lamm Wood at the Chicago Historical Society.

The interest and encouragement provided by Martin Marty and Peter Williams, both distinguished professors of religion and American studies, have been crucial to my project. Early support by Jeryldene Wood and Lee Sorensen was also important. Arthur Iorio and Gretchen and Jesse Seifert-Gram were always wonderful friends on my research trips to Illinois. I owe a debt of gratitude to Albert Ramp, Al Siewers, Nancy Beman Baker, and especially to Lawrence Schlack for their Chicago church-touring prowess and Charles Gregersen for his Bemanisms.

I must thank Marsha Burruss Ballard and Charles Hosmer at Principia College for research help and dialogue and Robert Craig for his informative tour of Maybeck's campus and his subsequent insights.

Thanks go to several people in New York—Seth Kaston and Sarah Cunningham at Union Theological Seminary; Janet Parks at the Avery Library; and Bill Ivey, Dror Faust, and Asher Aladjem. In particular I would like to express appreciation to Jack Scott and Eric Culver for their research help at First Church, New York. In Rochester, thanks to librarians at the Rochester Theological Institute and the Public Library's Special Collections; to the architects at Ungar, Kaplan, and Whitney; and to the Rochester Preservation Office.

I feel much gratitude for my contacts with Betty Ann Ridley, Kathleen Starrett, and the staff of the Daystar Foundation in Oklahoma City. Thanks also to Alex

Gewirts at the Bridwell Library at Southern Methodist University, Dallas, who was very helpful with the Corey Collection; and to the staffs at the University of Oklahoma Western History Collection; Duke University Library Special Collections; University of Arizona Library Special Collections; Chicago Historical Society; Missouri Historical Society; and New York Historical Society.

My appreciation goes to research assistants in Special Collections at Stanford University, the San Francisco Public Library, and the Bancroft Library at the University of California, Berkeley. Thanks also to others in California, especially to David Givens; Christopher Wagstaff; Eric Larmer; the Board of Directors of First Church, Berkeley; the Oakland Scottish Rite Temple and conservation officials in Oakland; the architects of MacKinlay, Winnacker, McNeil and Associates, Oakland; and especially to Alexander Schroeder.

Thanks especially to my desert friend and colleague Abigail Van Slyck for her stimulating discussions, comments, and insightful critiques of my work. I am also particularly grateful to Stephen Gottschalk for helpful comments on my introduction and to my father, Mack Ivey, for his advice and encouragement on earlier versions of the manuscript. Thanks go to John Tagg, Jane Williams, Stacie Widdifield, Julie Plax, Sarah Moore, Annmarie Adams, Jeanne Halgren Kilde, Betsy Fahlman, Julie Hansen, Alan Hess, Jacqueline Hucker, Kenneth Silver, William D. Moore, Jim Postell, Alfred Willis, Bill Marquand, Zurich Esposito, Joe Labate, Joyce Henderson, and the many other colleagues and friends who have supported the project with their helpful criticisms and comments. I am grateful to my colleagues at the University of Arizona for all their support; to Dean Maurice Sevigny for a summer research grant; and to all the graduate students in my seminars, especially Ann Marie Russell, Beth Hancock, Jodi Kelber, Ruth Keffer, Gretchen Gibbs, Cassandra Nelson, Kelly Lenz, and Kevin Justus. Thanks especially to Ricardo Lujan for hurrying around and for hanging on.

Clerks, Christian Science Reading Room librarians, and church members from around the country are the unsung heroes of this project. Christian Scientists on the Internet have also shared their stories with me. I am grateful to them all, from so many places, but particularly at First Church, Austin; First Church, Alameda; First Church, Baltimore; First Church, Berkeley; Second Church and Eleventh Church, Chicago; First Church, Colorado Springs; First Church and Third Church, Dallas; First Church, Denver; First Church, Evanston; First Church, Long Beach; First Church, Second Church, Third Church, and Fifth Church, New York; First Church and Third Church, Oakland; First Church, Palo Alto; First Church, Pasadena; First Church, Philadelphia; First Church, Providence; First Church, Rochester; First Church, Saint Louis; First Church, Salt Lake City; First Church, Second Church, Third Church, Fourth Church, and Fifth Church, San Francisco; First Church, San Leandro; First Church, Fourth Church, and Seventh Church, Seattle; First Church and Third Church, Tucson; and First Church, Vallejo. *Esse quam videri.*

ABBREVIATIONS

In the text:

COP	Committee on Publication
Journal	*Christian Science Journal*
Manual	*Manual of the Mother Church*
Sentinel	*Christian Science Sentinel*

In endnotes:

CHD	Archives of the Mother Church/ Church History Division, The First Church of Christ, Scientist, Boston

PRAYERS IN STONE

Introduction

The Mother Church of the Christian Science movement, the First Church of Christ, Scientist, in Boston, Massachusetts, was officially dedicated on January 6, 1895, only a week after its completion (fig. 1). According to various newspapers, five repeated services were held for between three thousand and five thousand visitors. A letter from an early pastor to Mary Baker Eddy, the founder of the church, was read aloud at each service. It closed with these words: "'*Laus deo,* it is done!' At last you begin to see the fruition of that you have worked, toiled, prayed for. The 'prayer in stone' is accomplished."[1]

A dedication tablet on the exterior of the tower proclaimed that the church was a testimonial to Mrs. Eddy (as she is referred to by Christian Scientists). An editorial in the January issue of the monthly *Christian Science Journal* commented on the accomplishments of the past year's labor: "think of the year's achievements in the erection of the Mother Church,—The First Church of Christ, Scientist, in Boston,— the Mother Vine, whose outspreading branches cover the true disciples everywhere! Read in its granite and marble and iron, the story of triumph and history! See in its solid walls the emblem of the unchanging Truth it typifies! And know that it stands for the second coming of Christ, whose mission now, as of old, is to 'Heal the sick, raise the dead, cleanse the lepers, cast out demons,' and redeem the world."[2]

The Christian Science building boom, which lasted into the early 1930s, was underway in earnest. In many cities and towns in the United States and Great Britain, Christian Science congregations began to consolidate their religious teachings and practices in built form as branches of the Mother Church. They also began to debate what types and styles of buildings would be appropriate not only for the func-

Figure 1. Franklin Welch, the Mother Church, The First Church of Christ, Scientist, Boston, 1894 (L. M. Holt, *Christian Science Church Architecture* [Los Angeles, 1908]).

tional aspects of their church services but also as the public face for a new American-based church. By the early twentieth century, many of the urban Christian Science congregations began to adopt the classical style. Though there was a diversity of church types in smaller towns and rural environments, it is this classical style that best tells the story of the Christian Science building movement because many social and religious meanings were ascribed to it by church members and a wider public. The standardization of this urban style of church set the religion apart from other Protestant churches while it also associated the religion with contemporary movements concerned with reform, city beautification, and the renewal of urban life. As the most visible members of the Christian Science movement, urban congregations had an impact beyond their numbers in shaping how their religion was perceived by others. This book is about these Christian Scientists, their churches, and the debates concerning the public representation of Christian Science in cities.

In the context of church building of the era, Christian Science solutions to church building were unique, largely because of the newness of the denomination. While congregations of many Protestant denominations were moving from the city core to newly forming suburbs, Christian Scientists located wherever their members were, without concern over earlier property entanglements. They often placed their churches in emerging fashionable residential districts or even near newly expanding civic centers. The size, design, and visibility of these attractive buildings sparked controversy among members of traditional Christian churches because the structures clearly positioned Christian Science in relation to larger, historical mainstream religions.

There were crucial differences between Christian Science churches and those of other religious groups. Although mainstream religions were also building in cities, none of them chose a representative architectural style as did the urban Christian Scientists. Most Protestant congregations adopted eclectic historical styles of architecture, which were never as denominationally unified as the style used in Christian Science churches. Other growing religious groups at the turn of the century, particularly Catholics and Jews, were faced with the architectural dilemma of either stylistically accommodating to their Protestant American contexts or segregating themselves through specifically ethnic architectural styles.[3]

Christian Science, on the other hand, was a rapidly expanding home-grown American religion that didn't need to consider its own historical traditions in church architecture since it had none. While the building of churches was originally authorized by Mrs. Eddy, the Mother Church leadership never mandated the style of branch churches. Christian Science churches were built entirely by the laity without recourse to the hierarchical decision-making characteristic of other religious groups. Individual congregations had to decide how they would represent themselves to the public, and many of them took the classical style as their model.

Typically, the urban Christian Science branch church was a central-plan building with a pedimented porch. This presented an authoritative public face, even though the Ionic column favored in many of the designs could be said to soften or even feminize the style, an interpretation held by Freemasons in the late nineteenth century.[4] The porch was frequently made of fine materials such as marble or terra-cotta. The building was often crowned by a low dome centered over an auditorium. There were usually three to five doors giving access to the interior. The typical interior was also classical in detailing and consisted of a large foyer created to foster sociability among church members, with at least three main entrances to the auditorium; a Sunday school underneath the auditorium; and offices for church business. The heaviness and authority of the exterior contrasted with the lightness and comfort in the domed auditorium. In fact, light dominated the uncluttered worship space. As a Protestant denomination, Christian Science continued much of the iconoclasm associated with the Puritans' rejection of symbols and other decoration in churches. Christian Science interiors were less elaborate and less ornamented than the interiors of the buildings of many Protestant denominations.

Christian Science emphasized the importance of the Word over the traditional rituals of both Catholicism and Protestantism. In Christian Science, God was immanent and the worship services were direct lessons in Christian Science theology. Therefore, Christian Scientists chose the amphitheater form similar to that of the pulpit-centered auditorium popular with some Methodist congregations, among others. This configuration emphasized a unity and intimacy of worship rather than hierarchy, a "gathering around" of believers who listened to a lesson-sermon read from a dual pulpit.

Christian Science interiors engaged the audience differently than did Protestant churches of the time. In classical churches, the large domes, often fitted with beautiful stained glass, dominated the experience of the worship space. Centralized entry tunnels leading from the large foyers positioned worshipers directly under these dramatic domes as they entered the auditoriums. The spaces were always calm and comfortable. The readers' platform, often framed by a decorative screen hiding organ pipes, was often adorned with cut flowers or potted plants rather than with Christian symbols.

Christian Science churches, then, were unique at the turn of the century and during the early twentieth century. A new challenging theology that promised physical healing, the standardization of new worship services, the locations of the buildings, and the use of the classical style all contributed to the building boom of a marginal group, one that created some of the most innovative Protestant architecture of the period.

Today numerous tour buses stop at the Christian Science Center on Massachusetts and Huntington Avenues in Boston's Back Bay (fig. 2). Disembarking tourists enter the Christian Science Publishing Society building, erected during the Depression years, between 1932 and 1935. The visitors traverse a suspended glass walkway through the thirty-foot globe called the Maparium, political boundaries still clearly outlined on it in richly colored stained glass. Guides offer them an issue of the Pulitzer Prize–winning international daily newspaper the *Christian Science Monitor* and invite them to peruse the church's multilingual publications displayed in an elegant dark oak and mahogany showroom. This is the way many people first experience the headquarters of Christian Science.

The significance of Christian Science's worldview becomes even more evident when visitors leave the Publishing Society building and examine the addition to the Mother Church known as the Extension. This monument, whose cornerstone was laid in 1904, symbolizes the centrality of the faith in this city. A grand Corinthian portico fronts the large domed edifice, which rises 224 feet above the street. South of the Extension, next to the older Horticultural Hall (1901), stands a poured-concrete Sunday school building (1971), a quarter circle in form. The facade of the Sunday school building draws the eye eastward to a 670-by-100-foot reflecting pool that covers a large underground parking garage. Trees and geometric gardens flank the southern edge of the pool. Anchoring the easternmost side of the complex, across from the long colonnaded Broadcasting Center (1973), is the modular 28-story Administration Building (1973), which resembles two great books resting back to back against one another. Between these buildings stands a beautiful circular fountain partially screened by an arc of linden trees. Finally, this urban spectacle centers one's attention back to the west, toward the intimate, Romanesque-style Mother Church of 1894, which stands in the shadow of the newer Extension.

In its entirety, this grand architectural display reminds us somewhat of the smaller Salt Lake City complex of the Church of Jesus Christ of Latter-day Saints, the other major religion founded in the United States. The Utah complex, with its pinnacled temple, intimidating corporate building, and long, low, vaulted tabernacle, is located within blocks of the grand domed state capitol, which, on higher ground, keeps a secular watch over the church. In contrast, the Christian Science Center more closely resembles a large utopian City Beautiful government center rather than a church complex. In fact, this is a matter of history: when the Mother Church Extension was completed in 1906, a journalist commented that its stately dome rivaled the golden statehouse dome of the Commonwealth of Massachusetts.[5]

The Boston ensemble of buildings suggests that Christian Science had a grand vision of its place in the urban environment. The Christian Science Center would dwarf the Salt Lake City complex, even though the membership of the Church of Jesus Christ of Latter-day Saints exceeds the Christian Science membership by millions. The scale and design of the Church Center support the notion that Christian Science has always been a religion most at home in an urban setting.

Figure 2. "View of the Mother Church and Christian Science Center, Boston," 1973, gelatin silver print, 8 × 10 in. (Courtesy Nicholas Nixon, photographer, and Zabriskie Gallery, New York).

The design of the Church Center and its modern components was carried out by Araldo Cossutta, of I. M. Pei's architectural office, after that firm's successful completion of the Boston Government Center master plan. The Christian Science Board of Directors, which had considered plans for expansion as early as the 1950s, believed that the firm's ideas for urban growth were consonant with their own. One of the stated objectives for the development of the sixteen-acre center, as described by Cossutta, was "to coordinate the Church planning efforts in concert with responsible organizations seeking the restoration of the Back Bay and thereby stimulate civic improvements throughout the district surrounding the Church Center."[6] Through the creation of grand vistas of the Mother Church buildings and the growing Back Bay skyscrapers beyond, the program for expansion helped to "spark a major renewal."[7]

This concept of urban renewal emerged early in Christian Science church building projects in large cities. The original Mother Church edifice referred stylistically to the nearest and newest civic space in Boston, Copley Square, where H. H. Richardson's Romanesque-style Trinity Church (1872–77) and McKim, Mead, and White's Renaissance revival Boston Public Library (1887–98) stood, buildings designed to educate the souls and minds of urban citizens. In the first decade of the twentieth century, the Mother Church expanded along with other cultural institutions in a new civic center at Massachusetts and Huntington Avenues, where the Symphony Hall (1900) and Horticultural Hall were built. The entire area later would be the site for urban renewal when the Christian Science Center project began in 1963 and was completed in 1975.

The architectural heritage of Christian Science, carefully nurtured in Boston, had a national and international scope. At the turn of the century, architecture became a symbol of the movement's aspirations to meet the needs of urban populations and to stimulate urban renewal in America's cities. Moreover, the architectural style and the solidity of the denomination's new edifices advertised what was, to the adherents of Christian Science, a new healing gospel that would unite humanity.

In the early part of the twentieth century, Christian Science was especially attractive to people living in growing cities, particularly to women. I will examine Christian Science architecture as a locus for the production of religious and social meanings by this generally Anglo middle-class urban group, whose members explored the changing economic, social, and gender relationships of the time. I will discuss also the self-representational strategies and practices in architecture and the press and their roles in the early years of Christian Science. Of necessity, this examination of Christian Science architecture is descriptive and interpretive, rather than exhaustive, since over two thousand branch churches of the Mother Church had been built by 1930. As a study of an indigenous and often misunderstood American-based religion, this book addresses the complex issues surrounding the creation and building of an American institution that has had considerable social and political influence and yet has created much controversy since its inception.

The Christian Science church emerged at an auspicious time, claiming to solve the problems of the individual in the city through a new radical and American-born spirituality. It suggested new methods of church work from its earliest days and soon institutionalized these, often through impressive urban architectures designed to attract the middle class and woo them from the fragmented Protestant visions of social change and urban flight.

Other economic and social forces played a part in the conceptual ferment of the period. For example, the strict hierarchical concepts that identified femininity with the domestic sphere and masculinity with the public sphere were being eroded by women's increasing public visibility and political adroitness. There were also wide-ranging debates on an array of family issues, particularly health care. Christian Science churches and reading rooms provided spaces where women could rethink traditional female roles and their own relationship to the public realm of business.

The Christian Science church addressed the changing status of women and, as a result, was particularly attractive to them. The church viewed itself as a prophetic institution that challenged traditional patriarchal views of women through its emphasis on the femininity of God. The church also supported free-market values and created a refuge for men interested in couching business success within a Christian rhetoric and moral practice.

Part of the success of the Christian Science movement lay in the opportunities it provided for urban middle-class citizens to create communities that emphasized Puritan morality in the workplace and at home. It also offered an intellectually challenging theology based on the idea that religious truth rested on principles demonstrable and scientifically provable in day-to-day human experience, which resulted in physical and moral healing. The phenomenal growth of Christian Science was proof to the membership that organized voluntary associations could "fight the good fight" against an increasingly monolithic medical establishment, successfully challenge a nearly hegemonic clergy, call women to the traditional areas of family hygiene and care of the sick, and provide females with substantial occupations as public practitioners of Christian Science.

As a growing institution, Christian Science established itself within complex social and economic conditions and became increasingly visible through the erection of churches that differed from traditional models of the day. Christian Scientists integrated themselves into the respectable social strata of the urban environment, often justifying their new and sometimes imposing edifices within the discourse of progressive ideals supported by civic federations, architects, and planners.

The architectural designs typical of the Christian Science movement attracted attention in the popular and professional press. These designs represented a unity of organization that was lacking in mainstream Protestantism. Although mainline Protestant churches strove for stability, the strong historical organizations already in place prevented them from moving toward a unity of practice and architectural expression. Christian Scientists soon became known for their unified approach to architecture even though this appearance of unity was debated within the church. In larger urban areas, congregations built edifices that often belied the congregations' numerical and financial strengths but demonstrated a commitment to the permanence and status of the rapidly growing religion.

These churches, the majority of them built in the classical revival style made popular by the great World's Columbian Exposition in Chicago in 1893, reflected the institutionalization of Christian Science ideals. However, debates by architects at the time concerning the appropriate architecture for Christian Science revealed an ambivalence toward institutional self-representation. Should church architecture be aligned with progressive civic movements in architecture and society or should it be based on Christian Science's continuity with historical and traditional Christendom? These are also questions I will consider.

Few people remember Mary Baker Eddy as the patron and major financier of one of the early century's most enigmatic building booms. As 1911 began, a *New York Times* story reflected on the habits of philanthropists in the past year. In the article, Mrs. Eddy was mentioned in the company of Andrew Carnegie, John D. Rockefeller, Henry Clay Frick, and John Pierpont Morgan. The article reported that at her death in 1910 she had bequeathed "$1,000,000 of her estate to various Christian Science churches and for the furtherance of the work of that denomination." This was a significant portion of her estate. One provision of her will, administered by its trustees, granted financial assistance to branch churches, intended for "the construction, remodeling, furnishing, or purchase of buildings to be used for Christian Science church services."[8] Her bequest contributed greatly to the subsequent Christian Science building boom.

The Christian Science building boom saw the erection of hundreds of buildings devoted to Christian Science worship and the spreading of the teachings contained in Mrs. Eddy's books. To the faithful, these new buildings were important educational and worship facilities designed to propagate American social and political ideals. Carol Norton, a Christian Science teacher, summarized this belief when he wrote in 1899: "Christian Science stands in every community for pure government, social purity, honest popular elections, business integrity, the purification of literature and journalism, and the elevation of the stage."[9]

The growth and success of the church in the early part of the present century seemed to indicate that the movement would quickly overtake the established Protestant denominations. Therefore, both Christian Scientists and architects asserted that the church's architectural styles not only represented the new institution but also contributed broadly to a new American architecture. In the early decades, the Christian Scientists occupied an influential space within the mix of government and religious building. This suggested that their buildings not only represented a new modern teaching for the twentieth century but were the very signs of urban renewal itself.

In my discussions of these events, I will not attempt to prove the theological truth or political correctness of Christian Science doctrine. My point of departure is the fact that Christian Science was a reform movement within Protestantism that was quickly made unwelcome by other denominations and also by the medical establishment. This rejection, along with Christian Science's rapid early growth, forced the new church to organize and establish itself within the city as an institution that expressed respectability, authority, and prestige if it was to survive the critical onslaughts of traditional churches and emerging medical institutions.

The Christian Science building movement represents a vivid example in American architectural history of the rise of a primarily urban religious practice and how it accommodated and also influenced the changing urban environment of the early twentieth century. Christian Science arose during a time of great change in American society, at a critical juncture in American economic, social, and cultural self-definition. The impressive Church Center in Boston continues to inculcate the religious and civic values of architectural expression important to the early movement.

NOTES

1. Mary Baker Eddy, *Pulpit and Press* (Boston: Christian Science Publishing Society, 1895), 44.

2. See *Christian Science Journal* 12, no. 10 (Jan. 1895): 448. The opening article included a discussion of the new church with illustrations (403–17). For the most thorough scholarly work on the Mother Church, see Margaret M. Pinkham, "The 'Miracle in Stone': The Building of the Mother Church, The First Church of Christ, Scientist, Boston, Massachusetts" (M.A. thesis, Boston University, 1994). See also the Church History pamphlet *1894, "Our prayer in stone"* (Boston: Christian Science Publishing Society, 1994).

3. An account of the complete historical context of church architecture in the United States is provided by Peter W. Williams, *Houses of God: Region, Religion, and Architecture in the United States* (Urbana: University of Illinois Press, 1997). See also Edward Joseph Weber, *Catholic Church Buildings, Their Planning and Furnishing* (New York: J. F. Wegner, 1927); Samuel Schafler, "The American Synagogue: A Sanctuary Transformed," *Journal of Religion* 69, no. 4 (Oct. 1989): 587; *Recent American Synagogue Architecture* (New York: Jewish Museum, 1963).

4. See Alan Gowans, "The Classical Symbol in the New Republic," in his *Images of American Living: Four Centuries of Architecture and Furniture as Cultural Expression* (New York: Harper and Row, 1976), 243–55; John Onians, *Bearers of Meaning: The Classical Orders in Antiquity, the Middle Ages, and the Renaissance* (Princeton: Princeton University Press, 1988), 14.

5. Frederick W. Coburn, "The New Christian Science Temple in Boston," *Indoors and Out* 4 (July 1906): 179.

6. Quoted in Lucille Aptekar and Joyce Cohen, "The Art of Architecture: The Christian Science Center, 1894–1990," mimeographed notes for exhibit, June 1–Sept. 7, 1990, Church History Division, The First Church of Christ, Scientist, CHD.

7. Ibid. *Architectural Forum* (Sept. 1973) said of the Church Center buildings that the "pours are nothing less than poetic" (31). Other articles on the Church Center include: F.W., "A Case History: Church Sponsored Community Renewal in Boston," *Progressive Architecture* (June 1966): 154–57; William Marlin, "Formed Up in Faith," *Architectural Forum* (Sept. 1973): 25–39; and idem, *I. M. Pei, National Center for Atmospheric Research, Boulder, Colorado, 1967; I. M. Pei and Partners and Araldo Cossutta, Christian Science Church Center, Boston, Massachusetts, 1973*, ed. and with photographs by Yukio Futagawa (Tokyo: ADA EDITA, 1976).

8. *New York Times,* Jan. 1, 1911. The trustees were authorized to donate or loan between 3 percent and 5 percent of the total cost of the property. See various circulars published for branch churches, for example, "Trustees Under the Will of Mary Baker Eddy, Circular Letter No. 2," Jan. 1, 1919, CHD.

9. Carol Norton, *The Christian Science Movement* (Boston: Christian Science Publishing Society, 1899), 19–20.

1 : Foundations

In November 1897, nearly ten thousand Christian Scientists and their friends arrived in Chicago from seventeen states. They came to attend the dedication services of First Church of Christ, Scientist, Chicago, the largest branch church built by the fledgling Christian Science movement (fig. 3). This building soon became the stylistic prototype for a series of conspicuous edifices nationwide. It was built in a monumental classical revival style reminiscent of that of the magnificent White City of the 1893 World's Columbian Exposition.

Chicago papers covered the dedication day with great interest (fig. 4). A reporter for the *Times-Herald* stated that the people attending were "brought hither by their enthusiasm and their desire to participate in what to them marked the dawn of a new religious epoch." One visitor was overheard to remark that the ceremonies were "almost like the World's Fair." The reporter summed up the church structure as coming "very near to realizing the ideal of a place of worship . . . certainly surpassed in beauty and qualities of utility by few if any churches in the West."[1] A *Chicago Evening Post* report noted that the building was an "artistic, pleasing and impressive" edifice and "a unique and bold departure from the conventional lines of ecclesiastical architecture."[2] The interior of the church was functional, unadorned by religious symbols, and lit by "electric stars" (fig. 5). It was a modern church building that represented a modern religion, founded in the United States only two decades earlier. Its solid architecture was particularly attractive in the changing cityscape of Chicago.

The church services were also noteworthy. During four identical dedication services, two lay readers, a man and a woman, read from the Bible and the Christian Science textbook, Mrs. Eddy's *Science and Health with Key to the Scriptures,* and repeated addresses written specifically for the occasion. They stood at a large readers' desk centered on a shallow platform and flanked by two seven-branched candelabra (fig. 6). Edward Kimball, a successful Christian Scientist who served the congregation as First Reader, said to those assembled: "You are here because you are involved in the history of a new era—the age of Christian Science! pre-eminently moral, pre-eminently Christian, and pre-eminently Godlike." Mrs. Ruth Ewing, the church's Second Reader, told the congregation: "It has been a noticeable characteristic remark from visitors of all classes who have come into this edifice since it was brought to a degree of progression nearing completion: It is so pure! We can but be glad of this first impression made upon the minds of the people. May this beautiful temple attract, invite, and inspire all who come within its portals to the thought of our God as Love 'who healeth all thy diseases.' "[3]

Figure 3. Solon Spencer Beman, First Church of Christ, Scientist, Chicago, 1897 (E. S. Van Horne, *Some Christian Science Churches* [Columbus, Ohio, 1912]).

IN A GREEK TEMPLE.

Chicago's First Christian Science Church Dedicated.

MESSAGE OF FOUNDER.

Mary Baker Eddy, Absent, Sends a Ringing Address.

SERVICES DAY AND EVENING.

Congregation Comes from All Over the Country.

HISTORY OF FAITH AND EDIFICE.

With a message from the mother and founder of their church, Mary Baker Eddy, who rejoiced with them over their new home, Christian Scientists of Chicago and a score of far away cities and States yesterday dedicated the beautiful white Greek temple at Drexel boulevard and Fortieth street, the First Church of Christ (Scientist) of Chicago, and the largest edifice of the Christian Scientists in the world.

With the message from the mother of the church came letters and messages from Christian Scientists in distant countries and from seemingly every nook and corner of the United States. Those who attended the dedication so far outnumbered even the large seating capacity of the church that the services had to be repeated four times, while the [illegible] vent a crush.

From early morning till late at night the yellow light was reflected down from the ivory and gold walls upon an almost constant audience, which was replaced between the four services almost imperceptibly. While those inside worshiped several hundred people stood outside the classic portico waiting for the doors to open and let them in.

One Service for Visitors.

Leaders in Christian Science have been coming to Chicago for the dedication from almost every State for the last four days. So many of these pilgrims were there that one of the four services, that at 11:45 o'clock, was held entirely for out of town visitors, and the 2,000 seats in the edifice were filled by them.

The dedicatory services were as simple as the brick architecture of the building itself, and as the weekly services of the new temple are planned to be hereafter. Besides the message from Mary Baker Eddy, whom age kept away from witnessing the triumph of her followers, there were but two addresses, read by the two readers of the church, Edward A. Kimball and Mrs. Ruth D. Ewing. Vocal music and organ solos made up the remainder of the services.

A feature of all four services was the congregation repeating the Lord's prayer, clause by clause, while the two readers of the church responded, also clause by clause, with the spiritual interpretation of the prayer by Mary Baker Eddy.

Mary Baker Eddy's Address.

The dedicatory address or message by Mary Baker Eddy, the discoverer and founder of Christian Science, was as follows:

[illegible]

Christianity which applies to all ages, and who dated time.

A spiritual understanding of the Scriptures restores their original tongue in the language of Spirit, that primordial standard of Truth.

Christian Science contains no element whatever of hypnotism or animal magnetism. It appeals alone to God, to the divine Principle or Life, Truth, and Love to whom all things are possible—and this Principle heals sin, sickness, disease, and death. It meets error with Truth, death with Life, hate with Love, and thus, and only thus, does it overcome evil and heal disease. The obstinate sinner, however, refuses to see this grand verity or to acknowledge it; for he knows not that in justice, as well as in mercy, God is Love.

With Sin and Sinners.

In our struggles with sin and sinners, when we drop compliance with their desires, insist on what we know is right and act accordingly, then the disguised or the self-satisfied mind, not ready to be uplifted, rebels, misconstrues our best motives and calls them unkind. But this is the cross, take it up; it wins the crown; and in the spirit of our great Exemplar pray: "Father forgive them, for they know not what they do."

No warfare exists between Divine Theology and Christian Science, for the latter solves the whence and why of the cosmos and defines noumena and phenomena spiritually, not materially. The specific quest of Christian Science is to settle all points beyond cavil on the biblical basis that God is All-in-all. Whereas philosophy and natural science, so-called, dealing with human hypotheses or material cause and effect, are aided only at long intervals with elementary truths, and ultimate in unsolved problems and outgrown proofless positions.

Progress is spiritual, it is the maturing conception of divine Love; it demonstrates the scientific sinless life of man and mortals' painless departure from matter to Spirit, not through death, but the true idea of Life, and Life not in matter, but Mind.

The Puritans possessed the motive of true religion, which, demonstrated on the Golden Rule, would have solved ere this the problem of religious liberty and human rights. It is "a consummation devoutly to be wished" that all nations shall speedily learn and practice the intermediate line of justice between the classes and masses of mankind, and thus exemplify in all things the universal equity of Christianity.

Thirty years ago Christian Science was discovered in America. Within those years it is estimated that Chicago has gained from a population of 238,000, to number 1,650,000 inhabitants.

The statistics of mortality show that thirty years ago the death rate was at its maximum. Since that time it has steadily decreased. It is authentically said that "one expositor of Daniel's dates fixed the year 1866 or 1867 for the return of Christ—the return of the Spiritual Idea to the material earth, or antipode of Heaven. It is a marked coincidence that those dates were the two first years of my discovery of Christian Science.

Thirty years ago Chicago had few Congregational churches. Today it is said to have a majority of these churches over any city in the United States.

Thirty years ago, at my request, I received from the Congregational church a letter of dismissal and recommendation to evangelical churches; thenceforth to exemplify my early love for this church—and a membership of forty years—by establishing a new old church whose foundations are the same, even Christ, Truth, as the chief cornerstone.

Growth of the Society.

In 1884 I taught a class in Christian Science and formed a Christian Scientist Association in Chicago. From this small sowing of the seed of Truth, which, when sown seemed the least among seeds, through God's blessing and the faithful labor of loyal students, sprang immortal fruits—the healing of the sick, reforming the sinner and the First Church of Christ, Scientist, with its large membership and majestic cathedral.

Humbly, gratefully, trustingly, I dedicate this beautiful house of worship to the God of Israel, the divine Love that reigneth above [illegible]

Figure 4. Chicago Tribune, November 15, 1897, report on the dedication of First Church of Christ, Scientist, Chicago (Chicago Historical Society Library).

One newspaperman reported that a feature most likely to attract the attention of strangers to Christian Science was the use of silent prayer, which had been adopted at the World's Parliament of Religions, an auxiliary congress held during the Columbian Exposition. He noted that the only prayer repeated audibly by the congregation was the Lord's Prayer, with a spiritual interpretation. Music was performed by a soloist and a quartet, and the congregation sang hymns. The service ended with a repetition of the scientific statement of being from *Science and Health,* which is still repeated every Sunday in Christian Science churches in its present version: "There is no life, truth, intelligence, nor substance in matter. All is infinite Mind and its infinite manifestation, for God is All-in-all. Spirit is immortal Truth; matter is mortal error. Spirit is the real and eternal; matter is the unreal and temporal. Spirit is God, and man is His image and likeness. Therefore man is not material; he is spiritual."[4]

All these features—the classical building facade, the sparely ornamented interior, the arrangement of the readers' platform, the religious language and forms of prayer used—clearly contrasted with the elements of a typical Protestant church and service. Who were these Christian Scientists, and why did they worship this way?

Figure 5. The spacious interior of First Church of Christ, Scientist, Chicago (Church History, Division of the First Church of Christ, Scientist, Boston, Massachusetts).

Origins, Growth, and Perceptions of Christian Science

Two decades prior to the erection of this important Chicago branch church, Christian Science had mostly a local appeal in the New England area. It began not in great cities but in the small factory towns of New England, where Mrs. Eddy wrote in isolation and taught a few students. Born in 1821, Mary Morse Baker was raised in rural New Hampshire in the Puritan religious tradition adopted by the Congregationalists (fig. 7). Although she rejected the Calvinist dogma of eternal damnation, it remained a strong influence even in her subsequent formulation of Christian Science and in the designs of branch churches.

Mrs. Eddy's early life was marked by personal struggle and difficulty, including the loss of her mother and favorite brother, who both died in her early adulthood. Her first husband, George Glover, died soon after they married. Her own ill health

Figure 6. The readers' desk, First Church of Christ, Scientist, Chicago (Church History, Division of the Church of Christ, Scientist, Boston).

Figure 7. Mary Baker Eddy, shown in 1891, around the time of the building of the Mother Church, photo by S. A. Bower (Church History, Division of the Church of Christ, Scientist, Boston).

caused her only son to be taken from her by his nursemaid. Her second marriage, to an itinerant dentist, Dr. Daniel Patterson, was a failure and ended in divorce, and her health deteriorated further, marked by acute nervous and physical weakness.

In her search for relief, Mrs. Eddy investigated a number of healing practices then available, including homeopathy and mesmerism. Particularly significant was her encounter with Phineas Quimby, a healer from Maine, whose ministrations had an important effect on her well-being. After being healed by him in 1862, she attempted to recast his healing methodology—which was based on mesmerism, suggestion, and massage techniques—into a Christian framework. However, it was only after she was severely injured in 1866 and not expected to live that she claimed to have discovered the decisive curative power of a spiritual understanding of the Scriptures. After reading an account of Jesus' healing, her health improved. She spent the next decade pondering the Bible, teaching small groups of students, and healing according to a new method, which was based on an understanding that life was in and of the Divine Mind, or Spirit, and that Jesus' teachings, correctly understood, revealed a scientific and spiritual mode of healing. She believed that she had discovered the spiritual meaning underlying the Gospels and wanted to bring people back to a living Christianity.

In 1875 in Lynn, Massachusetts, Mrs. Eddy published the complete statement of this methodology in her book *Science and Health*. Early attempts at proselytizing and organization were difficult. She did, however, create a Christian Science association of students in 1876. She was married in 1877 to Asa Eddy, but he was to die only five years later.

Finally, Mrs. Eddy and several faithful members of her association founded a church in 1879. They voted to name it the "Church of Christ, Scientist." Its function was to "commemorate the word and works of our Master, which should reinstate primitive Christianity and its lost element of healing."[5]

By 1881, the focus of the movement shifted to Boston, then the center of intellectual and religious life in America, where Mrs. Eddy chartered the Massachusetts Metaphysical College. In Boston she attracted attention among women and business people. Pupils of the college began the work of disseminating her teachings throughout the United States. Over the next decade, the Christian Science church grew at a rapid pace. In 1895 there were about 250 organizations, and by 1910 there were approximately 1,100 organizations. These were considered one centralized unity: the Mother Church in Boston with its branch churches spread throughout the country. The church had begun making converts in other nations, particularly Great Britain and Germany, and the Boston church soon became the center of an international organization. The church government was essentially federalist, with individual congregations enjoying democratic self-rule. In many American cities and towns, Christian Scientists were converting important citizens and erecting temples for worship. Congregations were forming at a rate of one or two per week.[6]

Meanwhile, intrigues and schisms confronted Mrs. Eddy's leadership. The long-established denominations had begun to criticize the new church in earnest by the

1880s. The growing medical establishment was also extremely critical of the healing methods of Christian Science. Challenges to Mrs. Eddy's authority even occurred within her own ranks, particularly among students who began teaching mystical versions of the increasingly popular mind-cure and calling them Christian Science.[7]

Mrs. Eddy's charismatic leadership and her organizational skills contributed to the growth and popularity of a theology at some variance with that of traditional churches. The theology expressed in Mrs. Eddy's writings through religious, literary, and even philosophical language emphasized that Jesus' life, death, and resurrection pointed to what she believed was the great fact of Being—that life and reality are spiritual. Jesus' healings were not supernatural; they followed naturally from the view that life was untainted by matter and its laws and was the reflection of divine Spirit. Comprehension of spiritual laws allowed access to a transformative power that healed the sick and reformed the sinner. The kingdom of heaven, moreover, which traditional churches reserved for after death, was immanently available as mortals gave up their beliefs of life in matter that were based on their assumed separation from God.

Mrs. Eddy continued to publish new editions of *Science and Health,* and in 1883 she established the monthly *Christian Science Journal.* In 1884 she taught a class in Chicago that helped solidify the movement in the Midwest. The National Christian Science Association was formed in 1886 and held meetings until 1890. In 1889 Mrs. Eddy dissolved much of the organization and moved out of Boston, finally settling in Concord, New Hampshire, in 1892.

Also in 1892, she reorganized the church, establishing the Boston church as the unique Mother Church. The first edifice of the Mother Church was built on land donated by Mrs. Eddy to the Christian Science Board of Directors. Work was underway in 1893, when Christian Science was represented at the World's Parliament of Religions in Chicago and attracted much attention. Meanwhile, Mrs. Eddy disseminated voluminous communications to students worldwide, giving them direction about their growing healing practices and advising them in organizational matters.

In 1895 a small volume of rules, entitled *Manual of the Mother Church,* was published. It established the standards of the organization and was continually revised up until Mrs. Eddy's death in 1910. Several periodicals were also begun: the *Christian Science Weekly,* soon renamed the *Christian Science Sentinel,* in 1898; *Der Herold der Christian Science,* in 1903; and the *Christian Science Monitor,* in 1908. This last publication was the international daily newspaper that gained worldwide respect for its well-reasoned, reform-minded reporting on national and international affairs.

In 1908 Mrs. Eddy moved to the Boston suburb of Chestnut Hill. At her death in 1910 at the age of eighty-nine she was a venerated though controversial international figure. Newspapers from around the nation and the world paid tribute and memorialized her accomplishments. Most commented on her organizational skills—her "spiritual empire" had spread across the globe. Some applauded her life as an example of a great American success story. "Out of nothing that is physical, no great fortune, no industrial invention, no inherited opportunity, Mrs. Eddy built up a great career," reported the *Chicago Post*.[8]

Mrs. Eddy viewed the church she founded as having an instrumental function in the lives of Christian Scientists. The church should make a difference in people's lives. It should educate them spiritually and provide them with a means of worship that they could assimilate into their experiences. Mrs. Eddy defined church, in part, as "that institution, which affords proof of its utility and is found elevating the race, rousing the dormant understanding from material beliefs to the apprehension of spiritual ideas and the demonstration of divine Science, thereby casting out devils, or error, and healing the sick."[9]

Two public services were instituted in the Christian Science church: the Sunday service and the evening prayer meeting, the latter first held on Fridays and by 1898 changed to the Wednesday evening testimony meeting. The Sunday services were subdued, meditative, literate, and solemn, just as they are today in Christian Science churches. In the early years of the movement, services were based loosely on Congregational models. The Sunday service consisted of hymns, responsive readings, prayer, a sacred solo, and a sermon. In 1895, the sermon was replaced with selections from the Bible and *Science and Health,* on subjects drawn from the International Bible Series, until new subjects were chosen by Mrs. Eddy and used beginning in 1898. It was also in 1895 that Mrs. Eddy ordained the Bible and *Science and Health* as impersonal pastors of the church. From that time forward, two readers, usually a man and a woman, appointed by the Christian Science Board of Directors in the case of the Mother Church and elected by local members in branch churches, served the congregations.[10] This not only solidified the place of Mrs. Eddy's writings in church services but also helped to unify and stabilize the services throughout the movement. The simplicity of worship was meant to ensure that Christian Scientists would not become entrenched in dogma and ritual.

Worship services developed into pure and uncomplicated affairs. On Sundays, now as then, the congregation enters the auditorium silently, often accompanied by an organ prelude. Scriptural selections are read by the First Reader, and the congregation joins together to sing a hymn from the *Christian Science Hymnal,* which features traditional hymn music with words that express Christian Science ideas. Silent prayer is followed by the audible repetition of the Lord's Prayer with its spiritual interpretation from *Science and Health.* After another congregational hymn and notices from the First Reader, a sacred solo is sung. Often, the words of the solo are from one of Mrs. Eddy's own poems, such as her "Communion Hymn," which opens: "Saw ye my Savior? Heard ye the glad sound? Felt ye the power of the Word?"[11] The congregation prepares to listen to both readers read the lesson-sermon from the *Christian Science Quarterly,* which consists of selected passages from the Bible and *Science and Health* that many have studied throughout the week. The service ends with an offertory, a hymn, and the repetition of "the scientific statement of being," with its correlative Scripture according to 1 John 3:1–3, followed by an organ postlude. Wednesday meetings, on the other hand, often include exuberant comments from members of an audience gathered to share testimonies on the benefits of Christian Science. After the singing of hymns and brief readings from the Bible and *Science and Health,* the First Reader opens the floor for testimonies and remarks on Christian Science from the congregation.

The standardized services, the equal representation of men and women in the pulpit, and an emphasis on the educated middle class ensured increasing interest in the church's social position by outsiders. By the early twentieth century, Christian Science churches were being built in fashionable residential neighborhoods or near new civic centers in many cities, and they were inventive and distinctive places of worship. Christian Science reading rooms began to appear in the business districts of cities and featured the *Christian Science Monitor* as well as religious literature. These were not only places for study but public reminders that the Christian Science church wanted to meet the spiritual and informational needs of urban populations in the everyday spaces of commerce.

The Christian Science church continued to grow rapidly, even after Mrs. Eddy's death. As Stephen Hasbrouck stated in 1912:

> With the Christian Science churches, the great problems are to find room for the people who throng their services, and collection boxes big enough to hold their offering for the support of the movement. A church which is of comparatively recent origin, which has attained a membership and following of 1,500,000 to 2,000,000; which is carrying on a successful ministry of relief from the bodily and mental sufferings of mankind, in accordance with Christ's commands; which has been building new churches and establishing new societies at the rate of two for every consecutive week during the past 19 years, must be reckoned with by organized Christianity, "and will be," says a brilliant satirist, "when it is too late."[12]

Hasbrouck's statistics were certainly inflated, but the denomination was enjoying increased popularity. Though actual membership was probably under 300,000, the numbers of people thronging the services were great. Clearly the growth and popularity signaled both a desire and a need for new buildings.[13]

From the beginning, Mrs. Eddy required that branch churches be organized according to multiplication and not division.[14] The church organized itself into a loose parish system, based on the general locales of its members.[15] In this regard, Mrs. Eddy established the uniform naming and numbering of branch churches in 1899. This system was consolidated as local congregations established literature distribution districts to be serviced by area churches.

Some Christian Science congregations located and built in what were becoming new ecclesiastical centers in fashionable residential districts. In 1903–4, for example, First Church, St. Louis, was built on what became known as "Holy Corners" and was a prominent addition to other religious structures built in the first decade of the century in that city (fig. 8).[16] First Church, Evanston (1912), located its classical edifice among the more traditional church architectures of several other Protestant denominations on the city green. These Christian Science churches were particularly distinctive within their urban settings.

As the denomination grew in large cities, new churches sometimes moved closer to the downtown areas even as traditional Protestant churches were leaving. Fifth Church, New York, for example, was built on the original location of St. Bartholomew's near Grand Central Station in 1921 (fig. 9).[17] The church was built literally and metaphorically on top of old ecclesiasticism and represented the new syndication of spirituality the congregation believed was needed in the commercial world. This branch church was intended to "provide a place where the constant light of Christian Science healing may shine through the world turmoil of a congested city."[18] Rather than build a traditional church edifice, the congregation supported a bond issue to build an office building. Inserted into it at street level was a grand and well-appointed classical-style church seating eighteen hundred. The building was the largest and most costly church/office building erected in the city at the time.[19]

Christian Science increasingly gained visibility through the erection of press-worthy church buildings. Certainly journalists were particularly influential in forming public opinion about Christian Science, and much of their coverage was negative and even hostile. Early strategies of representation, organized by the church's Committee on Publication (COP) in Boston and by committees in every state, were developed to "correct" the many periodical articles that Christian Scientists believed misrepresented their religion. As the defensive wing of the church, these committees—usually made up of male members of the church—responded promptly to negative statements. Early proactive articles by COP representatives on the growth

Figure 8. Mauran, Russell, Garden, First Church of Christ, Scientist, St. Louis, 1904 (Van Horne).

Figure 9. The Canadian-Pacific Building, Madison Avenue and Forty-fourth Street, containing the Fifth Church of Christ, Scientist, New York City, 1921 (*New York Evening Post*, January 24, 1920).

of the religion, often illustrated by images of new edifices, left the impression that the church was relatively wealthy and successful. Its teachings appeared to be aimed at specific educated social and economic groups who were ready to make spiritual and material investments. Christian Scientists, therefore, used their own publications and their architecture to counteract negative assertions in the press and to establish a respectable public face.

Church publications and the wide coverage by the popular press attracted many people to the church. One historian, Raymond Cunningham, observed that the proliferation of magazines, aimed at the middle class of this era, was responsible for bringing the story of Mary Baker Eddy and her church to thousands of readers. He suggested that around 1900 it was nearly impossible to be unaware of the sect due to popular coverage of the "recluse of Concord." Another study indicated that between 1890 and 1910 over 130 articles in the popular press were devoted to the new church.[20] Christian Science was often the subject of discussions in women's clubs, literary societies, and other social gatherings.[21]

Because of the urban concentration of its membership, Christian Science has often been called a religion of the great cities. But the true social makeup of Christian Science congregations has been difficult to ascertain due to the church's strict non-disclosure of membership information, a policy dictated by a *Manual* bylaw from 1908. Although demographic studies of the religion show that it also did well in cities with populations under a hundred thousand, Christian Science has been consistently aligned with the dynamically changing great cities at the turn of the century.[22]

Christian Science has also been characterized as a leisure-class sect that promoted physical health and capitalist success and has been described as the best organized and most conservative of the harmonial religions that arose in late nineteenth-century America.[23] On these points, many historians and sociologists concur. Kevin Christiano's study of religious diversity and social change in turn-of-the-century American cities revealed that the expanding American metropolis was a catalyst for the growth of religious groups like Christian Science, which specialized in the "spiritual needs of urban populations" and represented a "strong challenge to the prevailing Protestant establishment in nineteenth-century cities."[24] Sidney Stark and William Bainbridge studied the sociological makeup of the church and concluded that "Christian Scientists were recruited overwhelmingly from prosperous and genteel backgrounds."[25] However, Christian Science was also successful in less-populated areas and actually attracted the attention of middle-class working people. A 1912 critique of Christian Science suggested that its "gospel of healing; its religious message; its monistic idealism; its anti-materialistic spirit; its notable originator" and the "responsive practical mind of the American people" were the reasons for its success.[26]

The Membership

Christian Science was not a mystical or traditional faith. Its adherents claimed it was a demonstrable and practical form of Christianity, grounded in Mrs. Eddy's axiom that reality was radically spiritual and that this was provable in human experience in a scientific manner. As such its healing theology and its emphasis on morality in business affairs proved particularly attractive to city dwellers, who were challenged by the rapid changes in urban economics and culture. Christian Science offered a stabilizing lifestyle and projected a unity and rationality onto daily routine. The organization was particularly attractive to women as it conferred social status and provided opportunities to enter into the public practice of Christian

Science healing, for remuneration comparable to that of traditional medical treatment. Christian Science also appealed to business people. Judge Septimus Hanna, a church spokesman, suggested in the October 1896 issue of the *Christian Science Journal* that the "growth of Science among the businessmen here in Chicago is something marvelous, and all of them are able to give a solid reason for their being Scientists." Upon the organization of Fifth Church, Chicago, the *Times-Herald* summed up the growth of the movement: "It must be understood that Christian Science has drawn from the best elements of citizenship. Bankers, substantial businessmen, society people, and men and women of means have been attracted to it, and have cheerfully accepted its teachings and are testifying to-day of the good it has done them."[27]

The Christian Science church attempted to represent itself as a modern unifying alternative to a fractured Protestantism, and as the church whose teachings revealed the biblical laws of Christian healing and regeneration in a way that would make Christianity practical for all people. However, the solidity and spaciousness of branch churches in many large cities evoked much speculation in the popular and architectural presses about the social status and motives of church members. The appearance of prominent citizens in Christian Science services led many inside and outside the movement to believe that the congregations represented the business elite. In support of this idea, early urban Christian Scientists claimed that their religion initiated a new sense of well-being that contributed to business and social success. As one member summed up the enthusiasm held in common by many Christian Scientists: "There can be no doubt that Christian Science is having a decided and beneficial effect on the commerce, the religion, the literature and the art of the world today. It is broadening, uplifting, purifying, and spiritualizing the thoughts of hundreds of thousands of earth's workers in the professional, artistic and musical world. It is a stay to the capitalist and a strength to the toiler."[28] Many people who joined the church undoubtedly sought a religion that would give them stability and aid in their quest for social status. Then, as now, those in the middle class struggled not only to climb, but to keep from falling behind.

In traditional Protestant and Christian Science churches, business people made up the largest part of the congregations.[29] But many people who were attracted to Christian Science were "untraditional" members. The church attracted young city dwellers interested in spiritual rigor and occupational achievement. Single working women and men were attracted to its new intellectual language, its radical theology, and its methods, which projected a practical Christian means for personal healing and business success.[30]

Both friends and enemies of the church were quick to comment on the growing numbers of people attracted to the new religion and were interested in defining just who they were. Alfred Kohn, a physician, noted that Christian Scientists were generally as intellectual as any other class and included "judges of the bench, college professors, unsuccessful physicians, homeopaths and clear-headed businessmen, besides the usual number of faddist and emotional individuals."[31] William Johnston assured the readers of New York's *Broadway Magazine* that the Christian Science membership was comprised of "the most prominent and successful industrial, professional, and commercial men in the United States."[32]

The perception that Christian Scientists were wealthy worked against attracting the less fortunate workers in the city. Church officials projected a view of wealth and social prestige by citing influential and successful members in articles about the church, but they also claimed that Christian Science should attract all people. One critic stated, "whether it be that its appeal does not interest the lower classes, or that Christian Science is too expensive a luxury to indulge in, the fact is that the Christian Science congregations are largely composed of the well-to-do, with a fair sprinkling of educated men among them."[33]

However, the statistical evidence suggests that many middle-class citizens, not only those in the upper class, became Christian Scientists. An examination of the list of contributors to the building fund of what many Christian Scientists perceived to be the most wealthy branch church, First Church, New York (fig. 10), showed that approximately 30% were involved in engineering and building manufacture; 20% in banking and the financial markets; 15% in publishing and printing activities; 15% in luxury-goods manufacturing and retail; 10% in the garment industry; 5% in the food industry, and 5% in the legal professions.[34] In other words, the membership included a broad cross section of businesses that emerged in New York at the turn of the century. Some members were undoubtedly clerks, but few blue-collar workers donated to the building fund of First Church, and nearly all members contributed to the fund.

The increasing wealth in the American city, which fostered these professions, was generally endorsed by Protestantism and emphasized in Christian Science. The sentiment of many Protestant theologians was summed up in the idea that "it makes a man prosperous to be a Christian"—that "wealth" and "poverty" were only relative terms. Many successful business people believed that prosperity signaled spiritual affluence and required generous support of new cultural institutions, such as public libraries, churches, and museums. This belief in the link between wealth and spirituality ensured the spread of middle-class values of individualism, education, and the Protestant work ethic.

The men who became part of the expansion of big business and were attracted to Christian Science also saw themselves as part of a moral revolution that improved their business relationships and their profits.[35] In Christian Science, increasing prosperity was seen as a demonstration of one's immediate God-given "supply." Christian Science preserved the Puritan mores of industry, thrift, and success as manifestations of abundant grace and holiness. Georgine Milmine and Willa Cather, whose 1907–8 biography of Mrs. Eddy, serialized in *McClure's Magazine,* stirred up public controversy, reported that "worldly prosperity . . . plays an important part in the Christian Science religion to-day. It is, singularly enough, considered a sign of spirituality in a Christian Scientist. Poverty is believed to be an error, like sin, disease, and death." Milmine and Cather claimed that one of the advertisements for the first edition of *Science and Health* asserted that "men of business have said this science was of great advantage from a secular point of view."[36]

Business people were attracted to the church for a number of reasons. The church provided a place to forge new relationships among persons who approached business transactions similarly.[37] It offered a new arena for productive business affiliations as well as mutual support of others in the changing urban capitalist domain. The pragmatism of the Christian Science approach proved attractive to men. One prominent New York businessman thought that Christian Science "gives a business man that peace of mind, mental poise, freedom from worry, which are absolutely essential to business or professional success. To me it is all in all, an every-day, ever-present, practical help."[38] The standards of morality and business efficiency that

Figure 10. Carrère and Hastings, First Church of Christ, Scientist, New York City, 1903 (Van Horne).

Christian Science emphasized were often viewed as the primary strengths of the religion by outsiders.[39]

Most important, Christian Science churches did not focus on labor relationships and new labor movements, which occupied the minds of many evangelical ministers in the cities. Christian Scientists claimed to do away with the causes of poverty and said they helped the poor without actually supporting charitable institutions. They believed that the teachings of their church would eventually ameliorate all of the problems of the city. Distributing the literature that carried this promise of individual healing became the major means of proselytizing. Articles on business, the church, and "supply" filled the pages of the Christian Science periodicals in the years following the 1893 depression.[40] Christian Science lecturers often addressed thousands of people who gathered to hear about Christian Science's relationship to business, particularly as it supported the individualism of competitive business principles.[41] They claimed Christian Science would smooth the way for capitalist expansion. As a businessman from New York put it: "Christian Science will, I firmly believe, do more to solve labor troubles in America than any political influence which may be brought to bear. Then, as its work becomes international, it will help clear away the clouds and dissolve the bitterness and distrust that now exist between the nations of the world. Christian Science, you may be sure, will be a prime mover in promoting world-wide peace. It is inevitable."[42]

Christian Science claimed that it would lessen the negative effects of competition through its promise of brotherhood. However, one critic believed that Christian Science allowed business people to ignore the problems of labor that other churches increasingly confronted. He wrote:

> When the rich man enters a Christian Science church, his fine feelings are never jarred by hearing about poverty and misery. There is no such animal. On the way to church he may have heard some cussed IWW speaker on the street say that the rich had stolen their wealth from the poor laboring man; that wealth all belonged to labor; that labor had produced it all, and that the rich, by stealing it away by capitalistic methods, had caused the poverty and misery of the poor, the robbed. But just as soon as this prominent citizen gets into the shelter of the Mother's church, he hears just the opposite of this IWW and the Jesus stuff. He hears there is no such thing as misery and pain; therefore, he has caused no misery or pain. This is a consolation his soul has longed for and is now supplied. He hears that everything is good. That includes his conduct, of course, and that is a consolation to him. He hears that discontent is sinful, so he insists on his employees coming and listening to this pleasing doctrine. It prevents strikes and other disorders advocated by those foreign IWW and Socialists.[43]

In New York, the number of men *attending* Christian Science services was higher than in any other denomination, even though Christian Science was widely considered a religion of women. The Christian Scientists in New York had the highest male/female ratio, at 43:100.[44] Moreover, many of the people attending Christian Science services were not even members. According to a 1903 church census, reported in the

New York Herald, Christian Scientists enjoyed the highest proportion of attendance to membership, at 157.9:100.[45] The church particularly attracted men to reading rooms and Wednesday evening testimony meetings. One commentator quipped: "Think of it, fifteen hundred persons at one mid-week prayer meeting and nearly half of them men. This is one of the modern miracles to those outside the Christian Science Church."[46]

Christian Science gave the business person a sense of well-being and security as well as a confidence and certainty of status in the new religion. In addition to producing new opportunities for exchange within a moral atmosphere, it muted the socialist demands for labor's rights by a reiteration of positive and spiritually justified individualism.

Many critics disputed the claims of the moral idealism of Christian Science, asserting that it substituted greed for morality. Many criticized the new healing movement as being a mask for commerce.[47] Bradford Sherman, one of the early Christian Science workers in Chicago, wrote, "It was a common report in those days [circa 1884] 'If you wish to get rich you must enter into the Christian Science business.' "[48] But some staunch critics respected the business spirit that pervaded the church.[49] As Mark Twain, a hostile witness, put it: "The Christian Scientist has taken a force which has been lying idle in every member of the human race since time began, and has organized it, and backed the business with capital, and concentrated it at Boston headquarters in the hands of a small and very competent Trust, and there are results. Therein lies the promise that this monopoly is going to extend its commerce wide in the earth."[50]

Christian Science bolstered its image by publicly associating itself with the business elite. For example, a defensive article by Alfred Farlow, manager of the Committee on Publication, suggested that "many men prominent in social, political and business life are staunch friends of this movement, and stand ready to support it and defend it in every possible way, though they are not identified with it. They constitute a power for good, for the maintenance of justice, and for the preservation of individual rights, which, though perhaps overlooked, must nevertheless be reckoned with."[51] Farlow listed some of the "substantial business men who have been benefitted by Christian Science and who have accepted the teaching of Mrs. Eddy."[52] These were men of intelligence who were well qualified to judge the goodness of Christian Science. As the *Arena* editor B. O. Flower reiterated, "Its prominent members . . . are not the kind of men to sanction for a moment any subterfuge or attempt to deceive the public."[53] Many articles, including biographies of Mrs. Eddy, contained sections about prominent members of the church.[54]

Increasingly, however, critics and interested onlookers suspected that Christian Science was a religion only for the wealthy and often pointed to Christian Scientists' new large urban edifices as evidence. These buildings indicated that the Scientists enjoyed a degree of wealth not shared by all their Protestant neighbors. William Johnston suggested that if one happened by First Church, New York, on a Wednesday or Sunday:

You will note a block-long line of handsome automobiles and carriages before a magnificent church that cost one and one quarter million dollars. A steady line of well-dressed people is swinging through the doors. You will find within, a vast and beautiful auditorium, crowded to its doors, and its great galleries overflowing with people highly representative of the intelligence, activity, fashion and wealth of New York. And whoever you are, and whatever your belief, you will be greeted most cordially, and leave most pleased with yourself and with those whom you came to see and hear.[55]

Prominent edifices like First Church, New York, were said to "attest [to Christian Science's] wealthy, aristocratic, and numerous following."[56] The public profile of Christian Science, established by numerous reports in the society sections of New York newspapers about First Church, undoubtedly contributed to the idea that New York Christian Scientists were part of the wealthiest business elite.

Early in its history, however, the congregation of First Church, New York, had been inspired by much different aims. In November 1887 the two groups of New York Christian Scientists, mostly women, merged into one group with a vision of carrying the gospel of healing to the poor through the distribution of literature and free Christian Science treatment. The group quickly found that its quarters, though not well equipped, "had the advantage of being located near the aristocratic section of the city."[57] The small congregation met in several rented quarters in the late 1880s and early 1890s. Augusta Stetson, the organizer and early pastor of First Church, began to attract wealthy and influential citizens and even claimed to have healed members of the Vanderbilt and Huntington families, though this assertion may have been concocted to increase her prestige.[58] In 1896, when the congregation moved into its own building, the outgrown church home of a Protestant church leader, Rev. R. Heber Newton, its services attracted attention in the press. One reporter from the *New York World* who attended a service commented: "The audience did not disperse for nearly an hour. Beautiful women richly gowned, superb in beautiful coloring, swept up and down the aisles, stopping here and there chatting in groups, in twos and threes, and well groomed men taking their part in what was more like a reception at a Fifth Avenue mansion than the ending of a religious service."[59]

The vision of wealth and success supplied by Stetson's First Church and other New York churches influenced many subsequent stories about Christian Science throughout the movement.[60] The notion that Christian Scientists were of the wealthy, leisure class persisted, particularly when they were judged by edifices like First Church, New York. This contradicted the fact that most Christian Scientists in the larger nationwide movement were middle class.[61] But most Christian Scientists did try at least to appear well off. Stetson even appointed someone to supervise clothes distribution in a special room provided at her church, to keep the poorer members looking prosperous.[62] Stetson's church was "expensive and handsome, the music . . . good, the dressing of the congregation . . . extravagant, including a great display of jewels."[63] This personal adornment gave the impression of a well-to-do congregation, which would subsequently attract the wealthy.

Some commentators claimed that the success of Christian Science was based on its fashionable status in cities. M. M. Mangasarian explained that the "imposing edifices, the prosperous looking disciples, the number of automobiles in front of their churches, only prove that Christian Science is fashionable—that is all."[64] An Evangelical minister, Lathan Crandall, in 1899 asserted that most people became Christian Scientists because it was the most popular fad in an age of fads: "It is quite the proper thing in some cities to be an avowed believer in the new cult. In Chicago, for example, the congregation which meets in the building recently erected for the First Christian Science Church is not only large but well-dressed. It has in it many men and women of wealth and social standing. That this has its influence upon some is evident from the remark made by a Chicago Scientist while visiting in a small Illinois village. 'I should not care,' said she, 'to be a Christian Scientist in a small town!'"[65] James Snowden suggested that the large and costly churches left the impression that the Christian Scientists were wealthy people, but he pointed out that actually "few influential people of a city are found among them."[66]

While clearly some in the church appreciated the appearance of success, many economically struggling Christian Scientists viewed their newfound religion as a way of actually staying afloat in a difficult economic and social environment. Those who were even lower on the economic ladder often found the success orientation to be a source of aggravation—they had not "demonstrated" their God-given "supply" sufficiently. Since this was antagonistic to the spirit of Christian Science, many COP commentators tried to soften this success orientation, with mixed results. Alfred Farlow maintained that citizens from all classes who were "unsatisfied with the more material means and methods of attaining relief from human woe" should try Christian Science.[67] One church spokesman of First Church, New York, reiterated, "Carefully compiled congregational statistics show that, far from the wealthy predominating, the church attracts more greatly the small-salaried man and self-supporting woman, who say with one accord that their religion is a most practical seven-days-in-the-week religion, that it has helped them financially and in every way, and made life happier for themselves and those about them."[68] Another apologist suggested that a most casual observation of average Christian Science congregations would reveal that the members of the church are a "good, sound, average body of citizens, the 'plain people' that Lincoln held in his heart."[69]

Most observers of the day agreed that Christian Science should at least be taken seriously, in either a positive or negative sense.[70] The Reverend Heber Newton's 1899 book on what he called the "lusty and vigorous offspring" of Christianity suggested that the significant notable effects produced by Christian Science on the minds, bodies, and souls of many intelligent people, including cures of diseases and evil habits, as well as the "revival of real religion" in the lives of its adherents, demonstrated that it was "something more than the latest Boston fad."[71]

The Christian Science church truly stood out because it attracted an above-average number of women.[72] When the original building of the Mother Church was dedicated in 1895, a *Boston Globe* reporter commented that fully two-thirds of the "vast congregations" at the services were "strong, healthy, muscular women," who themselves viewed these attributes as "proof of the value of Christian Science as a gospel of health."[73] Estimates of female membership ranged from 72 to 90 percent.[74] Women, particularly married women, constituted the majority of patients for public practitioners.[75] Also, approximately 85 percent of professional Christian Science practitioners were women.[76]

The church attracted women because it provided them with a new public platform from which to discuss religion, health, and family issues. The church championed women's causes such as suffrage and supported women's rights to equality under the law. At the same time, the church offered them the opportunity to practice their spirituality in public as healers and readers, allowed them to travel in service to "the Cause," and gave them the chance to help build new churches.

The Christian Science church was an arena where the traditional familial role for women as healers was upheld and even emphasized. Its theology of the Father/Mother God favored concepts that many women found important to redefining their ideas about the role of religion in the modern world. The emphasis on masculinity in the public sphere of Christian Science was balanced by an emphasis in the Christian Science periodicals on more femininity in all spheres of life. Essays on women's issues and articles on suffrage and the suffrage movement were found in all the official periodicals.[77] Women in the public eye, such as Susan B. Anthony, Clara Barton, and Louisa May Alcott, expressed an interest in Christian Science and made laudatory comments about Mrs. Eddy. Some took classes taught by her students.[78]

This attention to women's issues was attractive to many young working women, as was the possibility of success in the Christian Science practice. Single women were also attracted to the emancipation principles upheld in Christian Science and the women's movement. Women who had economic problems could find strength in the discipline of Christian Science, which emphasized women's equality.

Married women were also drawn to Christian Science, with or without their husbands. Those who were empathetic but enslaved by their more traditional role at home were tied to their husbands' economic potential and had no control over their uncertainties. The changing socioeconomic order was perhaps more threatening to these women.[79] As their children left home to pursue economic independence, their role of family nurturer became less significant. However, when these women joined in the official classes and activities of the Christian Science church, they achieved a quasi-official status, not unlike that seen in some masculine-dominated lodges.[80] Women had the opportunity to take up positions of importance through the system of rotating offices established by branch church governments.

Christian Science offered a religion, and a public profession, that emphasized the Motherhood of God, the sharing of moral and spiritual values between practitioner and patient, and the concept of divine guidance achieved through the affirmation of spiritual and ethical precepts rather than through traditional intercessory prayer.[81] Women practitioners took their nurturing skills, developed in the home, and created public practices that emphasized the strength of maternal and traditional bourgeois feminine characteristics such as spirituality, patience, purity, virtue, gentility, refinement, and love. They believed these were the qualities that the everyday working world needed.

The increasing popularity of Christian Science required that teachers, many of them women, be willing to relocate to other cities. Christian Science, thus, allowed women the opportunity to travel as emissaries of the new religion. In 1885, a Chicago student told the readers of the *Journal* that after riding days and nights through "utter desolation and barrenness" she reached Los Angeles, a city of forty thousand inhabitants. It was "overrun with the sick and dying, from all parts of the United States, who come here to get health. . . . They come; but very few are benefitted. What a field for labor,—for Science. There is no other location where so much good can be done. When one is healed, he returns home with the glad news that the climate does not heal, but Truth. . . . Coming from all parts of the country, invalids will carry the knowledge of our Science to as many points. How many laborers are needed here!"[82] An 1888 issue of the short-lived *Chicago Christian Scientist* (published 1887–90) included an appealing travelogue from a female Christian Scientist who noted the gentility and hospitality of the Christian Scientists across the West, and the relative ease of the crossing to California.[83]

The Christian Science church provided professional practitioners in the healing role. These practitioners were thought to be vehicles for divine guidance in the healing process. More than counselors, they nonetheless fulfilled this therapeutic position. They were listed in the *Christian Science Journal* and were available to take cases on an individual basis. By 1901, Christian Science practitioners in Los Angeles numbered over one hundred, nearly a third of the number of registered nurses in the city.[84]

Another attraction of Christian Science to women was the opportunity to have a real say in the designs and features of church buildings. Women were the first to build branch churches. The first Christian Science edifice was built in Oconto, Wisconsin, in 1886 by the women of the church, one of whose husband donated the land for the small wood-frame building (fig. 11). Bradford Sherman, a Chicago church organizer, believed that they had done so because it was their "natural inheritance" to do church work.[85] But Christian Science women were often innovative in their demands. Eleven Christian Science students, mostly those of Oakland teacher Francis Fluno, started the church in Berkeley, California. When the bylaws were adopted in 1905, twenty-eight of the twenty-nine members were women.[86] By 1909 a building committee consulted twelve architects and unanimously chose Bernard Maybeck.[87] Though Maybeck was at first hesitant to accept the commission from the group of church women, he was impressed by their enthusiasm and sincerity and agreed to design a simple and honest church building for them, though he thought they wouldn't like it (fig. 12). The women requested a progressive and individual design that was sincere and honest as well as comfortable and homelike.[88] Christian Science ideals of femininity had increasing importance in the designs of branch churches, particularly on the interior appointments.

The Christian Science church emphasized the theological importance of femininity. The church's symbolic and descriptive representations of the feminine were fair-

Figure 11. First Church of Christ, Scientist, Oconto, Wisconsin, 1886 (Van Horne).

ly traditional. Women should be muselike, contrite, pure, and noble.[89] The *Christian Science Sentinel* represented this ideal on its covers from 1906 to 1966 through a drawing of two classically idealized young women carrying burning lamps of knowledge and wisdom, and included the quote from Longfellow, "A Lady with a Lamp Shall Stand in the Great History of the Land, A Noble Type of Good Heroic Womanhood."

In theory at least, Christian Science proclaimed that women were equal to men. Mrs. Eddy stated that "in divine Science, we have not as much authority for considering God masculine, as we have for considering Him feminine, for Love imparts the clearest idea of Deity."[90] Mrs. Eddy also suggested that women had "a special adaptability to lead on Christian Science" and were well suited to its practice.[91] She "placed woman by the side of man in the pulpit as co-worker and co-equal" when she ordained the Bible and *Science and Health* as the impersonal pastor of the church in 1895, and instituted readers.[92] This ideal infuriated several of Mrs. Eddy's fundamentalist critics, who believed in a literal interpretation of the biblical injunction forbidding women to speak in church. One Baptist critic, the Reverend Isaac Haldeman, wrote, "Christian Science is a perversion of divine order! God has ordained that man shall be the head of a woman. God has ordained that man and not woman shall be the office bearer, the messenger and teacher in the church. Christian Science reverses this order. *Christian Science is a female system.* Its founder is a female, its teachers and healers are females. Here and there are a few men prominent in it, but these seem to be in their characteristics *feminine* rather than masculine. It was through a woman the devil brought sin into the world, it is through a woman he would spread damnation in the world."[93] Mary Baker Eddy was sometimes deemed the anti-Christ, especially because of her emphasis on femininity.[94]

In complete contrast, other critics argued that Christian Science theology reflected positive feminine characteristics, though these were rarely viewed as leading to public leadership. For example, Arthur Brown, a Unitarian seminarian, suggested that the great appeal of Christian Science was the belief that it would reform the world into the kingdom of God, "not by doing . . . [but] by *feeling*." He thought Christian Science was a subjective religion that produced no passion for justice or public spirit by its systematization of feminine sentimentality. He believed that this sub-

Figure 12. Entry to Bernard Maybeck's First Church of Christ, Scientist, Berkeley, 1911 (Paul Ivey).

jectivism paralleled the introspection of the leisure class, whose mentality had become "sensitive to its own states": "Your manual laborer never, so far as I have been able to learn, becomes a 'Scientist,' nor does the mechanic, or in fact, any man whose mind is forced to be mainly objective."[95]

Many women, however, were attracted to Christian Science precisely because they believed that their intellectuality and spirituality would be valued above and beyond their often limited social opportunities. They believed Christian Science inculcated a feminine philosophy. Joel Rufus Mosley told the readers of *Cosmopolitan Magazine* that Mrs. Eddy's system was Platonic and related to the "modern doctrine of subjective idealism as developed by Berkeley, Kant, Hegel, and their successors," suggesting that women could also understand and utilize philosophy.[96]

Some critics, such as Elbert Hubbard, founder of the Roycrofters, believed that Christian Science was successful because it was a women's religion that embodied the traits of the founder's personality.[97] However, the so-called feminine sensibilities of Christian Science teaching were also used to discredit Christian Science as a serious religion. One critic suggested, "The femininity of Christian Science is at once its strength and its weakness. It undoubtedly has drawn unto itself many strong men, but its distinguishing qualities are not those of virility and robustness. It is a religion of softness; and in this respect it fits into the mood of this ease-loving age. It seeks to cushion life's hard duties, and to provide an escape from pain and self-denial—and that is a palatable thing to unrenewed human nature."[98] The historian Donald Meyer would later characterize the entire movements of a broader "mind-cure," including Christian Science, to the ubiquity of women and the troubled souls of *fin de siècle* females.[99]

Criticisms of Christian Science practitioners from medical doctors also took on a specific gender bias. Whereas men who were tried in courts for Christian Science healing were often exonerated because of their public prominence, women were convicted due, apparently, solely to their sex.[100] The message from the medical establishment of the time was that women could not be entrusted with the healing of the sick in their care, and women medical students were rare.[101] But Mrs. Eddy was adamant that the female element in Christian Science was of positive benefit to society. Christian Science conferred a high social status on women as spiritual healers and teachers.[102]

Although women made up the majority of members and established themselves in the public practice of Christian Science healing, men were more prominent in the public business affairs of the church and were most visible as public ambassadors of Christian Science.[103] Mrs. Eddy specifically wanted the COP, the front-line defensive wing of the church, to be comprised of men.[104] The overwhelming majority of the directors and trustees were men. The First Readers in the Mother Church and in branch churches, who read from *Science and Health,* were usually male, though by tradition, not church policy. As a result, the organization's publicity itself sometimes took on a certain masculine character, which Mrs. Eddy was compelled to restrain. Its style was rational, sometimes aggressive, even confrontational in nature.

Although business acumen was applauded in the Christian Science periodicals, a business sense that was exclusively worldly and masculine in orientation was viewed with suspicion because it did not represent the unity of the public and private spheres, of masculine strength tempered by feminine intuition and love, that was so important to the Christian Science vision.[105]

Some critics of Christian Science attacked the concept of gender equality that Mrs. Eddy proposed. Other outside observers commented positively on the rational and intellectual sensibility of Christian Science as it was associated with successful businessmen. Some commentators stated that Christian Scientists were intellectually disciplined, thought out their problems, and were philosophers at heart. Many of the new examples of classicizing architecture being built by the denomination were thought to be rational and progressive, that is, masculinist in their appeal. Rational, reformatory, and business ideals were increasingly expressed through the classical style of civic architecture.

The interiors of branch churches, however, expressed what could be called the comfort and efficiency of the Christian home. Earlier in the nineteenth century, important writers on women's issues such as Catharine Beecher and Harriet Beecher Stowe had exhorted women to be the ministers of the home. The Beecher sisters' own homes were designed to maximize efficiency. Christine Frederick, an important domestic engineer, had also suggested that the arrangement of spaces in the home be based on their functions and the efficiency of movement between them.[106] Mrs. Eddy's own rigorous and disciplined homelife, described in numerous magazine articles and personal reminiscences, also suggested a new and important model for efficient femininity. In Christian Science, these ideals of the home were brought into the public place of worship and became the model for the efficient and functional organization of the interior spaces in branch churches. The interest in advancing the ideals of femininity, however, was balanced by the need to strengthen the public face of the Christian Science movement in the city.

In the city, architectural prominence became an important element in suggesting Christian Science's social position and conveying its ideals of public worship. During the building-boom years, Christian Science men and women found themselves drawn into broad-ranging debates about the social and reform function of contemporary church architecture in the urban environment. Architecture was the most important agent in the representation of the religion to a critical public. As one Minneapolis church member reported, after the congregation built a small classical frame building to serve as a Christian Science headquarters at the Minnesota State Fair in 1902: "Everything about our building presented a most pleasing appearance and gave an impression of the substantiality and permanency of Christian Science."[107] This "substantiality and permanency" became of utmost importance in the erection of new branch churches designed to impel the Christian Science vision of healing and gender equality into the modern city.

The Christian Science church was founded with little fanfare. By the early twentieth century, however, the public's attraction to its teachings and the growth of

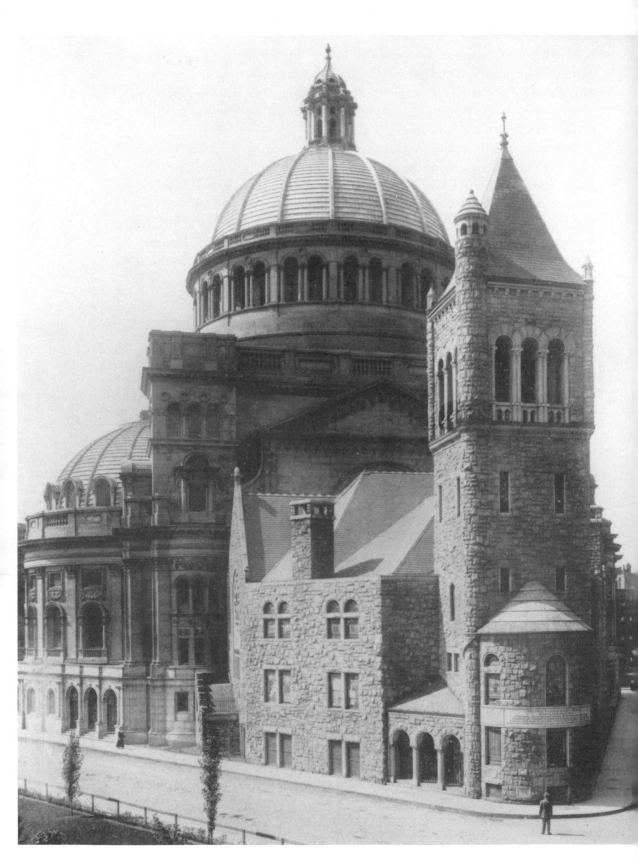

Figure 13. The Mother Church with Extension (1906) in rear (Van Horne).

church membership demanded that congregations create public spaces for worship that upheld and even proclaimed the church's functional, theological, and gender ideals. A great love of Christian Science compelled its adherents to erect gleaming branches of the Mother Church to represent the new teaching, and these edifices were conspicuous and attractive. As Wilder Quint put it, the "plain people" of the Christian Science movement were, thankfully, "endowed with the great gift of good taste, so that their services for art are very real and worthy of highest praise."[108] Soon after the completion of the Mother Church in Boston in 1894, the Christian Science movement had a visible model. When the Extension of the Mother Church was completed in 1906 (fig. 13), the movement had an even more dramatic and monumental model of a public worship space to follow in urban church designs. The building boom was underway.

NOTES

1. *Chicago Times-Herald,* Nov. 15, 1897.

2. Quoted in the *Christian Science Journal* 15 (1897–98): 633.

3. Mary Baker Eddy's *Science and Health, with Key to the Scriptures* (Boston: Christian Science Publishing Society, 1875, 1906, 1971) went through hundreds of editions before her death. The final authorized version is from 1906. All references to this work in the present book are from this edition. The church readers were quoted in the *Chicago Times-Herald,* Nov. 15, 1897. The December 1897 number of the *Christian Science Journal* also included the dedication addresses.

4. Eddy, *Science and Health,* 468.

5. Mary Baker Eddy, *Manual of the Mother Church, The First Church of Christ, Scientist, in Boston, Massachusetts,* 89th ed. (Boston: Christian Science Publishing Society, 1908), 17. Hereafter cited as the *Manual;* all references are from this edition.

6. Henrietta Williams claimed that "new churches have been organizing at the rate of from four to six each month, while church attendance shows an average yearly increase of about forty per cent." Williams, "The Founder of Christian Science," *New England Magazine* 21 (Nov. 1899): 305.

7. See, for instance, Ursula N. Gestefeld, *Statement of Christian Science* (Chicago: Ursula N. Gestefeld, 1889), or Emma Curtis Hopkins's magazine, *Christian Metaphysician,* published in Chicago, 1887–97. For a broad overview of mind-cure and New Thought see Charles S. Braden, *Spirits in Rebellion: The Rise and Development of New Thought* (Dallas: Southern Methodist University, 1963). See also Gail Harley, "Emma Curtis Hopkins: 'Forgotten Founder' of New Thought" (Ph.D. diss., Florida State University, 1991).

8. Quoted in *Editorial Comments on the Life and Work of Mary Baker Eddy, Discoverer and Founder of Christian Science, and Author of the Christian Science Textbook, "Science and Health with Key to the Scriptures"* (Boston: Christian Science Publishing Society, 1911), 21–22. This volume gathered various quotes from the press dealing with the life and work of Mrs. Eddy.

9. Eddy, *Science and Health,* 583.

10. For the institution of readers in the Mother Church see Eddy, *Manual,* articles 2 and 3, 29–33.

11. See "Communion Hymn," numbered variously 298, 299, 300, 301, 302, with different musical arrangements, in the *Christian Science Hymnal* (Boston: Christian Science Publishing Society, 1932).

12. Stephen Hasbrouck, *Altar Fires Relighted: A Study from a Non-Partisan Standpoint of Movements and Tendencies at Work in the Religious Life of To-Day* (New York: Burnett, 1912), 329–30.

13. On urban mobility see Stephen Thernstrom, *Progress and Poverty: Social Mobility in a Nineteenth-Century City* (Cambridge, Mass.: Harvard University Press, 1965). On the growth of suburbia see Kenneth T. Jackson, *Crabgrass Frontier: The Suburbanization of the United States* (New

York: Oxford University Press, 1985); Robert Fishman, *Bourgeois Utopias: The Rise and Fall of Suburbia* (New York: Basic Books, 1987).

14. See May 15, 1947, letter to the Chicago Christian Scientist Perry Radcliffe, of Ninth Church, CHD. Also see *Christian Science Sentinel,* Feb. 19, 1910, concerning Science churches as "the outgrowth of multiplication and not division."

15. In 1912, a joint committee of Churches of Christ, Scientist, in Portland issued a letter suggesting that "the greatest good to the greatest number would be attained through each member attending and becoming a member of the Church in his own district." Districts were then defined for the five branch churches. Field Collection, CHD. (All branch church documents are located in the Field Collection and Archives in the Church History Division, the First Church of Christ, Scientist, Boston.)

16. On First Church, St. Louis, see *Brickbuilder* 13 (Sept. 1904).

17. According to William G. Wirth, "St. Bartholomew's Church, one of New York City's most fashionable worshiping places, was recently purchased by the Christian Scientists at a rumored cost of $3,000,000. This edifice is to be removed, and a mammoth and costly Scientist church built on its site. Christian Scientists, in cities where their membership will warrant it, are very extravagant in church building." Wirth, *Christian Science X-Rayed* (Mountain View, Calif.: Pacific Press, 1921), 58.

18. Letter to the membership from the Board of Trustees of Fifth Church, Jan. 29, 1920, 2, CHD.

19. The church and office building were to be completed in 1921 for $8,500,000. See the *New York Evening Post,* Jan. 24, 1920, 1. This first-page story reported that the Scientists had effectively rented $15,000,000 in office space for only $99. The rent was $1 per year on a 99-year contract. The author compared the transaction to old Peter Minuit's purchase of Manhattan Island from the Indians for $24. In return for its lease the church sold $2,000,000 in bonds secured by the building. See *Architecture and Building* 54 (Jan. 1922): 6–7.

20. Raymond J. Cunningham, "The Impact of Christian Science on the American Churches, 1880–1910," *American Historical Review* 72 (1967): 887. See also Eugene Wood, "What the Public Wants to Read," *Atlantic Monthly,* June 8, 1901, 911; Frank L. Mott, "The Magazine Revolution and Popular Ideas in the Nineties," *Proceedings of the American Antiquarian Society* 64 (Apr. 1954): 195–214.

21. See Georgine Milmine, *The Life of Mary Baker G. Eddy and the History of Christian Science* (New York: Doubleday, Page, 1909, 1937), 370.

22. See Eddy, *Manual,* article 8, section 28, 48; A. J. Lamme III, "From Boston in One Hundred Years: Christian Science in 1970," *Professional Geographer* 23 (1971): 329–32. For a broader study see Lamme's "Spatial and Ecological Characteristics of the Diffusion of Christian Science in the United States 1875–1910" (Ph.D. diss., Syracuse University, 1968). A précis of the dissertation is Lamme's *Christian Science in the U.S.A., 1900–1910: A Distributional Study* (Syracuse: Syracuse University, 1975). See also Harold Pfautz, "A Case Study of an Urban Religious Movement: Christian Science," in *Contributions to Urban Sociology,* ed. Ernest W. Burgess and Donald J. Bogue (Chicago: University of Chicago Press, 1964), 284–303; and Leender Pieter Van Der Does, *Christian Science als Sociaal Vershinsel* (Delft, 1933). Mrs. Eddy in the early 1890s encouraged her students to locate in large cities, but she was equally interested in Christian Science's taking hold in rural areas. See Mary Baker Eddy, *Retrospection and Introspection* (Boston: Christian Science Publishing Society, 1892), 82.

23. See, for instance, Sydney Ahlstrom's classic treatment of Christian Science in *A Religious History of the American People* (New Haven: Yale University Press, 1972). Stephen Gottschalk's *The Emergence of Christian Science in American Religious Life* (Berkeley: University of California Press, 1973) attempts to mitigate Ahlstrom's account. See also Stephen Gottschalk, "Christian Science," *The Encyclopedia of Religion,* ed. Mircea Eliade (New York: Macmillan, 1987), 3:442–46; idem, "Christian Science and Harmonialism," in *The Encyclopedia of the American Religious Experience,* ed. Charles H. Lippy and Peter W. Williams (New York: Scribner, 1988), 2:901–16; Edwin Scott Gaustad, *Dissent in American Religion* (Chicago: University of Chicago Press, 1973); Martin Mar-

ty, *Modern American Religion,* vol. 1: *The Irony of It All, 1893–1919* (Chicago: University of Chicago Press, 1986). The most imaginative approach to Christian Science theology is found in Mary Farrell Bednarowski's *New Religions and the Theological Imagination in America* (Bloomington: Indiana University Press, 1989). For academic critiques of Christian Science see Charles Braden, *Christian Science Today, Power, Policy, Practice* (Dallas: Southern Methodist University Press, 1958), and Stuart E. Knee, *Christian Science in the Age of Mary Baker Eddy* (Westport, Conn.: Greenwood, 1994).

24. Kevin J. Christiano, *Religious Diversity and Social Change: American Cities, 1890–1906* (New York: Cambridge University Press, 1987), 3, 148.

25. Sidney Stark and William Bainbridge, *The Future of Religion: Secularization, Revival and Culture Formation* (Berkeley: University of California Press, 1985), 409. Stark and Bainbridge also note, "New religious movements will vary to the extent that they draw privileged followers. The more the emphasis is on ideas, on complex culture, the more that recruitment will be restricted to persons of considerable privilege and sophistication. Here Christian Science stands out. Its emphasis is on a highly abstract and counterintuitive doctrine. It eschews all emotionalism in its services, which more closely resemble a study session than a worship ceremony. Not surprisingly, it has appealed almost exclusively to people of considerable wealth and social standing" (ibid.).

26. Edgar Jones, "A Criticism of Christian Science Values" (Ph.D. diss., University of Denver, 1912), 136.

27. Hanna quoted in the *Christian Science Journal* 14, no. 7 (Oct. 1896): 343; *Times-Herald* quoted in the *Christian Science Sentinel* 2, no. 31 (Apr. 5, 1900).

28. George Shaw Cook, "Growth of Christian Science in America: What Christian Science Is Accomplishing," *Fine Arts Journal* (May 1907): 201.

29. The evangelical reformer Samuel Lane Loomis agreed with Washington Gladden, also a reformer, who commented in 1886 that even with free church pews and accessibility to the working class, only one-tenth of the families on his church rolls belonged to this class. See Samuel Lane Loomis, *Modern Cities and Their Religious Problems* (New York: Baker and Taylor 1887), 82; Washington Gladden, *Applied Christianity: Moral Aspects of Social Questions* (Boston: Houghton Mifflin, 1886), 209; Josiah Strong, *The New Era, or The Coming Kingdom* (New York: Baker and Taylor, 1893), 207.

30. See Strong, *The New Era,* 196. See also Thomas W. Wilby, *What Is Christian Science?* (New York: John Lane, 1915), 160–62.

31. Alfred D. Kohn, *Christian Science from a Physician's Standpoint* (Chicago: Privately printed, 1906), 2.

32. William A. Johnston, "Christian Science in New York: History of the New York Organizations," *Broadway Magazine* 18, no. 2 (May 1907): 157.

33. A. M. Bellwald, *Christian Science and the Catholic Faith* (New York: Macmillan, 1922), 24.

34. Among the membership were manufacturers and suppliers of large machines and construction materials such as Corliss engines, roadmaking steam rollers, locomotive heating, elevators, hydraulic mining machines, sheet metal, wholesale lumber, and glass. Superintendents and clerks from Western Union, Standard Adding Machine Company, United States Glass, Jersey City Light, and Union Oil were members. The membership also included a general construction contractor and engineers for the railroad and the gas, water, and electric works. There were those who manufactured and sold straw hats, biscuits, jewelry, badges and lodge supplies, bookbindings, rubber, twines, cords, and yarn, tin cans, pails and boxes, and watch cases. There were architects, artists, piano and organ salesmen, musicians, and actors. The world of printing was well represented in the membership by several commercial lithographers and stationers and the printers of bulletins for the Bigelow Company, International Sunshine Society, and Junior League. Publishers, editors, journalists, and advertising salesmen covering fields as different as railroad engineering, music, dry goods, and international advertisement had joined the church. The garment industry was represented by merchants, importers, and retailers of tailoring goods, wools, silks and linens, and ready-to-wear clothing. Members in the food industry represented a large farm as well as meat

packing and the retail grocery business. The financial services, including banking, insurance, and stock exchange commodities on Wall Street, were also well represented.

35. See Winfred Ernest Garrison, *The March of Faith: The Story of Religion in America since 1865* (New York: Harper, 1933), 60.

36. Milmine, *Life of Mary Baker G. Eddy*, 209–10. Milmine's book published the serialization from *McClure's*. On the authorship issues surrounding this text see Brent Bohlke, "Willa Cather and the Life of Mary Baker G. Eddy," *American Literature* 54, no. 2 (1982): 288–94.

37. See Alfred Farlow, "Christian Science in Business Life," *American Business Man* 11 (May 1908): 155–57, in which the author concluded: "It seems to us that a Christian Scientist can judge better as to his real advancement by noting how many of his pet sins he is escaping, rather than by counting the amount of money he is gaining." See also Remington Edwards Twitchell, "An Analysis of the Published Writings of Mary Baker Eddy to Determine Metaphysical Concepts That Christian Scientists Might Apply to Selected Business and Personal Financial Problems" (Ph.D. diss., New York University, 1977).

38. Quoted in Johnston, "Christian Science in New York," 165. As Johnston reported in his article, an exposé of Christian Science in New York for the *Broadway Magazine,* he met "the president and vice-president of two of the largest industrial enterprises in the United States. Both were clean-cut, hard-headed, brainy and energetic men of middle age, well-educated and traveled, carefully dressed, excellent representatives in every way of American success" (166).

39. For example, see Lyman Powell, *Mary Baker Eddy: A Life-Size Portrait* (Boston: Christian Science Publishing Society, 1930), 256–57.

40. For example, see "Christian Science in the Business World," parts 1 and 2, *Christian Science Journal* 12, no. 11 (Feb. 1895): 477–82, and no. 12 (Mar. 1895): 497–502.

41. For discussion of Christian Science and its relationship to business, see Bicknell Young, *Christian Science: Its Principle and Rule in Business* (Boston: Christian Science Publishing Society, 1917).

42. Johnston, "Christian Science in New York," 166.

43. Hugo Hume, *The Superior American Religions* (Los Angeles: Libertarian Publishing Co., 1928), 91.

44. The lowest male/female ratio belonged to the Episcopalians; men comprised just 29 percent of their membership. See "Void of Ritual, Oratory and Glamour, Christian Scientists Fill First Church," *New York Herald,* Feb. 19, 1912.

45. The proportion of attendance to membership among some other denominations was: Methodists, 138.7:100; Unitarians, 114.8:100; and Roman Catholics, 64.2:100. See "How New York Goes to Church, Completed Census of Attendance on Four Sundays," *New York Herald,* Dec. 15, 1903. The Christian Science church was comparatively small, with just over 2,100 members, but it had 3,366 people attending. The Episcopalians, for example, had nearly 50,000 members but only 39,000 attending. The Roman Catholics had over 510,000 members with only 289,000 attending services.

46. Johnston, "Christian Science in New York," 161. See also George Shaw Cook, "Christian Science in Chicago," *American Queen* (Apr. 1907): 9. Kohn, *Christian Science from a Physician's Standpoint,* writes: "It is perhaps the only denomination in which the male attendance outnumbers the female, and it is steadily growing in spite of ridicule, in spite of advancing medical science (53 churches last year); for the potent reason that it is the only modern religion which offers a remedy for both spiritual and bodily ills; and happiness and perfect contentment besides" (2). In the early days of the movement, businessmen in several cities sometimes gathered to discuss Christian Science and business. See Edward Kimball, *Lectures and Articles on Christian Science* (Chesterton, Ind.: Edna K. Wait, 1921), 475–76. See also letter, J. U. Higinbotham to Mary Baker Eddy, June 25, 1903, *Christian Science Journal* 21 (1903–4): 292.

47. See Francis Edward Marsten, *The Mask of Christian Science* (New York: American Tract Society, 1909), and Herbert N. Casson, *The Crime of Credulity* (New York: Peter Eckler, 1901), 101. In one evangelical tract, a practitioner allegedly told a young woman that she would earn "two

or three hundred pounds between now and Christmas. . . . Ours is a better profession than teaching, Miss Harwood. I can tell you my husband finds me a help in piling up his fortune." Anne Harwood, *An English View of Christian Science: An Exposure* (Chicago: Fleming H. Revell, 1899), 47, 52. Harwood explained that the only class of people whom the Christian Scientists "do cure are the rich, idle women who fancy they have all manner of diseases, when really there is nothing the matter with them" (52).

48. Bradford Sherman, *Historical Sketch of the Introduction of Christian Science in Chicago and the West* (Chicago: F. M. Leyda, 1915).

49. See James Campbell, *What Christian Science Means and What We Can Learn From It* (New York: Abingdon Press, 1920). As Campbell puts it: "One thing that renders the organization compact and strong is the commercial spirit which pervades it; a spirit to which this commercial age is peculiarly responsible. Its leaders, readers, and practitioners constitute an inner circle or guild bound together by a common interest in supporting a system which gives them good financial returns" (77).

50. Mark Twain (Samuel Clemens), *Christian Science* (New York: Harper, 1899, 1907), 86. The prevalence of new business methods in the organization caused Twain to dub it a trust. The conflation of Christian Science and business provoked some exasperated responses, like this one from William McCracken, representative of the New York COP:

That the business affairs of the Christian Science denomination are on a sound financial footing, is conceded. Is there any fault to find with that? Is it not rather a welcome mark of stability and good faith that this denomination can meet all its liabilities as they grow, can erect its own churches and at its own cost, maintain free reading rooms and free lectures, to which the public have access without charge? Is it not a virtue that it needs no fairs, bazaars, etc., and that none of its churches are dedicated until paid for? If the Christian Science denomination called upon those who have not had the benefits of its Christian healing to contribute towards its expenses, or if it were in debt and unable to pay its way, the status of its business affairs might be justly criticized, but under present conditions there is no such pretext. There is no doubt that executive and business skills are needed to manage the affairs of so great and active an organization; but because this management succeeds, is it necessary to call the denomination a "trust," a "bargain counter" or a "factory?"

See W. D. McCracken, *Mrs. Eddy's Relation to Christian Science: A Reply to Mark Twain* (New York: North American Review, 1903), 3. See also Glenn Kratzer, *The Christian Science Church* (Chicago: Privately printed, 1914), on the church's early administration.

51. Alfred Farlow, "A Glance at the Personnel of the Christian Science Movement: A Statement of Mrs. Eddy's Faith, and the Names of Some Prominent People Who Believe in It," *Human Life* 4 (Jan. 1907): 5.

52. Farlow's list included, among others, John Crowell, associate editor of the *Wall Street Journal;* Mr. Hayne Davis, arbitrator and secretary to the American delegation to the thirteenth and fourteenth Inter-Parliamentary Conferences; a president of a New York City Bank; a vice-president of another bank; a prominent businessman associated with the Van Camp Packing Company; the mayors of Oswego and Indianapolis; judges at various levels; an Indiana state representative; attorneys; a prominent musician; a manager with Western Union and Wisconsin Telephone; and the "noted Chicago Capitalist, Frank Bush."

53. B. O. Flower, "The Recent Reckless and Irresponsible Attacks on Christian Science and Its Founder, with a Survey of the Christian Science Movement," *Arena* 37, no. 206 (Jan. 1907): 59–60.

54. Powell, *Mary Baker Eddy: A Life Size Portrait,* 257–98. Powell pointed out that several businessmen, including Clarence Howard of St. Louis, of the Commonwealth Steel Company of Granite, Illinois, and William Delaven Baldwin, chairman of the board of the Otis Elevator Company, had utilized Christian Science precepts in the organization of their businesses. Charles Klein, a Broadway playwright, had also found relief in Christian Science. Powell believed, in fact,

that "no field has been more productive of a type of Christian Science than the stage" (258). Klein had produced several plays on Broadway. When he was approached in church by Johnston and asked about his feelings he replied that "there's the spirit of Broadway here [in the church]. I mean Broadway the street, as it typifies this great city, which in turn typifies the New World—progress, discovery, mental and physical evolution, in short the spirit of the twentieth century, the determination to get at the real gist of things and then apply them to a practical end." Johnston, "Christian Science in New York," 165. Johnston explored the makeup of the church membership in New York and noted that Charles E. Finley, president of the Aetna National Bank; Colonel Robert C. Clowrey, president of the Western Union Company; and Henry D. Esterbrook, a well-known attorney, were all associated with Christian Science. While at a Wednesday evening meeting Johnston had seen David Bispham, a well-known baritone, and Whitney Mockredge, a tenor; William Norris, a comedian; H. Clay Barnaby, a famous "Bostonian"; Mary Ellen Lease, a lecturer; and Clara Louis Burnham, an author. But he queried: "Who are some others? New Yorkers want names." A spokesman replied that no names were given out due to public doubt and contempt: "So, in deference to the many members in high and responsible places of public trust, we say nothing of their connection with us, in order that they, too, may not be misunderstood." But Johnston was further informed "in the same quiet confident manner, New York would marvel if it knew them all" (164–65). In England, many converts were people prominent in education and social circles, some even related to royalty. See Bryan Wilson, *Sects and Society: A Sociological Study of the Elim Tabernacle, Christian Science, and Christadelphians* (Berkeley: University of California, 1961); Charles Adolphus Murray, Seventh Earl of Dunmore, *Prophecy: Fulfillment: Revelation* (Boston: Christian Science Publishing Society, 1908).

55. Johnston, "Christian Science in New York," 156. Most assuredly, Johnston joined the church after his enthusiastic investigation.

56. Marsten, *The Mask of Christian Science,* 50.

57. Altman K. Swihart, *Since Mrs. Eddy* (New York: Henry Holt, 1931), 12. The first location was above the Caswell and Massey's Drugstore at Fifth Avenue and Forty-seventh street. See also Sarah Gardner Cunningham, "A New Order: Augusta Emma Simmons Stetson and the Origins of Christian Science in New York City, 1886–1910" (Ph.D. diss., Union Theological Seminary, New York, 1994).

58. Swihart, *Since Mrs. Eddy,* 43. See also Arnold Bloome, *A Voice Is Calling* (New York: Putnam, 1926), 155.

59. *New York World,* Dec. 15, 1908.

60. See, for instance, Charles Pease, *Exposé of Christian Science Methods and Teaching Prevailing in the First Church, C.S., New York City* (New York: Restoration Publishing Co., 1905), 40.

61. See Pierre Janet, *Psychological Healing,* trans. Eden and Cedar Paul (New York: Macmillan, 1925): "Christian Science has a message of joy for all; it exalts health, vanity, and material prosperity, as lofty virtues. . . . It thus ministers to the sense of satisfaction and well-being characteristic of the prosperous classes of the United States" (88). The Rt. Honorable H. A. L. Fisher characterized Christian Science as "a religion of the rich, the eupeptic, the vivacious." H. A. L. Fisher, *Our New Religion* (London: Ernest Benn, 1929), 175. John Elward Brown noted, in his *In the Cult Kingdom: Mormonism, Eddyism and Russellism* (Siloam Springs, Ark.: International Federation Publishing Co., 1915): "Eddyism . . . makes its appeal, almost wholly, to those who have a degree of learning and a measure of refinement. Amongst the idle classes, and especially those who desire a religion that carried with it a great deal of show, but which requires no self denial, Christian Science runs riot. Los Angeles is the greatest Christian Science city in the world, and largely because Los Angeles has more men and women of wealth and idleness than any other city in the world" (20).

62. Swihart writes, in *Since Mrs. Eddy:* "A great supply of hats, coats, shoes was always on hand, and at times even beautiful fur coats were given out. In this way the poorer members were enabled to share in the prosperity of others. In some cases the more expensive clothing was furnished by rich women whose husbands would not give the money for the cause of Christian Science but

allowed them to buy all the clothes they wished. These women gladly provided all that Mrs. Stetson desired along this line" (45). See also Edward Franden Dakin, *Mrs. Eddy: The Biography of a Virginal Mind* (New York: Scribner, 1929), 352; Robert Peel, *Mary Baker Eddy: The Years of Authority* (New York: Holt, Rinehart, and Winston, 1977), 410 n. 64.

63. Pease, *Exposé of Christian Science Methods,* 49.

64. M. M. Mangasarian, *What Is Christian Science?* (Chicago: Independent Religious Society, 1921), 48. Mangasarian observed: "It was not long ago when judges condemned innocent women as witches and sentenced them to be tortured to death. Did that make witchcraft a fact, or can it be quoted to justify the belief in witchcraft? The late chief justice of the United States was Catholic. What does that prove?" (49). See also Father Cyril Buotich, who preached a series of lectures at St. Boniface, San Francisco, and concluded: "In the wake of its victories have arisen Christian Scientist churches in every city of size and importance . . . [where] the magnificence of the majority of these structures and their grandeur of architecture, as well as the luxurious limousines parked in their vicinities . . . [are] representatives of the so-called circles of society and aristocracy of wealth." Rev. Cyril Buotich, *Christian Science, An Apostasy from Science and Christology: A Course of Lectures* (San Francisco: St. Boniface, 1916).

65. Lathan A. Crandall, "Its Growth," in *Searchlights on Christian Science* (Chicago: Fleming H. Revell Company, 1899), 67.

66. James Snowden, *The Truth About Christian Science* (Philadelphia: Westminster Press, 1921), 219.

67. Farlow, "A Glance at the Personnel of the Christian Science Movement," 5.

68. Quoted in Johnston, "Christian Science in New York," 163.

69. Wilder D. Quint, "The Growth of Christian Science," *New England Magazine* 47 (Sept. 1909–Feb. 1910): 317.

70. According to Oliver Huckel, *Christian Science and Common Sense: A Contribution toward a Rational Explanation of the Phenomena of Mental Healing* (Baltimore: Arundel Press, 1899), "This movement has assumed such propositions that it cannot be laughed away as the latest Boston fad, or the latest popular humbug" (12).

71. R. Heber Newton, *Christian Science: The Truths of Spiritual Healing and Their Contribution to the Growth of Orthodoxy* (New York: Putnam, 1899), 1–3.

72. Rodney Stark and William Bainbridge, *The Future of Religion: Secularization, Revival, and Cult Formation* (Berkeley: University of California Press, 1985), 237. By the 1926 national census Christian Science appeared to be 75 percent female and 94 percent urban. Female members made up 55.7 percent of mainstream religions. An attempt to explain this attraction is found in Joseph Kelly Johnson, "Christian Science: A Case Study of a Religion as a Form of Adjustment Behavior" (Ph.D. diss., Washington University, St. Louis, 1938). Johnson called Christian Science a "woman's religion for women" (15).

73. *Boston Globe,* Jan. 6, 1895.

74. Wirth, *Christian Science X-Rayed,* 89. Wirth put the female membership at 72 percent. See also Harwood, *An English View of Christian Science,* 18, where it is noted that four-fifths of the congregation in London were women. The *Boston Globe* for June 8, 1899, reported that nine-tenths of the congregation at weekly testimony meetings were women.

75. See John Schwenke, "An Analysis of the Contributions of Christian Science to the Basic Human Needs of People Living in Modern Urban Society, with Special Emphasis on Evidence Collected in the Chicago Metropolitan Area" (B.D. thesis, Chicago Theological Seminary, 1948), 124.

76. Arthur T. Brown, "The Psychological Reasons for the Appeal of Christian Science" (B.D. thesis, Meadville Theological School, Chicago, 1919), 169. On the personal life of a Christian Science practitioner see Cynthia Grant Tucker, *A Woman's Ministry* (Philadelphia: Temple University Press, 1984).

77. Sibyl Wilbur, *The Life of Mary Baker Eddy* (New York: Human Life Publishing Co., 1907), 296. Alice Stone Blackwell, editor of the suffrage-supporting *Women's Journal,* had contributed

an article on suffrage to the April 1887 issue of *Christian Science Journal.* See Margery Fox, "Protest in Piety: Christian Science Revisited," *International Journal of Women's Studies* 1, no. 4 (1978): 401–16.

78. See Robert Peel, *Mary Baker Eddy: The Years of Trial* (New York: Holt, Rinehart, and Winston, 1971), 223; Powell, *Mary Baker Eddy: A Life-Size Portrait,* 137; *Christian Science Sentinel* 10, no. 20 (Jan. 18, 1908): 383–84.

79. This idea was explored thoroughly in Johnson, "Christian Science," 11–15, and Schwenke, "An Analysis of the Contributions of Christian Science," 141.

80. See Schwenke, "An Analysis of the Contributions of Christian Science," 233. See also William D. Moore, "The Masonic Lodge Room, 1870–1930: A Sacred Space of Masculine Spiritual Hierarchy," in *Gender, Class, and Shelter: Perspectives in Vernacular Architecture,* vol. 5, ed. Elizabeth Collins Cromley and Carter L. Hudgins (Knoxville: University of Tennessee Press, 1995), 26–39.

81. As Schwenke, "An Analysis of the Contributions of Christian Science," remarks: "The practitioner was an agent of Divine Truth in a most intimate and thorough way, that the lives and fortunes of many people actually depended upon her" (232).

82. *Christian Science Journal* 3 (1885–86): 205–6.

83. C. J. Thatcher, *Chicago Christian Scientist* 2, no. 3 (Aug. 1888): 62–64. Thatcher wrote from Monterey, on July 15, 1888. On her trip from Chicago to Los Angeles she made stops at a spacious Denver home as well as in Canon City, Salt Lake City, and Oakland. The message of the article: these cities need teachers.

> Our teachers go into communities much as do cyclones and tornadoes; they flow through "mortal mind," uproot the stagnant beliefs, and lock horns with Satan, make the lions of carnality growl and cause a howl from the "old fogies" of ecclesiasticism; then "ship the town" to other fields that are green or yellow for harvesting, and leave the dazed, dumfounded converts alone to fight it out on any line they see fit. . . . To speak of the work in this city [Oakland], is to echo what is true of many other cities. The Truth is marching on, and the Pacific coast is by no means behind the age, in Christian Science. All are imbued with the same spirit, and welcome new comers with a cordiality which speaks well for the brotherhood of man. From here we go to the south part of the state, where we expect to behold of the marvelous beauties of this land towards the setting sun (64).

See also Tucker, *A Woman's Ministry.*

84. Quoted in Sandra S. Frankiel, *California's Spiritual Frontiers: Religious Alternatives in Anglo-Protestantism, 1850–1910* (Berkeley: University of California Press, 1988), 68.

85. Sherman, *Historical Sketch,* 2. Laura and Victoria Sargent and several students built a small frame church on property that Victoria Sargent's husband donated to the small congregation. The church was occupied in late 1886. See William Curtis Coffman et al., Student's Association, *A Biographical Sketch of Victoria H. Sargent, CSD, and Laura E. Sargent, CSD* (Green Bay, Wis.: Privately printed, 1953); "Christian Scientists' First Church—Oconto, Wisconsin," *Milwaukee Journal,* June 14, 1952.

86. See *Christian Science Sentinel,* Dec. 23, 1905.

87. "History of First Church of Christ, Scientist, Berkeley," undated ms., CHD. Quoted in Esther McCoy, *Five California Architects* (New York: Reinhold, 1960), 24, and Kenneth H. Cardwell, *Bernard Maybeck: Artisan, Architect, Artist* (Salt Lake City: Peregrine Smith, 1977), 122. For coverage of the church building in the press, see "$50,000 Church to Be Built by Christian Scientists," *San Francisco Call,* Sept. 24, 1910.

88. Documents on the History of First Church, Berkeley, Field Collection, CHD.

89. Carol Norton, a young Christian Science teacher from New York, declared that the new man, which Christian Science would compel into being, would be theologian, reformer, statesman, and idealist. But the new woman "will be a greater revelation to the world in many respects than the new man. She will be noble with grace and strength, she will reflect the motherhood of

God, proclaim infinite compassion of the divine maternity, uplift the race in chastity, equality." Carol Norton, *Woman's Cause* (Boston: Christian Science Publishing Society, 1895), 49.

90. Eddy, *Science and Health,* 517.

91. Mary Baker Eddy, *Miscellaneous Writings, 1883–1896* (Boston: Christian Science Publishing Society, 1896), 210. Recently, scholars have addressed what the historian of religion Susan Lindley in 1984 called the "ambiguous feminism" of Mary Baker Eddy. One suggested that Mrs. Eddy's ideal was encapsulated in the Victorian concept of "sentimental womanhood," akin to Brown's argument concerning femininity as feeling; one thought that her vision was an integration of traditional ideas of masculinity and femininity; another stated that Mrs. Eddy's God was androgynous. Susan Hill Lindley, "The Ambiguous Feminism of Mary Baker Eddy," *Journal of Religion* 64 (July 1984): 318–31. See also Gail Parker, "Mary Baker Eddy and Sentimental Womanhood," *New England Quarterly* 43 (Mar. 1970): 11; Mary Farrell Bednarowski, "Outside the Mainstream: Women's Religion and Women Religious Leaders in Nineteenth Century America," *Journal of the American Academy of Religion* 48 (June 1980): 209; Susan Setta, "Denial of the Female, Affirmation of the Feminine: The Father-Mother God of Mary Baker Eddy," in *Beyond Androcentrism: New Essays on Women and Religion,* ed. Rita M. Gross (Missoula: University of Montana Press, 1977). Parker argues for sentimental womanhood as Eddy's ideal; Bednarowksi explores Eddy's notions as suggesting an androgynous God; Setta views Eddy as integrating masculinity and femininity. See also Jean A. McDonald, "Mary Baker Eddy and the Nineteenth-Century 'Public Woman': A Feminist Reappraisal," *Journal of Feminist Studies in Religion* 2, no. 1 (Spring 1986): 89–111; Amanda Porterfield, *Feminine Spirituality in America: From Sarah Edwards to Martha Graham* (Philadelphia: Temple University Press, 1980); Penny Hansen, "Woman's Hour: Feminist Implications of Mary Baker Eddy's Christian Science Movement, 1885–1910" (Ph.D. diss., University of California, Irvine, 1981). Mrs. Eddy's own writings suggest that she believed that women had basic inalienable rights that had not been recognized or protected by law. See Eddy, *Science and Health,* 63. As Lindley summarized in her article ("Ambiguous Feminism," 328):

> On the one hand, some of her ideas might be identified as religiously radical: her dual image of God; her own role as a religious founder; the possibilities she opened for other women, both in terms of religious leadership and of an alternative spirituality; her break with much of traditional—and patriarchal—Christianity. On the other hand, Eddy could be aligned with the "conservative" wing of nineteenth-century religious feminism, insofar as she seems to have endorsed a peculiar (and superior) nature and role for women, just as she raised few questions of the prevailing moral patterns and assumptions of her day. Yet although she argues for a broad and positive impact on society at large from the emergence of women and the feminine, her primary concern and vision were personal, even individualistic, and spiritual. Despite a secondary concern with issues like suffrage and economic rights for women, it is striking how limited were the practical and political implications of her form of conservative feminism.

92. Norton, *Woman's Cause,* 49.

93. I. M. Haldeman, *An Analysis of Christian Science, Based on Its Own Statements* (Philadelphia School of the Bible, 1909), 33–34. Also see Haldeman's "Christian Science and Woman's Place in the Church," in his *Christian Science in the Light of Holy Scripture* (New York: Fleming H. Revell 1909). Haldeman writes, "The woman is the symbol of the Church in submission to Christ, owning His headship, obeying His will, her desire subject unto Him, not giving, but receiving from Him" (320–21).

94. Knee, *Christian Science in the Age of Mary Baker Eddy,* 77.

95. Brown, "Psychological Reasons," 168–72.

96. Joel Rufus Mosely, "Christian Science Idealism," *Cosmopolitan Magazine,* July 1907, 330. For a more complete study of Christian Science and its relationship to Western philosophy, see Henry W. Stieger, *Christian Science and Philosophy* (New York: Philosophical Library, 1948).

97. Elbert Hubbard, *Little Journeys to the Homes of Great Teachers* (Aurora, N.Y.: Roycroft, 1908), 137–38. For a similar viewpoint, see also Hume, *The Superior American Religions,* 81.

98. Campbell, *What Christian Science Means*, 12.

99. See Donald Meyer, *The Positive Thinkers: A Study of the American Quest for Health, Wealth and Personal Power from Mary Baker Eddy to Norman Vincent Peale* (Garden City, N.J.: Doubleday 1965), 46–59. For other treatments of women and health, see Ann Douglas Wood, "'The Fashionable Diseases': Women's Complaints and Their Treatment in Nineteenth-Century America," *Journal of Interdisciplinary History* 4 (Summer 1973): 25–52; Carroll Smith-Rosenberg, *Disorderly Conduct: Visions of Gender in Victorian America* (New York: Oxford University Press, 1985).

100. In the case of E. M. Buswell, of Beatrice, Nebraska, the defense attorney had little trouble enlisting several prominent citizens on the jury to come to his defense: "You gentlemen of the jury, know that he is a man whose personal character is above reproach; a man who has lived among us for a score of years, identified with the country's growth, with all that is best in the country, morally and every other way, a man against whom naught can be said." Quoted in Thomas Johnsen, "Christian Scientists and the Medical Profession: A Historical Perspective," *Medical Heritage* (Jan.–Feb. 1986): 73. For another apologetic account see Norman Beasley, *Cross and Crown* (New York: Duell, Sloan and Pearce, 1952). For other cases after 1910, see appendixes in Beasley's *The Continuing Spirit* (New York: Duell, Sloan and Pearce, 1956), 329–47. See *Harper's Weekly* 41 (Dec. 25, 1897): 1283; other references to Christian Science and medicine include *Washington Times*, Aug. 2, 1897; F. J. Carroll, *Georgia Journal of Medicine and Surgery* 5 (1899): 368; *New Haven Register*, July 16, 1899; "Persecuting a Cult," *Christian Science Sentinel* 1, no. 46 (1899): 6; "A Test for 'Christian Scientists,'" *Journal of the American Medical Association* 34 (1900): 759; Frederick W. Peabody, *The Religio-Medical Masquerade: A Complete Exposure of Christian Science* (Boston: Fleming H. Revell, 1910). On the trial of two female Christian science practitioners charged with practicing medicine without a license, see *Christian Science and the Practice of Medicine* (Milwaukee, 1900); T. M. Koon to Della Pierce, M.D., Dec. 18, 1895, Archives and Manuscripts Department, Chicago Historical Society. See also other important books on alternative women's health/spirituality movements, such as Susan E. Cayleff, *Wash and Be Healed: The Water-Cure Movement and Women's Health* (Philadelphia: Temple University Press, 1987), and Ann Braude, *Radical Spirits: Spiritualism and Women's Rights in Nineteenth-Century America* (Boston: Beacon Press, 1989).

101. See Mary Roth Walsh, *"Doctors Wanted, No Women Need Apply": Sexual Barriers in the Medical Profession, 1835–1975* (New Haven: Yale University Press, 1979); John S. Haller Jr., *American Medicine in Transition, 1840–1910* (Urbana: University of Illinois Press, 1981); Joseph F. Kett, *The Formation of the American Medical Profession: The Role of Institutions, 1780–1860* (New Haven: Yale University Press, 1968); Richard Harrison Shryock, *Medicine and Society in America, 1660–1960* (New York: New York University Press, 1960); idem, *Medical Licensing in America, 1650–1965* (Baltimore: Johns Hopkins University Press, 1967); Martin Kaufman, *American Medical Education: The Formative Years, 1765–1910* (Westport, Conn.: Greenwood Press, 1976); Paul Starr, *The Social Transformation of American Medicine* (New York: Basic Books, 1928); Catherine Albanese, "Physic and Metaphysic in Nineteenth-Century America: Medical Sectarians and Religious Healing," *Church History* 55 (1986): 489–502; Robert C. Fuller, *Alternative Medicine and American Religious Life* (New York: Oxford University Press, 1989).

102. Eddy, *Miscellaneous Writings*, 294–95.

103. In response to a letter to her in 1910, which expressed the idea that there was a "grave need for more men in Christian Science practice," Mrs. Eddy replied: "I have not infrequently hinted at this. However, if the occasion demands it, I will repeat that men are very important factors in our field of labor for Christian Science. The male element is a strong supporting arm to religion as well as to politics, and we need in our ranks of divine energy, the strong, the faithful, the untiring spiritual armament." Mary Baker Eddy, *The First Church of Christ Scientist and Miscellany* (Boston: Christian Science Publishing Society, 1913), 355.

104. See Eddy, *Manual*, 99.

105. Robert Peel, Mrs. Eddy's biographer, outlined this sort of masculine/feminine argument briefly in his *Health and Medicine in the Christian Science Tradition: Principle, Practice, and Chal-*

lenge (New York: Crossroads Press, 1989), 128–33. See also, Peel, *Mary Baker Eddy: The Years of Authority,* 15–16.

106. See Catharine E. Beecher and Harriet Beecher Stowe, *The American Woman's Home* (New York: J. B. Ford, 1869); Christine Frederick, *The New Housekeeping: Efficiency Studies in Home Management* (Garden City, N.Y.: Doubleday, Page, 1914); Christine Frederick, *Household Engineering: Scientific Management in the Home* (Chicago: American School of Home Economics, 1923); Dolores Hayden, *The Grand Domestic Revolution* (Cambridge, Mass.: MIT Press, 1981), 55–58; Kathryn Kish Sklar, *Catharine Beecher: A Study in American Domesticity* (New Haven: Yale University Press, 1973); David P. Handlin, *The American Home: Architecture and Society, 1815–1915* (Boston: Little, Brown, 1979).

107. See *Christian Science Sentinel* 5, no. 9 (Oct. 30, 1902): 140. See also *Christian Science Sentinel* 4, no. 50 (Aug. 14, 1902): 802.

108. Quint, "The Growth of Christian Science," 315.

AUST DUC

FRESH
AIR
INTAKE

GOD IS LOVE AND HE THAT DWELLETH IN LOVE DWELLETH IN GOD AND GOD IN HIM

2 : The Early Building Boom

The Christian Science building boom that began attracting attention in the popular and architectural press in the early twentieth century started rather modestly in Boston in 1894 with the erection of the Mother Church. It gained momentum with the construction of several prominent churches, such as First Church, Chicago, in 1897, and First Church, New York, in 1903, and culminated in the building of the Extension of the Mother Church in 1906. Of these four conspicuous models, the Boston and Chicago churches influenced the designs of the larger urban branch churches subsequently built throughout the country.

The Mother Church

In the late 1880s, Christian Scientists in Boston began to consider building their own church edifice. The congregation had met for several years in rented halls. This was a common practice of new Christian Science groups, who often met in private parlors until increasing memberships necessitated moving to larger quarters. As noted earlier, the first church erected specifically for Christian Science worship was a small frame church built by women students in Oconto, Wisconsin, in 1886.[1] Scientists in Toledo and Buffalo purchased extant buildings from other denominations, while Scientists in Scranton; Denver; Weeping Water, Nebraska; and Jamestown, New York, built their own edifices between 1891 and 1893. These were usually modest churches with Romanesque or Gothic details, featuring short towers. However, most Christian Science congregations in the 1880s and 1890s continued to be opportunistic in the use of various buildings, renting spaces in public halls or acquiring auditoriums from other denominations. By the late 1890s, however, the organization was firmly centralized in Boston and a phase of consolidation began.

The church focused its efforts to find its niche in the religious landscape of urban and suburban America. In Boston in late 1886 a concert was held to raise funds for the new church edifice. Cards were sold and a fair was held to solicit money for the building fund. The *Christian Science Journal* reminded the members, "let no one say as an excuse for not giving, that this is a material work, and that Christian Scientists do not need a church *building*."[2]

By late 1891 the *Christian Science Journal* published a drawing of a proposed combined church and publishing society, designed by a local architect, Arthur Gray, to be built of brick and located on land purchased by Mrs. Eddy. It was modest in size and would cost approximately fifty thousand dollars.[3] Land for the church was deeded to the Christian Science Board of Directors in 1892, and Mrs. Eddy directed the board to build a church edifice there within five years. On December 23, 1893, the board of directors sent a letter to all Christian Scientists stressing the importance of building this edifice. The church would be a "fitting symbol in the footsteps of our progress" and should be "accomplished as soon as possible."[4] However, Gray's design was rejected by Mrs. Eddy and the board, who thought that a stone church would be more appropriate. Competing plans were then drawn by both Gray and Franklin I. Welch, of Malden, Massachusetts.

The question of the style of the church was considered an important one. As an early church historian pointed out, "To have made the church edifice inside and out of severe lines with no expression of beauty, would have been indicative of a rigid Puritanical spirit, repellent to the younger generation coming into Science and looking for that which was modern in construction and decoration."[5]

Increasingly, the Boston church was conceived of in terms of the central position it would occupy in the movement. The building proposed by Gray was deemed not monumental enough to represent the church headquarters. Consequently, Welch's design for a church edifice alone was chosen instead.[6] (Other professional architects, hired later to help complete the edifice, regarded Welch with some disdain, as this was his first commission.) The church would be built with New Hampshire granite, from Mrs. Eddy's home state. The cornerstone was laid on May 21, 1894. The building was located on a kite-shaped lot at Falmouth and Norway Streets, in the Back Bay, in a residential apartment-block neighborhood with few amenities such as restaurants or hotels.[7] It was a decidedly Romanesque-style church, punctuated with a tower that contained tubular chimes and rose 126 feet at the narrowest point of the property (fig. 14).

There are good historical accounts of the building problems that were encountered. Joseph Armstrong, a board member who oversaw the work, together with Edward P. Bates, the contractor for the church's heating and ventilation systems, left first-hand accounts of the project.[8] The many difficulties included rising prices of materials, design flaws in the truss systems, plastering problems, delivery and build-

Figure 14. The Mother Church with floor plans (*American Architect and Building News,* May 25, 1895).

ing delays, and contract troubles. New fireproofing codes—which posed challenges to the builders—had just been instituted and the Mother Church was one of the first churches required to conform to them.

The octagonal, finely detailed auditorium seated eleven hundred people. The interior appointments were the work of Frederick Comstock, who later became well known for several conspicuous church designs. Mrs. Eddy commented to the board that the "costly finish" of the interior was of "a good type" and advised them to make "additional touches" to the exterior. She insisted that the church should be completed in 1894.[9] The church was fitted with art glass windows by Phipps and Slocum of Boston that bore biblical and symbolic images. The rose window on the south side of the auditorium, designed with the assistance of the directors, depicted the perfect "city foursquare" from the Revelation of St. John. Frescoes, illuminated texts from the Bible and *Science and Health,* and other decorations embellished the interior walls. Stunning electric standards were placed on the platform that would support the readers' desks, and 144 electric bulbs lit a sunburst of art glass in the auditorium ceiling, a seven-pointed crystal star in its center. The church featured an excellent, well-built pipe organ, which later became the standard for hundreds of prominent branch churches. The building included offices, a well-appointed apartment for Mrs. Eddy (which elicited sharp words from her critics), and a large Sunday school room with adjacent classrooms. A writer in a 1905 issue of the *Craftsman* commented on the excellent acoustics and ventilation, the modern, simple use of mosaic and marble, and the distinctive rose-colored interior, as well as the "sociability" of the foyer.[10]

The church took only seven months to build (fig. 15). The property and building cost the young denomination almost $250,000. The *Boston Herald* announced that the Scientists had erected "one of the most remarkable church buildings in the city," a structure whose "massive strength" asserted that it had been "built to endure for centuries."[11] One critic underscored this by referring to the church as the "armory of metaphysics."[12] The building was oversubscribed and was fully paid for upon its dedication, a practice that became standard in the movement.

After the completion of the Mother Church, Christian Science building projects throughout the United States began to increase. Most of these projects were small, featuring auditoriums that would seat between 250 and 500 people. This was the first phase of the building boom. In 1895 a Gothic-style church was erected in St. Louis, the first Christian Science church in Missouri. Smaller wood-frame churches were built in Bunch, Iowa, and in Stillwater, Oklahoma. In 1896 Scientists in Providence, Rhode Island, and Rock Island, Illinois, erected small churches, the first in their respective states. Besides building new structures, Christian Science congregations in the late 1890s continued to adapt extant buildings for their own use. First Church, New York, bought a large edifice formerly occupied by All Souls Protestant Episcopal Church. In 1897 over ten churches acquired property and occupied or built edifices. The most impressive of the new buildings was First Church, Chicago, which was the largest Protestant church in the city. Scientists in other large cities were also buying property or edifices. Mrs. Eddy herself bought and refitted a small hall in

Figure 15. Contemporary illustration of the annual meeting of the Mother Church, 1899 (*Boston Globe,* June 3, 1899).

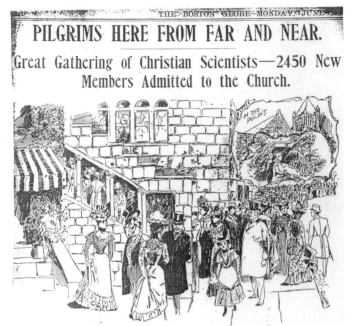

Concord, New Hampshire, her home town. By 1898, over thirty-two buildings, some of them quite impressive, had been dedicated to the Christian Science cause all over the United States. The *Christian Science Journal* announced that "Christian Scientists regard the present as an era of church building . . . known to and endorsed by our Leader, the Rev. Mary Baker Eddy, in words of heartiest commendation."[13]

Several of the early Christian Science churches used the same style as the Mother Church and had similar interior qualities. The church building in Salt Lake City of 1898, for example, integrated beautifully detailed interior woodwork and art glass with a Richardsonian Romanesque exterior designed by Walter E. Ware (fig. 16). First Church, Oakland, designed by the prominent Bay Area architect Henry A. Schulze and constructed in 1901–2, was the first edifice erected for Christian Science worship in California. It was built in a Romanesque-revival style, of lava stone, with stained glass windows and Craftsman-inspired interior details (fig. 17). The large exterior doors were held with elaborate iron hinges, the upper one branched to form the initials "C.S."[14] The *Journal* reported that the Oakland church possessed the atmosphere of a large private mansion. The character of many of these early buildings clearly indicated the Scientists' desire to create churches for new adherents with homelike and comforting elements similar to those of the Mother Church, but with selected features associated with their earlier church affiliations.[15]

Mrs. Eddy did not attempt to control the types or styles of church edifices. Although she applauded the erection of churches, her main concern was directed toward the practical demonstration of the teachings of Christian Science in healing and changing lives. The "Church," for Mrs. Eddy, was a spiritual idea distinct from the "edifices" that represented it. Margaret Williamson suggested that the most im-

Figure 16. Walter E. Ware, First Church of Christ, Scientist, Salt Lake City, 1898 (Holt).

Figure 17. Henry A. Schulze, First Church of Christ, Scientist, Oakland, 1902 (Holt).

portant attribute for Mrs. Eddy was the "churchly character" of a building, "unmistakably designed for religious worship."[16] When students in the White Mountains resort town of Fabyans, New Hampshire, asked Mrs. Eddy to counsel them on the possibility of building a church to be used only during the summer months, she approved of the project.[17] Dedicated in the summer of 1898, this was the first Christian Science church in New Hampshire. However, when the congregation sent pictures of the small church, Mrs. Eddy responded that "they send me pictures of their churches with no spires pointing heavenward!" a reaction that caused the students to request designs for a tower. Next year the tower was in place. This episode was cited as a precedent in the debates that soon arose concerning appropriate styles of architecture to represent the new church.[18]

Mrs. Eddy's opinions about church style were pertinent in the erection of First Church, Concord, New Hampshire (figs. 18 and 19). The local board of directors, headed by a former Universalist minister, Irving Tomlinson, supported the building of a large church befitting the resident city of the church's founder. In 1903, Tomlinson announced that a new church edifice was being donated by Mrs. Eddy, to be built on the site of the small Christian Science Hall that she had refurbished in 1897.[19] The architects, Francis Allen and Frederic Collins of Boston, designed a large English Gothic–revival church with a high spire. The building was completed in 1904. E. Noyes Whitcomb of Boston was the builder. Brick and local Concord granite were the primary building materials. The interior included hand-carved pews and woodwork of Indiana oak. The walls, old rose in color, were pierced by a series of stained glass windows that illustrated Jesus' healings. The glass had been fabricated in England. A reading room and rooms for officers of the church were included, as was an apartment designed exclusively for Mrs. Eddy's use, although she visited the church only once.[20] The original plan was for a $100,000 church but the final cost, supported by contributions from Christian Scientists from throughout the movement, was over $250,000.[21] As Tomlinson later told the architect Elmer Grey:

> That which impressed me most in the noble church at Concord was that it fulfills a type. As I entered and stood within, waiting for the first distinct impression, I felt strength, beauty, historic associations of Christian architecture, and in the midst of it all a simplicity that just escaped severity. Here, I said, is the fruition and fulfillment, in type, of the Puritan ideal—its rugged strength, its unswerving fidelity to conviction, its severe ideal of righteousness, all this is suggested, and yet there is added to it, freedom and beauty. That which our thought is to seek and hold shall be, and is not only the things that are "true," "honest," "just," and "pure," but likewise, what our sterner ancestors omitted— the things that are "lovely" and of "good report."[22]

The Concord edifice inspired other Christian Science architects. First Church, San Francisco, whose membership had been meeting since 1889, decided to erect a building in Pacific Heights late in 1903. The congregation, which met in a Jewish temple, voted unanimously to build a church in a "modified gothic" style. They suggested that a competition among six leading architects, including Myron Hunt, Ernest

Coxhead, and John Galen Howard, would benefit the church, but they subsequently invited only Howard to submit a proposal because the other architects balked at competing. Howard had recently begun work on the University of California at Berkeley. For the church, he projected a large Gothic structure that would cost almost $200,000. However, the 1906 earthquake shattered the congregation's plans to build. The Scientists continued to hold services on the site of their razed temple, with "glistening stars" for a roof. When they decided in 1909 to build a 1,200-seat church, they chose Edgar Mathews, a church member whose architectural career consisted largely of residential commissions. He designed a less-expensive but "substantial"

Figure 18. Francis Allen and Frederic Collins, First Church of Christ, Scientist, Concord, New Hampshire, 1904 (Van Horne).

Figure 19. Interior of First Church of Christ, Scientist, Concord (Holt).

Romanesque/Byzantine edifice, which was completed in 1913 and was featured in the September issue of the *Pacific Coast Architect* that year (fig. 20). Mathews, who also designed the 1917 Third Church, San Francisco, later said that Mrs. Eddy's traditional Concord church had inspired him. Both the color scheme and the use of decorative terra-cotta tiles with floral and cross-and-crown motifs attracted comment.[23] The prominent church architect and gothicist Ralph Adams Cram included six plates showing the church in his 1915 publication *American Churches.*

Chicago Churches

By 1897, the most monumental building yet erected by the Christian Scientists in the United States was nearly completed in Chicago. The importance of this branch church as a model was publicized throughout the movement and congregations of new churches began to choose the classical style to present their public face. The *Chicago Evening Post* reported, "The present is recognized among Christian Scientists as distinctly an era of church building, and the fact that the Chicago congregation has already outgrown its new house of worship—the largest church edifice in the city—is believed to indicate the erection, in the near future, of other church buildings of this denomination on the North and West sides of Chicago. Scores of cities and towns in all sections of the Union are the scenes of preparations for church building on the part of resident Christian Scientists."[24]

In 1895, the growing Chicago Christian Science congregation had moved into Louis Sullivan's Auditorium Building. In January 1896 a message was received from

Mrs. Eddy stating that the time had come for Scientists to own their own edifices.[25] At the beginning of the congregation's second year in the Auditorium, a Conference Committee was established with members from throughout the city to decide on a strategy for action.

Mrs. Eddy suggested that the church be built in a good residential area, but many local Scientists wanted to locate it in a business district. The Conference Committee originally wanted to secure a lot downtown but found it prohibitively expensive. With the recommendation to purchase a cheaper lot, to hold fast to the "divine order" to possess an edifice, the congregation unanimously adopted a resolution to raise money for the erection of a church through subscriptions, with the question of location and building plans submitted to a vote. The congregation was fully engaged in all decisions involving the building of the church, hence a truly democratic organization was being developed. The democratic nature of branch churches, still being worked out by Mrs. Eddy in revisions to the *Manual,* was derived from the Chicago experience.[26]

The Conference Committee selected a site on fashionable Drexel Boulevard near Oakwood, giving as their reasons "the excellent transportation and the fact that it

Figure 20. Edgar Mathews, First Church of Christ, Scientist, San Francisco, 1913 (Church History, Division of the Church of Christ, Scientist, Boston).

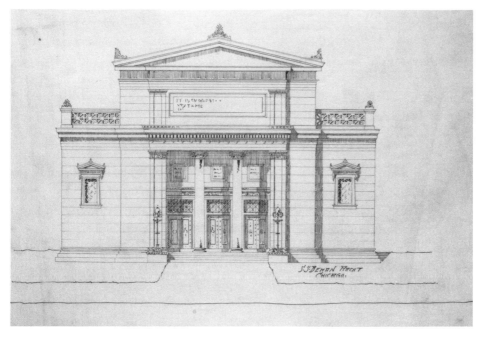

Figure 21. Solon Spencer Beman, west elevation for the First Church of Christ, Scientist, 4017 South Drexel Boulevard, Chicago, ink on linen, 1897, 46.3 × 36.5 cm, gift of Jeremy C. Beman, RX17381 (Photograph © 1998, The Art Institute of Chicago, All Rights Reserved).

[is] one of the best residence sections on the south side." A building committee was also appointed at this time. Twelve leading architects were asked to submit plans for a church to seat fifteen hundred and "to contain a large vestibule hall corresponding somewhat to the foyer in the Auditorium."[27] Each architect was invited by the committee to have an evening meeting where he and the committee discussed the design. The committee unanimously chose the design submitted by the Chicago architect Solon Spencer Beman (fig. 21), and the congregation members concurred. Beman offered to donate the plans, if accepted, to the church, in gratitude for the healing of his wife's invalidism through Christian Science, but the committee declined the offer.

Beman's design was for a classical church, modeled on the Merchant Tailors building he had produced for the World's Columbian Exposition (fig. 22). Charles Jenkins wrote in an 1897 issue of the Chicago *Architectural Reviewer* that the Merchant Tailors Building was a "delightful little bit of Ionic architecture . . . charmingly located on one of the lagoons and was approachable either by water or land. . . . Few, indeed, were the visitors to the Exposition who did not select this little gem, small as it seemed in the midst of such immense buildings, and speak of it as one of the beauty spots of that grand architectural display."[28] Beman's First Church included a semicircular arrangement of tiered theater seating, derived from Louis Sullivan's Auditorium, and a large foyer as requested. In his proposal, Beman wrote that he had chosen the Erechtheion of the Athenian acropolis as a prototype. He claimed that his studies of the basic principles of Christian Science led him to a model that would express "elements of dignity, strength, refinement, and beauty by crystallizing these high sentiments that your teaching inculcate into the architectural harmony," rather than to more traditional ecclesiastic forms.[29]

Construction began after the laying of the cornerstone on April 21, 1897. The church, adjacent to a small park and across from a large parkway, was completed in less than eight months. Exterior innovations were matched and exceeded by interior ones. Beman's church was noted for its excellent acoustics. Also innovative were the tiered theater seating and the open spaces created by the absence of supporting columns, which allowed all participants to see and be seen. The auditorium was illuminated by "electric stars" that lit up the Tiffany glass dome.[30]

The constructing of the church was discussed in the Chicago press, and the building was nationally recognized. It was the first major church to be erected after the Mother Church in Boston, and because of this, interested Christian Scientists and their friends from around the country sent contributions to the building fund, much as they had for the Mother Church. In summing up the building, the local church history suggested, "The beautiful proportions of this auditorium, the graceful curves and noble height of the ceiling, the simplicity and unity of the classic decoration, the harmony of the windows conforming to the architectural lines of the roof and the walls, all combine to produce what the architect sought, an atmosphere of beauty, dignity, and peace."[31]

Figure 22. Solon Spencer Beman, design for the Merchant Tailors Building at the World's Columbian Exposition, 1893 (Chicago Historical Society, ICHi-13690).

The building was completed and dedicated free of debt in November 1897. It had cost the congregation of thirteen hundred contributors over $108,000. The minutes of the board stated that Mrs. Eddy "wished this to be a notable occasion,"[32] so a special dedication service was planned and repeated four times to between eight thousand and ten thousand people.

A year later, the congregation had outgrown its building. Consequently, a Second Church was organized in November 1898, scarcely one year after the opening of First Church. While holding services at a synagogue, the congregation experienced a growth of 200 percent and was expected to fill its new edifice immediately upon its completion.[33] In December 1898, a Third Church was duly organized. First Church, however, continued to be a large and prosperous church. By 1907 it had spawned four more branch churches.

The Conference Committee of the three Chicago Churches of Christ, Scientist, met to consider possible sites and plans for its two new church buildings. The *American Contractor* of April 15, 1899, published commission notices and related that Solon Beman had designed a building for Second Church, to be built at the corner of Wrightwood and Pine Grove Avenues, and the architect Hugh Garden had been chosen for his "competitive plans" for the Third Church.

The Second Church was built rapidly and along the same lines as First Church (fig. 23). The ground was broken in August and the cornerstone was laid on November 20, 1899. On April 7, 1901, the *Times-Herald* published a description of the building in an article celebrating the Easter dedication ceremonies of the previous day.

> The exterior is characterized by a simplicity and breadth of treatment at once impressive and dignified, and is imbued with the subtle charm and refinement of the most beautiful of Greek order, the Ionic of the Erechtheion of the Acropolis, a temple which all writers agree was almost faultless in its art. Ascending a broad flight of granite steps, the recessed portico or loggia is reached. This recess, while serving as a covered way, is really for the purpose of isolating the colonnade and providing for contrasting lights and shadows, necessary accompaniments to the harmony of classical architecture. At either end of the steps are beautiful bronze tripods sustaining the lamps. From this loggia five double doorways of mahogany open into the outer vestibule, passing through which one enters an extensive foyer . . . [so large] that almost the entire congregation can be comfortably accommodated in it. It is a well-lighted and cheerful place, and is provided with large fireplaces. The auditorium extends above this lower foyer. . . . Upon reaching the auditorium one finds himself standing under a noble arched ceiling, in the center of which is a stained-glass dome. This dome is thirty-five feet in diameter, and is richly paneled and ornamented. The platform and readers' desk are placed in the center of the north side, and form the common focus point from which the aisles generally radiate, and the seats bank up. The organ loft is back of the platform and over the readers' rooms, and opens upon the main auditorium in the form of an ornamental, arched, open plaster screen. The auditorium is decorated in ivory as a field, with all plastic ornaments in gold. The most substantial construction has been employed, steel trusses being used to support the roof and ceiling, and they in turn are supported on steel columns. . . . The auditorium will seat 1,450 persons. . . . The foyer and vestibule are paved with marble mosaic and generally

Figure 23. Beman's Second Church of Christ, Scientist, Chicago (*Twentieth Century Magazine* 4, no. 21 [1910]).

wainscoted with marble. There are about 6,000 square feet of mosaic flooring. The windows are filled with handsome leaded stained glass.[34]

The cost of the building, including organ and furnishings was nearly $120,000, but at the time of dedication over $240,000 had been raised for both Second and Third Church building projects. Over 4,000 persons contributed to the building funds.[35]

The Second Church held four nearly identical dedication services, with over ten thousand attending. Readers from all the other branches were invited to read at one of the services, making it a citywide celebration. The services were similar to the ones held a few years earlier at First Church. The *Inter-Ocean* reported:

> There was no pomp, no allegory, no symbolism, no mystery, no ecstasy of appeal in the music, in the sermons nor in the calm exercises. No incense, no candles, no splendid vestments, marked the progress of the dedication. The sunlight, during the three day services, filled the wide space of the classic white interior, and at night a thousand incandescent lamps illumined the edifice. The first test proved the perfect acoustic properties of the auditorium. The great crowds were attended by thirty ushers and during the intervals between services every nook and corner of the building was examined and approved by visitors.[36]

During the services, addresses were read by several prominent officials, and one included a rhapsodic description of the building: "In this assembly there is no one who has mused and loved and worshipped in this great auditorium long before human eye was gladdened by its perfect symmetry. We see it now; like a benediction, an exquisite symphony in form and color, it rests about us all. And yet this dream of beauty was all the architect's own, held in the sanctuary of thought, until, in the very genius of love's generosity, he drew the veil and permitted us to see its stately, yet everchanging, always restful lines and catch the pure melody in its song-fretted dome."[37]

New York Churches

Within the competitive and charged urban environment of New York, to build a church enhanced the local stature of a congregation. This was particularly true in the formation and building of First Church and Second Church, New York. The two congregations first competed for the same site but ended up building within fifty blocks of one another on prestigious Central Park West.[38]

By 1898, both Augusta Stetson of First Church and Laura Lathrop of Second Church, chief organizers of their respective congregations, were fighting over two properties within a two-block span and then the same property on Sixty-eighth Street.[39] Lathrop's Second Church finally bought the Sixty-eighth Street property and the congregation hired Frederick Comstock, a Hartford architect, to design a church that represented in white marble the "city foursquare" of the Apocalypse.[40] Comstock, who had studied architecture under William Robert Ware at MIT, had been employed as an associate architect for the original Mother Church building and subsequently designed several other Christian Science churches in the East and Midwest, such as First Church, St. Joseph, Missouri (1897–1907, fig. 24), as well as many schools, private homes, and hotels.[41]

The building of Second Church began in 1899 with a "congregational miracle." Some members claimed that an incorrect inscription on the ten-ton granite cornerstone had been changed through prayer.[42] After several on-site problems, alterations to enlarge the original plan, and increasing costs, the building—a cube approximately 110 feet on each side—was completed in 1901 (fig. 25).[43] Though Stetson's congregation was becoming popular and press-worthy, Lathrop's congregation succeeded in building a beautiful modern church, with reception areas and offices in which Christian Science practitioners could meet patients from 9:00 A.M. to 5:00 P.M. (a practice officially abandoned throughout the movement in 1909).[44]

Upon the building's completion, the *New York World* claimed that the membership of Second Church was about to occupy an edifice "not often surpassed in religious architecture since the days of classic Greece and Rome."[45] Mrs. Wilson Woodrow, writing in *Metropolitan Magazine,* described the "traditionless, magnificent temple" as one that appealed to the imagination: "Enter that great white marble edifice, the Second Church of Christ, Scientist, fronting the Park on Sixty-eighth

Figure 24. Frederick Comstock, First Church of Christ, Scientist, St. Joseph, Missouri, 1907 (Church History, Division of the Church of Christ, Scientist, Boston).

street, New York City; without, it is purely, chastely splendid; within, glowing with light and color. In all its harmony of matchless material and perfect taste, it is a fitting external expression of inner peace and harmony; but it is more than that. What built that church was not the $550,000 which it actually cost, but a great faith which never doubted and an unwavering enthusiasm which ignored all obstacles." The price tag made Second Church the most expensive Christian Science edifice built up to that time.[46] The church was paid for and dedicated in 1911, the year after Mrs. Eddy's death. According to the *New York Sun,* Second Church, New York, was the second-largest beneficiary under her will.[47]

The prominent architectural firm of Carrère and Hastings was hired by First Church, New York, to build what proved to be the most conspicuous branch church in the movement (figs. 10, 26). It was a lucrative though frustrating commission.[48] The mandates of Augusta Stetson, the powerful teacher who controlled the church, were increasingly grandiose, and the architects constantly had to change their designs to please her. It was what many viewed as a competition to outdo not only Second Church, New York, but also the original Mother Church in Boston.[49]

Carrère and Hastings were hired in late 1899 to build an auditorium that would seat 2,200 on a site at Ninety-sixth Street and Central Park West. Charles Cottrell, a Christian Scientist, was appointed the superintendent of construction and contractor of decorative and interior work. Hastings was responsible for the building, possibly because his wife was a member of the Christian Science church.[50] The firm submitted initial plans to the building committee of the church in 1900. What had begun as a $300,000 project continued to increase in cost, which aggravated both the architects and the building contractors. First, the committee rejected the brick and Indiana limestone specified by the architects in favor of white Concord granite from Mrs. Eddy's home state, an addition costing $400,000 alone. The architects then produced drawings for a $550,000 church with Sunday school and offices in the basement. Stetson and her trustees decided, however, that "Sunday-school children [should] be taught in light sunny rooms." The plans were changed accordingly, and the Sunday school, twenty-five practitioner's offices, and other offices were placed above the auditorium. This necessitated including two plushly decorated elevators, which at the time were an expensive departure in church construction, bringing the cost to $750,000. Seating for the choir was changed and the building

Figure 25. Frederick Comstock, Second Church of Christ, Scientist, New York City, 1901 (Van Horne).

Figure 26. Carrère and Hastings, interior, First Church of Christ, Scientist, New York City (Holt).

committee decided that even the hat and umbrella stands should be more "artistic." There were long pages of complaints from the committee to the contractors and architects. The last major required change was the addition of a pyramid on top of a tall steeple, which was added to the architect's short baroque tower. The pyramid was meant to represent spiritual man. On June 14, 1903, the first services were held in the building, and by Thanksgiving Day, five months later, the church was dedicated, free of debt.[51]

Mrs. Eddy was concerned about all the publicity being given to First Church, New York. In a dedication letter to the congregation, she reminded her followers that the "temple but foreshadows the idea of God—the 'house not made with hands, eternal in the heavens,' while a silent grand man or woman healing sickness and destroying sin builds a heaven-reacher."[52] Nevertheless, this church edifice was by far the most impressive one built by the Christian Science denomination. This was not lost on Mrs. Stetson. She wrote to Mrs. Eddy before the dedication, "The church is attracting a great deal of attention. . . . The edifice is only a type, I know, but a better symbol than the old church, for the love that through us has laid in the outstretched hands of God one million two hundred and fifty thousand dollars prove that much of self-love and trust in money has been destroyed."[53] Some of Mrs. Stetson's students made more esoteric statements, likening the edifice to Stetson's "consciousness of church, extended in symbol."[54] In Mrs. Stetson's dedication address, she told the assembled audience that "from the first inception of this temple, conception has constantly unfolded, revealing greater beauty in architecture, decoration, symmetry and harmony; until the Love which has been manifested as money has reached the sum of $1,185,000," a demonstration of what Stetson called the "limitless affluence of our Father-Mother God."[55] The congregation dedicated the church as a "Tribute of Love" to Mrs. Eddy.

The church was quite imposing. Cottrell described the Concord granite from which it was built as "glistening silvery white . . . so uniform in color and quality as at once to give one the impression that the whole must have been cut from one huge perfect block." All of the white granite used for the building had to be hand cut because of its extreme hardness.[56] Stylistically, the building was a composite design. It was conceived as three large blocks, according to the regular aisled basilica type. The exterior of the central block contained two large fluted Ionic columns *in antis.* A baroque tower, its steeple reaching two hundred feet above the street, rose from the huge central cornice. The side aisles terminated in pavilions that housed elliptical spiral staircases (fig. 27).[57] The central nave terminated in a large rectangular block penetrated by a large window, its etched glass depicting "Jesus and Mary in the Garden after the Resurrection." The glass was often claimed to be from John LaFarge's studio. In the entry hung heavy velvet curtains through which worshipers entered the foyer, which had a decorative floor and wall patterns in several varieties of marble. The interior plasterwork decorations and gilded light fixtures were molded in a Louis XVI style.[58]

Figure 27. Architect's cutaway rendering of First Church, New York City (Ivey).

The readers' platform beneath the organ pipes reflected an earlier arrangement that included a place for a choir. The organ front of First Church was the central motif of the large platform framed in a proscenium arch. The organ case was quite elaborate: the pipes were of Etruscan gold, framed by walnut woodwork, with ivory and gold mounts. Circassian walnut pews and Italian and French walnut decorative carvings filled the auditorium, and there were several kinds of imported marble in the church. The six chandeliers, inspired by those at Versailles, each carried seventy-eight electric lights.[59]

Responses to the building were varied. One Christian Science critic, Omen Washburn, called the church an example of the meetinghouse; another saw in the design the influence of Christopher Wren. Some architectural historians have suggested that the "blocky composition" and sense of solidity showed an indebtedness to Nicholas Hawksmoor or the Scottish architect Alexander "Greek" Thomson.[60] Montgomery Schuyler, the leading architectural critic in the United States, writing in 1903 about new churches in New York, stated that the architect had assumed as his prototype the meetinghouse,

> and a very good substantial meeting-house he has made. We do not know a more successful treatment of this type in New York. . . . It must be admitted that the present edifice is a very favorable specimen of its species. It owes its impressiveness mainly to its unusual massiveness. . . . Upon the whole, regarded from its own point of view, this is a very successful performance. This emphasis of the substructure of the tower is very common in the church work of the British Renaissance. To say that it is as well done here as in any of the historical examples, done at a time when the style was as nearly vernacular as it could become, and when it was the only medium for whatever there was of architectural talent, is high praise, but not higher than it seems to us the building deserves.[61]

Another critic, writing in *Architectural Review,* was more bombastic: "The whole thing possesses a degree of force and power that is astonishing. As for the building itself, it is as clever a piece of evolution as one could ask. There is something of the New England meeting house, something of the French *projet,* a touch of what one might call 'Mormonesque,' and a hint of spontaneous generation, all of which works well together, and succeeds admirably as an architectural expression of a concrete idea that can scarcely claim voicing through architectural precedents."[62] Certainly Washburn summed up the monument: "The result is a building of the highest import at least to Christian Scientists. If we may not speak of a cathedral, in this case, we certainly possess the metropolitan church."[63] Carrère and Hastings also completed a prominent branch church for the congregation of First Church, Philadelphia, in 1910 (fig. 28).[64]

Third Church, New York, was built several years later, in the Georgian style (fig. 29). The congregation had first established itself in Harlem but soon found a building site on Park Avenue, in the southernmost part of its literature distribution zone. It purchased the property for $500,000 in 1920.[65] The cornerstone was laid on Christmas Day 1922, and the edifice, which seated fifteen hundred, was completed in late

Figure 28. Carrère and Hastings, First Church of Christ, Scientist, Philadelphia, 1910 (Van Horne).

Figure 29. Delano and Aldrich, Third Church of Christ, Scientist, New York City, 1923 (Church History, Division of the Church of Christ, Scientist, Boston).

1923 at a cost of over $550,000. The membership had wanted to build a "symbol of beauty," "representative of the finest type of architecture," which "would show it at a glance to be unmistakably a structure devoted to the service of religion, and not a bank," but without an ecclesiastical appearance.[66] The architects, Delano and Aldrich, decided to build the congregation a dignified Georgian meetinghouse. It was a particularly lavish example of the type, with a large glass chandelier hanging in the center of the low dome.

The Christian Scientists in Manhattan conceived some of the most elaborate edifices in the movement, second only to those that would be built in London in the 1920s and 1930s. A competitive spirit of commerce marked these building projects. The congregations were made up of the emerging urban middle class and were influenced by the business ethos of a growing commercial capital. The selection of specific sites in affluent neighborhoods or business districts, followed by the erection of edifices specifically appropriate to these areas, illustrates both the patterns of urban development and the desire of Christian Scientists to represent themselves appropriately as a new religion for the city.

The building and press-worthiness of First Church, New York, undoubtedly contributed to the idea that Stetson was competing with the Mother Church for prominence. By 1908, she even expressed her desire to build a branch church of First Church, New York. Mrs. Eddy responded that the Mother Church was unique and rebuked her in the *Christian Science Sentinel:* "Are you striving, in Christian Science, to be the best Christian on earth, or are you striving to have the most costly edifice on the earth?"[67] Many observers undoubtedly believed that the Mother Church should "go one better" than Stetson's church.[68]

The Mother Church Extension

As early as April 1896, the congregation of the Mother Church had exceeded its seating capacity.[69] By 1901, the movement as a whole was rapidly expanding; 105 new churches had been added and memberships were increasing. At the annual meeting in 1902, a motion was passed by the ten thousand Christian Scientists attending to build a new two million dollar auditorium for the Mother Church.[70] In the words of Judge Ewing, an important Christian Science lecturer: "As we have the best church in the world, and as we have the best expression of the religion of Jesus Christ, let us have the best material symbol of both of these, and in the best city in the world."[71] The congregation informed Mrs. Eddy of its vote and she replied in late July that she was "bankrupt in thanks."[72] By August 1902, Solon Beman, architect of First Church and Second Church, Chicago, volunteered his architectural expertise for the project, through lawyers from Chicago who had connections with Boston church officials.

After successive land purchases, the Christian Scientists owned an entire city block in the Back Bay by 1903.[73] By March 1904, Mrs. Eddy made an amendment to a *Manual* bylaw to prevent the demolition or removal of the original Mother Church.[74] The area around the Mother Church was becoming a revitalized civic center, with the erection of several other prominent buildings, including Symphony Hall, the Horticultural Society, St. James Theater, and the New England Conservatory of Music. The stately Mother Church Extension contributed architecturally to this burgeoning area. The cornerstone for the Extension was laid on July 16, 1904, Mrs. Eddy's eighty-third birthday. The Christian Science periodicals of the day, particularly in 1905, asked for contributions throughout the period of construction. Branch church congregations, many in the process of building themselves, gave generously and regularly to the fund, often giving up their entire building funds to this purpose, convinced that their bounty would increase in giving.[75]

In the building of the Mother Church Extension, the board of directors first used the services of E. Noyes Whitcomb, who had been employed as a builder to complete First Church, Concord. He was impressed by a new Protestant church in Fairhaven, Massachusetts, designed by the Boston architect Charles Brigham, which was recognized as an outstanding new design.[76] Brigham, already experienced in building public buildings, such as the Art Museum in Copley Square, was hired by the board of directors to design the Extension of the Mother Church.[77]

According to Brigham's chief assistant, Charles C. Coveney, the building was considered first as a problem of space, and then as a problem of style. An unobstructed floor area was the most important consideration in the design of the new church. Within six months, starting in June 1903, the architects projected over 150 drawings and plans for a separate huge auditorium church.[78] They finally proposed that the Extension be contiguous with the Mother Church and adopted a modified mosque plan, with a large domed rotunda on a square base. The initial design had been Byzantine in style and included two towers on the St. Paul Street facade that were reminiscent of minarets. The large domes and semidomes reminded some architects of Hagia Sophia (532–37) and the Ottoman mosque of Sultan Ahmet Cami (1609–17). In the design process, however, Eastern features were replaced by classical ones throughout, with the exception of the domical ceilings. Elsewhere, "the revived classical architecture of the Renaissance in Italy" was the inspiration, particularly for the exterior treatment of the dome (figs. 13, 30).[79]

When Whitcomb died suddenly, the board of directors invited Solon Beman to replace him in 1905. Beman's position would be as an associate, but he was hesitant to take it because it went against the spirit of the American Institute of Architects (AIA) rules concerning architectural professionalism and ethics.[80] Beman was an architect, not a builder. Mrs. Eddy implored him to accept and he finally relented.[81] When Brigham became ill and went to Bermuda on the advice of his physician, the board of directors requested that Beman come to Boston at once. This left Beman in charge. Mrs. Eddy wrote Beman and thanked him for his skill and wisdom when he advised strengthening the edifice.[82]

It was Beman who suggested the structure's design be classicized. He chose to minimize its references to Eastern prototypes, because, to him, they connoted not rational but mystical and oriental interpretations. He wrote to the board of directors in late 1905 regarding four dome turrets on the corners of the square domical roofs over the staircase pavilions, which had appeared in the original design. These, he believed, disturbed the dignity of the Extension's "noble form" and detracted from the "symmetrical balance of the central composition." The dome should stand alone. He continued:

> This composition is most inspiring with its massy lines of living force carrying the eye with them right up the soaring dome to the beautiful lantern or belfry which crowns the summit of this graceful mountain of architectural art. Nothing is much finer than its splendid contours, its impressive majesty and the charm of its fascinating variety,—all sufficient in themselves without the aid of forced and extraneous features, which could only tend to detract and scatter instead of enhance and unify its mass and emphasize its greatness, not to say jeopardize the integrity of its art. This building is to take its place among the enduring architectural monuments of the country and nothing flippant or trivial should have place in this stately structure.[83]

Figure 30. Interior, Mother Church Extension (Holt).

Mrs. Eddy herself responded to this letter, saying that it was "quite sufficient to determine the style of The Mother Church building. . . . We all bow to your skill in this matter."[84]

Despite a labor strike over the concrete work for the building, the huge steel and stone structure was built rapidly.[85] The building rose 224 feet above the street at the apex of the dome, which had a diameter of 82 feet. One writer noted that this made it four-sevenths the diameter of the dome of St. Peter's in Rome.[86] The primary building material was Bedford limestone from Indiana. Knoxville marble was used for a decorative facade on St. Paul Street. Like the original Mother Church edifice, the Extension was fireproof, and it exceeded many building codes. The steel construction, modern ventilation and lighting systems, and the huge auditorium seating nearly five thousand drew comments from the architectural and popular press. The building, bearing a testimonial inscription to Mrs. Eddy in stone, was completed and dedicated, free of debt, by the annual meeting in June 1906. To many, it visibly declared that Christian Science had, indeed, arrived as major force in American religious life.

Critics agreed that the interior of the church was a departure from tradition and were impressed by the evenly diffused light and "cheerfulness" of its effects. The interior of the church created, according to Coveney, an atmosphere of "quiet, simplicity, restfulness." Frederick Coburn told the readers of *Indoors and Out* that what the auditorium lacked in picturesqueness it made up for in comfort. He thought the space was restful, the ornamentation conventional and monotonous, but the overall colors warm. The mahogany of the pews was tempered by cool green cushions.[87]

Upon its completion, Mrs. Eddy applauded the new structure even though she never visited it.[88] She wrote, "The modest edifice of The Mother Church of Christ, Scientist, began with the cross; its excelsior extension is the crown. . . . Its crowning ultimate rises to a mental monument, a superstructure high above the work of men's hands, even the outcome of their hearts, giving to the material a spiritual significance—the speed, beauty, and achievements of goodness. Methinks this church is the one edifice on earth which most prefigures self-abnegation, hope, faith; love catching a glimpse of glory."[89]

Newspapers worldwide noted the dedication service and described the new building.[90] The architectural press soon began to consider the importance of this new temple complex, although many writers were highly critical of the Extension's size and architectural style. For example, in April 1907, Harriet Monroe wrote about the Extension, which was represented in the twentieth annual exhibition of the Chicago Architectural Club. Nearly all the entries emphasized classical revival architecture. The focus was almost exclusively on projects representing the precepts of the City Beautiful movement, which advocated the integration of classical buildings with formalized gardens and grounds. Thirty-four architects from Chicago and twenty-four from other cities exhibited designs, most of which met with Monroe's approval. Along with Daniel Burnham's new City Beautiful plans for San Francisco, his firm's plan for Union Station in Washington, D.C., some watercolors of the restoration and elaboration of L'Enfant's Washington, and some drawings and models of other large public buildings, there was a rendering of the new Extension. To Monroe, that was "probably the most important building shown," but it was "the most depraved example of renaissance design, tortured and misapplied. . . . The enormous Christian Science Church of Boston, [is] shown by Brigham, Coveney, and Bisbee of that city. With millions to spend upon a monumental work, these architects have defaced their city with an enormous, domed monstrosity."[91]

Within a decade, the church block was balanced by the inclusion of a large park facing the south facades of the original Mother Church and the Extension, creating a grander City Beautiful context for the complex. As Myra Lord later described it: "The dome of this stately edifice swells out against the sky-line high above the adjacent buildings and by the generous gift of one of its members the church now has a fitting approach from Huntington Avenue, through the beautiful sunken garden which from day to day is a joy to the city dwellers weary of brick walls and dusty streets."[92]

Some critics believed that the Extension, though not comparable with the "renowned buildings of antiquity," effectively competed with Bulfinch's gilt-domed State House.[93] One stated simply that "the dome of the Christian Science Temple is a concession to the . . . American taste [which] inclines strongly to domes," pointing out that all states except Louisiana had capitols with domes.[94] But this, after all, was not a state capitol, but a church whose prominence bothered many critics of Christian Science. Dr. Alfred Kohn, lecturing against the growth of the movement, realized that the edifice revealed the "force of such stupendous magnitude as Christian Science has assumed."[95]

Others felt less threatened by the church and believed that the architecture represented a modern adaptation of style and form that could be utilized in a "church, clubhouse or city hall"—as a universal public architecture. Coburn viewed the Extension as an innovation in religious architecture, since traditional churches still used conventional features such as steeples, "even in districts where they are certain sooner or later to be completely overtopped by skyscrapers."[96] He suggested that the Christian Science church was poised to produce a new modern church architecture. A critic in *Architectural Review* disagreed with him specifically: "For a religion which is in itself modern the selection of a suitable architectural style is a hard problem. No kinship can be claimed with Italy or France; the structure should have been essentially American and essentially Modern. As a matter of fact, it is neither, unless the use of a steel frame hidden away in the stonework brands it American." Certainly the shape of the lot and the original edifice of the Mother Church created difficulties for the architects, and the critic concluded that perhaps these factors were "largely responsible for the bewildering pile of loosely related motive of which the structure is made up."[97]

Other important public commissions in Boston were compared to the Extension. Ironically, Shepley, Rutan, and Coolidge's Harvard Medical School buildings, which reminded one critic of a classically styled "white city of healing," located merely blocks away on the Fenway, were also completed at the time of the dedication of the Mother Church Extension.[98] Apparently, new practitioners in both medicine and religion, in this case competitors in the healing arena, demanded new architectures.

By 1906, then, the classical style appeared to many urban Christian Scientists to be a triumphant expression appropriate for prominent Christian Science branch churches. However, debates concerning the religious and civic values of church styles and interiors emerged soon after the completion of the Extension of the Mother Church. Central to these debates was theorizing about how the Christian Science church would establish its respectability in cities, where it was meeting increasingly hostile criticism. How could the church's architectural presence contribute to the burgeoning North American cities?

NOTES

1. For a brief history of this church see "Christian Scientists' First Church—Oconto, Wisconsin," *Milwaukee Journal,* June 14, 1952.

2. *Christian Science Journal* 5 (1887–88): 427.

3. William Lyman Johnson, *The History of the Christian Science Movement,* vol. 1 (Brookline, Mass.: Zion Research Foundation, 1920), 460.

4. Open letter from Christian Science Board of Directors, Wm. B. Johnson, Secretary, 62 Boylston Street, Boston, Mass., Dec. 23d, 1893, Christian Science ephemera collection, Principia College, Elsah, Illinois.

5. Johnson, *History of the Christian Science Movement,* vol. 1, 429.

6. Ibid., 461. Riding on the success of the commission, Welch designed at least two plans for schools and two library plans, but he did not, as was sometimes reported, design nearly all the Christian Science churches in New England. He did design First Church, Manchester, New Hampshire, in 1902.

7. Ibid., 503.

8. See Joseph Armstrong, *The Mother Church* (Boston: Christian Science Publishing Society, 1897), and Edward Bates, "Reminiscences Concerning the Construction of the Mother Church," personal memoir, ms., 1918, CHD.

9. Johnson, *History of the Christian Science Movement,* vol. 1, 430. For another account see Robert Peel, *Mary Baker Eddy: The Years of Authority* (New York: Holt, Rinehart, and Winston, 1977), 67–72.

10. *Craftsman* 7 (Mar. 1905): 690–91.

11. *Boston Herald,* Dec. 24, 1894.

12. Gordon Clark, *The Church of St. Bunco: A Drastic Treatment of a Copyrighted Religion—un-Christian Non-science* (New York: Abbey Press, 1901), 123.

13. *Christian Science Journal* 10 (Jan. 1898): 653.

14. William Marnell, *A Biography of Francis J. Fluno, M.D., C.S.D.* (Oakland: Privately printed, 1933), 11–12. Pastor Fluno believed that his branch was "the swellest church on the coast" (12). Fluno felt that the church, "governed by Infinite Mind . . . must then express harmony and perfection in every detail and accessory, combining commodious and convenient interior with structural beauty and substantiality" (16). This was rhetoric typical of those involved in the building boom. For a discussion of the building, see Annalee Adams, "Christian Science Church Provides Glimpse into History," *Oakland Tribune,* Feb. 2, 1997.

15. There were some other big-city churches built in the Gothic style throughout the building boom, for example: First Church, Toledo (1900); Second Church, Minneapolis (c. 1908); First Church, Brooklyn (1909); and Fifth Church, Minneapolis (1914).

16. Margaret Williamson, *The Mother Church Extension* (Boston: Christian Science Publishing Society, 1939), 33. According to Williamson, Mrs. Eddy "liked best the beautiful things which she knew and understood" (33).

17. See Emma Shipman, "The History of the Christian Science Church in the White Mountains, Near Fabyans, New Hampshire," undated ms., CHD, 2. The story of the New Hampshire project is also recounted in "White Mountain House," *White Mountain Life* 2, no. 6 (Aug. 11, 1898).

18. In 1905, when Alfred Farlow, head of the Committee on Publication in Boston, was preparing an article on the architecture of Christian Science, he wrote to Mrs. Eddy, asking if she would mind if he included this paragraph: "It is said that when Mrs. Eddy, the Discoverer of Christian Science, was shown a plan for a simple little church devoid of a spire, to be erected by Christian Scientists at a summer resort in the White Mountains, she remarked: I should like to see something on it pointing upward, and out of respect for her modest suggestion a tower was added to the original plan." Quoted in Alfred Farlow, "Christian Science Church Architecture," *New England Magazine* 32 (Mar. 1905): 44. Mrs. Eddy wrote back that she did not object to the paragraph. See her letter to Farlow, Jan. 3, 1905, CHD.

19. "History of First Church of Christ, Scientist, Concord," undated ms., 10–14, CHD. On the Concord church see also "Cornerstone Laid at Concord," *Christian Science Journal* 21, no. 5 (Aug. 1903): 297–99; "Dedication of the Church in Concord," ibid. 22, no. 5 (Aug. 1904): 257–74.

20. See an account of this sole visit in *Christian Science Sentinel* 8 (1905): 54.

21. Peel, *Mary Baker Eddy: The Years of Authority,* 455 n. 7.

22. Elmer Grey, "Christian Science Church Edifices and What They Stand For," *Fine Arts Journal* (Oct. 1907): 49–50.

23. Mathews mentions the Concord church in a letter to an unnamed recipient, Feb. 20, 1936, CHD. The edifice was featured in *American Architect* 104, no. 1962 (July 30, 1913): 45–46, and also in *Pacific Coast Architect* 5, no. 6 (Sept. 1913): 254. On the dedication of the building, including an account of the church after the earthquake, see also *San Francisco Examiner,* Nov. 24, 1913, and *San Francisco Chronicle,* Nov. 24, 1913. Later descriptions appear in *San Francisco News,* Jan. 18, 1930, and Eric L. Larmer, "A History of the Building of First Church of Christ, Scientist, San Francisco, California" (student paper, Community College of San Francisco, 1991). For other descriptions, see Theresa Gordon Beyer, "The Development of a California Style: Regionalism and the Spanish Colonial Revival in Southern California 1890–1930," *Precis IV, American Architecture: In Search of Traditions* (New York: Columbia University Press, 1983), 18–21; Ruth Hendricks Willard, *Sacred Places of San Francisco* (Novato, Calif.: Presidio Press, 1985), 152–53. Edgar Mathews's aesthetic was influenced by his brother Arthur Mathews, who became a well-known Arts and Crafts furniture designer and painter in the California Decorative style. See Richard Longstreth, *On the Edge of the World: Four Architects in San Francisco at the Turn of the Century* (Cambridge, Mass.: MIT Press, 1983), 306–9.

24. *Chicago Evening Post,* Nov. 14, 1897; also quoted in the *Christian Science Journal* 15 (1897): 633.

25. Letter from Mrs. Eddy to Mr. Edward Kimball, Jan. 10, 1896. Quoted in "Resumé of the Establishing of First Church of Christ, Scientist, Chicago," undated ms., CHD. Also see "History of First Church of Christ, Scientist, Chicago," ms., 1939, CHD.

26. See Mary Baker Eddy, *Manual of the Mother Church* (Boston: Christian Science Publishing Society, 1895, 1908) (hereafter *Manual*), article 23, section 10, 74, and idem, *The First Church of Christ Scientist and Miscellany* (Boston: Christian Science Publishing Society, 1913) (hereafter *Miscellany*), 246–47. Ary Johannes Lamme, writing in "Spatial and Ecological Characteristics of the Diffusion of Christian Science in the United States, 1875–1910" (Ph.D. diss., Syracuse University, 1968), notes that "Mrs. Eddy recommended the way that Chicago had gone about establishing additional churches" (163). Also see Bicknell Young's letter to Miss Anna T. Robinson, Jan. 28, 1938, CHD: "I think it can be established chronologically that Mrs. Eddy's statement to the effect that the Christian Science movement is essentially democratic followed the demonstration

of a democratic church in Chicago,—the very first of its kind in the world." On Bicknell Young, see Edward Kimball, *Lectures and Articles on Christian Science* (Chesterton, Ind.: Edna K. Wait, 1921), 11; Charles Braden, *Christian Science Today: Power, Policy, Practice* (Dallas: Southern Methodist University Press, 1958), 328; Kenneth L. Cannon II, "Brigham Bicknell Young, Musical Christian Scientist," *Utah Historical Quarterly* 50, no. 2 (Spring 1982): 124–38.

27. Both committees are quoted in "History of First Church of Christ, Scientist, Chicago," 39. The *American Contractor* of April 15, 1899, indicated that only eleven architects submitted designs for First Church. S. S. Beman and Hugh Garden must have been two of these architects. Beman was the unanimous choice for First Church in 1896, with Garden gaining an honorable mention. Two years later, by the time the congregations were thinking of building, the Conference Committee decided to choose from the submissions they already had. Doubtless the expense of holding another competition was taken into consideration, and with plans already submitted from the First Church competition, the committee could easily find a well-qualified architect for the job. Garden had possibly submitted a rendering to the committee during the first competition. In the *Chicago Sketch Club Annual* of 1897 we find two drawings, one exterior, one interior, of a "Project for First Church of Christ." This is probably the project drawing from the First Church competition. There is no explicit reference to Christian Science; however, the exterior rendering is of a classical structure with a dome, and the interior view shows a low dome with tiered auditorium seating—two elements that became characteristic of Christian Science architecture.

28. Charles E. Jenkins, "Solon Spencer Beman," *Architectural Reviewer* 1 (Feb. 1897): 92–93.

29. Beman also wrote in his proposal: "I was influenced through a study, though superficial, of the basic principles of your beautiful faith, to depart from the forms most common to ecclesiastic structure, and to endeavor to give expression in the design to those elements of dignity, strength, refinement, and beauty by crystallizing these high sentiments that your teaching inculcate into the architectural harmony. To this end I chose the Greek art of the age of Pericles, which is marked by the achievement of the greatest perfection in the art of architecture that the world has ever witnessed, and it is from that order which found such high expression in the Erechtheion of the Athenian Acropolis that I have made my adaptation." Quoted in "History of First Church of Christ, Scientist, Chicago," 40.

30. Quoted from the *Chicago Times-Herald,* in the *Christian Science Journal* 15 (1897–98): 635. As late as 1899, another reporter noted that the edifice was "as well provided for as any church in the city"; in fact, it was "far better provided for than most, inasmuch as its edifice is after a fashion of its own devising and as elegant as it is appropriate." "Christian Science's Rapid Growth," unattributed newspaper clipping, c. 1900, CHD.

31. "History of First Church of Christ, Scientist, Chicago," 43–44.

32. Ibid., appendix, "Additional Items Concerning the Church Edifice," 44.

33. See "To Dedicate a Church," *Chicago Times-Herald,* Apr. 7, 1901, and *Chicago Inter-Ocean,* Apr. 7, 1901.

34. "To Dedicate a Church."

35. Ibid.

36. *Chicago Inter-Ocean,* Apr. 7, 1901.

37. From "Dedication Addresses of Second Church of Christ, Scientist, Chicago," undated ms., Field Collection, CHD.

38. *Christian Science Journal* 15, no. 10 (Jan. 1898): 587.

39. See Doc. 5225, Doc. 1605, Document Collection, CHD. There was also a resolution of May 23, 1898, by Second Church, notifying First Church to stay away from the Sixty-eighth Street and Central Park West site.

40. "History of Second Church of Christ, Scientist, New York City," undated ms., CHD, 10.

41. Comstock was born at Ballston Spa, New York, in 1866, and was educated at Union College, Schenectady, New York, and at Columbia University. He built several commercial buildings, public buildings, libraries, and churches, mostly in Connecticut. See *American Architect and Building News* 964 (June 16, 1894) for his accepted design for First Presbyterian Church in New

Haven. See also *American Architect and Building News* 1066 (Apr. 30, 1898) and *American Architect and Building News* (May 14, 1898) for other Comstock church designs. Comstock designed First Church, Junction City, Kansas (1901); First Church, Grand Forks, North Dakota (1901); First Church, Orange, New Jersey (1901); First Church, Florence, Colorado (1902); and First Church, St. Joseph, Missouri (1897–1907).

42. See "Christian Scientists Say That a Miracle Was Wrought Here," *New York World,* Apr. 8, 1901.

43. See "History of Second Church of Christ, Scientist, New York City," undated ms., CHD, 7. See also *New York World,* Apr. 8, 1901; *New York Sun,* Nov. 12, 1932.

44. See Eddy, *Manual,* article 23, section 11, 74.

45. Quoted in the *Christian Science Sentinel* (Mar. 14, 1901): 447.

46. Mrs. Wilson Woodrow, "Christian Science and What It Means. A Plain Exposition of the Newest Religious Cult, Which Numbers among Its Enrolled Adherents One Million Intelligent Persons," *Metropolitan Magazine* 14, no. 1 (July 1901): 76–83. Though they contributed to national building projects in Boston, as did other branch churches, the members at Second Church were not as affluent as Stetson's congregation and could not pay off their mortgage. Therefore they could not officially dedicate the building, as had become the tradition in the movement. Several very strong missives on correct prayer and generosity were circulated to the membership in an attempt to rectify this situation. See Eddy, *Miscellany,* 201. In an undated document, probably from between 1907 and 1909, a series of numbered reasons told "WHY THIS INDEBTEDNESS SHOULD BE PAID AT ONCE." One of the nine reasons listed was, "Because it is manifestly anomalous and unscientific for a Christian Science Church to be in debt." See Church File, CHD. Woodrow reported that the membership of Second Church was not quite four hundred persons, of whom a very few were wealthy, while many of them were of moderate circumstances. The church represented not only the "extreme of liberality" but also "actual sacrifice and self-denial." Woodrow reported that one member of the church sold her collection of beautiful jewels so she could raise her contribution ("Christian Science and What It Means," 78–79). The two daughters of William G. Fargo, of the Wells-Fargo Express Company, each gave $90,000. In addition, one of the daughters, Mrs. Balliat, gave the church the organ in gratitude for a healing of her young son in Christian Science. Actors and actresses who were members of the congregation contributed the readers' desk, and Mrs. Lathrop and her son "each gave all they possess, reserving only sufficient funds to cover their living expenses, and they have each further pledged themselves for $20,000 apiece, to be paid within two years" (ibid., 79).

47. See "History of Second Church of Christ, Scientist, New York City," undated ms., CHD, 10–15. See also *Christian Science Journal* 31 (May 1911): 71–83.

48. Carrère and Hastings took their 5% for the building, 2½% on elevators and electric lighting and plumbing contracts, and 7½% on interior decorations. They made over $33,500 on the building alone, and with additional expenses they made a total of approximately $52,000. "Church Records, First Church of Christ, Scientist, New York," undated ms., First Church of Christ, Scientist, New York.

49. See Altman K. Swihart, *Since Mrs. Eddy* (New York: Henry Holt, 1931), 6; Edwin Franden Dakin, *Mrs. Eddy: The Biography of a Virginal Mind* (New York: Scribner, 1929), 178. See also Augusta E. Stetson, *Reminiscences, Sermons and Correspondence Proving Adherence to the Principle of Christian Science as Taught by Mary Baker Eddy, 1894–1913* (New York: Putnam, 1913). See also *Letters of Mary Baker Eddy to Augusta E. Stetson, C.S.D., 1889–1909,* reproduced from the Manuscript Collection of the Huntington Library, San Marino, California (Cuyahoga Falls, Ohio, 1990).

50. See David Gray, *Thomas Hastings, Architect* (Boston: Houghton Mifflin, 1933); "Life of Hastings," *Architectural Forum* 60 (Mar. 1934), supplement 26.

51. "History of First Church of Christ, Scientist, New York," undated ms., CHD, 11.

52. See entire letter in *Christian Science Journal* 21 (1903–4): 585. See also *Christian Science Sentinel* (May 30, 1903).

53. Augusta E. Stetson, *Vital Issues in Christian Science: A Record* (New York: Putnam, 1914), 170.

54. Arnold Bloome, *A Voice Is Calling* (New York: Putnam, 1926), 67. For other reactions, see Sibyl Marvin Huse, *Christ's Offering of Spiritual Generation* (New York: Putnam, Knickerbocker Press, 1921), 32, 38.

55. Augusta Stetson, "Church Records, First Church of Christ, Scientist, New York," undated ms., First Church of Christ, Scientist, New York.

56. Charles H. Cottrell, "Description of the New Building," *Architectural Record* (Feb. 1904): 165.

57. See H. M. Riseley, "A New Million Dollar Church," *National Magazine* 19, no. 6 (Mar. 1904): 707–9.

58. Ibid., 709; Jean-Pierre Isbouts, "Carrère and Hastings, Architects to an Era" (Ph.D. diss., Kunsthistorisch Instituut, Rijksuniversiteit, Leiden, 1980). As Isbouts describes it: "The entire configuration reflects an organic flow of load and support and creates the impression of a spatial continuum from wall to wall. The feature of a giant barrel vault gathering the main momentum is stressed by its low point of origin, springing from individual piers on head-level. Hastings aimed at an effect which rivalled the space-gathering monumentality of Roman architecture, similar to intentions he formulated a decade before: '. . . to combine the dignified and monumental character of the interior of the old Roman basilicas with the requirements of a modern church'" (146).

59. See Cottrell, "Description of the New Building," 171.

60. Omen Washburn, "The Architecture of a Christian Science Church," *Architectural Record* (Feb. 1904): 159. For a description of the church, see Robert Stern, Gregory Gilmartin, and John Massengale, *New York 1900: Metropolitan Architecture and Urbanism, 1890–1915* (New York: Rizzoli, 1983), 395. A discussion of the broader context in British architecture can be found in Andrew Landale Drummond, *The Church Architecture of Protestantism* (Edinburgh: T. and T. Clark, 1934), 50. Thomson's classical revival designs were well adapted to the worship requirements of Presbyterianism, also a nonliturgical denomination that needed a basic auditorium.

61. Montgomery Schuyler, "Recent Church Building in New York," *Architectural Record* 13 (June 1903): 527–30.

62. "The First Church of Christ, Scientist, New York City," *Architectural Review* 12 (Sept. 1905): 254–55.

63. Washburn, "The Architecture of a Christian Science Church," 160–61.

64. The *Philadelphia North American* (June 26, 1910) noted that the church, with its "splendid light," was inspired by the Italian Renaissance. The large auditorium had a dome 80 feet in diameter and an oculus 50 feet above the floor. The auditorium seated 1,200 and was particularly distinctive because of the beautiful dull-gold-colored iron and blue crystal chandeliers designed by Violet Oakley, a church member and well-known artist, working with artisans from Tiffany and Company. Carrère and Hastings created what the architectural historian George Thomas has called one of the three best pieces of church architecture in Philadelphia. See Eric Roberts, *Daily Pennsylvanian,* Nov. 5, 1982. A much earlier writer for *Architecture* was not as generous: "Whether the undeniable beauty of the design of the First Church of Christ, Scientist, Philadelphia. . . . atones for its introduction into a city whose characteristics are so purely Colonial as that of Philadelphia, seems to me an open question, and perhaps for any other purpose than that of a Christian Science church it would not have been attempted; but that sect, without traditional architecture, seems to demand that their buildings be treated in a manner to differentiate them from surrounding work, even though the result be inharmonious." *Architecture* 23, no. 4 (Apr. 15, 1911): 168. See also William Edgar Moran, "Plan and Design of Christian Science Churches," *Architectural Forum* (Apr. 1924): 148, and the *Architectural Record* (Jan. 1910).

65. "The History of Third Church of Christ, Scientist, New York City, 1891–1953," ms., 1953, CHD.

66. Ibid., 8. For references to the architecture of Third Church, see *Architectural Forum* 40 (Feb. 1924): 85, plates 17–21. See also *Architecture and Building* 56 (Mar. 1924): 19–20, plates 57–59; "Third

Church of Christ, Scientist Is a Striking Edifice," *Real Estate Record and Guide* 113 (Feb. 2, 1924): 9; *American Architect* 129 (Jan. 1926); Robert Stern, Gregory Gilmartin, and Thomas Mellins, *New York 1930: Architecture and Urbanism between Two World Wars* (New York: Rizzoli, 1987), 163; Eugene Clute, *The Practical Requirement of Modern Buildings* (New York: Pencil Points Press, 1928), 61. G. H. Edgell, *American Architecture To-Day* (New York: Scribner, 1928), 214–17, described both First and Third Church, New York, and concluded, "One feels that the sect is young and its architecture is still in the stage of experiment."

67. Quoted in Peel, *Mary Baker Eddy: The Years of Authority,* 334–35. For accounts in greater depth, see Swihart, *Since Mrs. Eddy,* 59–66; and Dakin, *Mrs. Eddy,* 472–80.

68. See, for example, Herbert Thurston, *Christian Science* (New York: Paulist Press, 1925), 25–26.

69. Williamson, *Mother Church Extension,* 5.

70. Eddy, *Miscellany,* 7.

71. Ibid., 8.

72. Ibid., 9.

73. Williamson, *Mother Church Extension,* 16.

74. Eddy, *Manual,* article 34, 102–3.

75. For example, the Christian Scientists in St. Louis, after spending over $189,000 for the two church edifices for their First Church congregation, still contributed over $28,000 toward the building of the Extension. See "Fifty Years of Progress, A Brief Record of the Organized Movement of Christian Science in the St. Louis Field," ms., 1944, CHD.

76. Bliss Knapp, *The Destiny of the Mother Church* (Boston: Privately printed, 1947), 42.

77. For the history of architecture in Boston, see Douglass Shand-Tucci, *Built in Boston: City and Suburb 1800–1950* (Amherst: University of Massachusetts Press, 1988); Walter Muir Whitehill, *Boston: A Topographical History* (Cambridge, Mass.: Belknap Press of Harvard University Press, 1968).

78. Charles Coveney, "The Designing and Building of the Mother Church Extension, Boston, Massachusetts," ms., 1934, CHD. Various designs were suggested, including a large basilica in the shape of a tau cross, with a large tower; a Byzantine cross with rotunda—one version with twin towers on the Falmouth Street facade, with stairway turrets not unlike those of St. Paul's Cathedral; a huge Greek cross that seated five thousand; and other modified plans based on these ideas.

79. Ibid., 18. Williamson (*Mother Church Extension,* 32–33) claimed that Hagia Sophia had inspired the form of the auditorium, and either Brunelleschi's dome of Santa Maria del Fiore in Florence or Michelangelo's St. Peter's had suggested the dome. Chester Lindsay Churchill, architect of the present Christian Science Publishing Society building, has likened the form of the Mother Church to Longhena's Santa Maria della Salute in Venice. Quoted in Lucille Aptekar and Joyce Cohen, "The Art of Architecture: The Christian Science Center, 1894–1990," mimeographed notes for exhibit, June 1–Sept. 7, 1990, Church History Division, The First Church of Christ, Scientist, Boston, CHD.

80. See Beman's letters to Archibald McLellan, June 14, 1905, and letter from McLellan to Mrs. Eddy, June 15, 1905, gathered in "Documents which describe the work of architect, Solon Spencer Beman," CHD. On definitions of professional practice and ethics, differences between architects and builders, and the increasing standardization of architectural forms and contracts, see Henry H. Saylor, *The A.I.A.'s First Hundred Years* (Washington, D.C.: Octagon, 1957).

81. Mary Baker Eddy Papers, vol. 74, p. 45, no. 10492, Correspondence from Solon S. Beman, Mrs. Eddy, and the Board of Directors, CHD. Also see Williamson, *Mother Church Extension,* 29.

82. Mary Baker Eddy Papers, vol. 74, p. 45, no. 10493. Mrs. Eddy also suggested that there be fewer "picture" windows in the Extension. See Williamson, *Mother Church Extension,* 33. Also see letter, Mary Baker Eddy to Archibald McLellan, Nov. 29, 1905, Papers of William E. Chandler, New Hampshire Historical Society, Concord, New Hampshire; in this letter she suggested that Beman should "decide this question as well as all others relative to our Church Extension."

83. Quoted in "Documents which describe the work of architect, Solon Spencer Beman," CHD.

84. Mary Baker Eddy Papers, vol. 74, p. 49, no. 10494.

85. See *American Architect,* no. 1630 (Mar. 23, 1907): 114, concerning a labor dispute at the building site.

86. Frederick W. Coburn, "The New Christian Science Temple in Boston," *Indoors and Out* 4 (July 1906): 174–79.

87. Ibid., 178. The Extension was featured in *American Architect and Building News* 90, no. 1598 (Aug. 11, 1906).

88. Mrs. Eddy, who had traveled to the original Mother Church building only three times, would never attend a service or actually visit the Extension. See Peel, *Mary Baker Eddy: The Years of Authority,* 321. Adam Dickey, *Memoirs of Mary Baker Eddy* (Boston: Marymount Press, 1927), claimed, "It was a long drive from her home to The Mother Church, and only once did she take the time to drive to Falmouth and St. Paul Streets, and then she did not alight, but had her first view of the Mother Church from her carriage" (72).

89. Eddy, *Miscellany,* 6.

90. See Eddy, *Miscellany,* 65–100, for reports from newspapers.

91. Harriet Monroe, "Architectural Exhibition at Art Institute Limited but Interesting," *Chicago Illinois Examiner* (Apr. 6, 1907).

92. Myra Lord, *Mary Baker Eddy: A Concise Story of Her Life and Work* (Boston: Davis and Bond, 1918), 55.

93. Coburn, "The New Christian Science Temple in Boston," 179. He continued: "Often its lines are softened in the haze that hangs over the city so that it seems to belong, not to prosaic Boston, but to a realm of romance. It is indeed the dream-like embodiment of Mrs. Eddy's grandiose dream" (ibid.).

94. Quoted in the *Springfield Union* (July 29, 1907).

95. Alfred D. Kohn, *Christian Science from a Physician's Standpoint* (Chicago: Privately printed, 1906), 1.

96. Coburn, "The New Christian Science Temple in Boston," 176.

97. *Architectural Review* (Aug. 1906): 116.

98. Coburn, "The New Christian Science Temple in Boston," 179.

3 : The Public Face
of Christian Science

The theology of Christian Science was powerful in its promises and grandiloquence, enabling the church to flourish and attract followers into its congregational life. Christian Science's support of business ideals and women's spirituality in the changing city undoubtedly appealed to many urban dwellers. The city itself was the most visible stage for Christian Science activities, and the church's rapid success in the city led to intensified criticisms from other denominations and the medical establishment. Despite such criticism, however, urban reform ideals supported by Protestant church leaders and sociologists intersected with Christian Science congregational concerns for building new churches to attract and heal city dwellers and resolve their problems. Ideals held by civic federations and city planners, among them City Beautiful proponents, dovetailed with the theology of Christian Science and the concepts underlying the architectural styles of urban Christian Science buildings. How did Christian Science succeed in the city in spite of harsh criticisms? How were its new buildings configured by the urban congregations to suggest reform ideals held in common with other Protestants and broader civic reform movements?

Christian Science in Its Urban Setting

Christian Science emerged in an American culture marked by tensions of increased social and cultural differentiation brought about by the rigors of capitalism, especially increased industrialization, wealth, immigration, and the rise of a mobile, urban work force. As cities grew, the attraction of a better standard of living was greater than ever before in the United States. People moved from the rural areas as techniques of farming required less manpower. The cities offered entertainment, technological advancements, and better distribution of consumable products. Immigrants, particularly those from Ireland and Germany, swelled the populations of cities, joining men and women who moved to urban centers from rural America. Yet, with those who advanced economically and socially in the cities were those who did not. Poverty was rampant in many neighborhoods.

The economic and social crises of the day created economic and psychological anxieties that challenged the traditional American population. In tandem with a broader longing for a return to uncontested Protestant values of individualism, work, and morality in the city, there was a rising "anti-modernism," as T. J. Jackson Lears puts it, whose adherents were ambivalent about newness and material progress and wanted to redeem the Protestant vision of a uniracial genteel society out of secular culture.[1] Christian Science functioned successfully within this social context because its beliefs actually emphasized earlier ideals of self-reliance along with a work ethic. The attention given to practical spiritual healing also had, according to the historian Robert Cross, a special attraction as it "purveyed a singularly straightened version of Christianity to a peculiarly middle-class segment of the urban population."[2] Therefore, Christian Science was perhaps limited in its appeal as it emphasized the importance of maintaining the traditional social cohesion and economic power of a largely Anglo population in a period of economic and social change.

Christian Science characterized itself as a modern teaching, but it held on to long-established concepts of individual self-reliance and the often gender-specific roles of men and women in traditional public and private spheres. At the same time, Christian Science embraced the economic and social progress that challenged these very notions of identity. The values that the Christian Scientists claimed as their own recalled an earlier Protestantism, even Puritanism. But Christian Science addressed what Lears has called the paradigmatic change from a Protestant to a therapeutic worldview, that is, from salvation as self-denial to salvation as self-fulfillment. Christian Science taught that the denial of self as material was a first step in realizing that self-fulfillment was spiritual. Proofs of Christian Science's claims included a regenerated, healthy body and mental attitude, a renewed morality, and a unified sense of spiritual selfhood not fragmented into matter and spirit.[3] Attractive Christian Science periodicals overflowed with testimonies to its benefits.

The growth of Christian Science took place during a crucial transition in American religious life as well. The late nineteenth century was a time of challenge within Protestantism. Traditional Protestant churches were confronted by the changing population and economic class of city dwellers, as well as by the shifts in urban demographics that immigration and industrialization produced. Values that had seemed congruent with the Protestant and middle-class vision of individualism, the family, and the free market were radically challenged by large numbers of immigrants, many of whom were Catholic.[4]

Protestant church leaders filled bookshop shelves with writings concerning urban blight, suffering, and dislocation. Most of these publications addressed the need to strengthen Protestantism's hold in light of influences such as immigration, "Romanism," wealth, materialism, intemperance, and socialism.[5] In her *Message to the Mother Church 1902*, Mrs. Eddy commented that during the last decade there had been a transition "from stern Protestantism to doubtful liberalism," and the 1890s had witnessed the loosening of the old Calvinist grasp on Protestant seminaries with the rise of liberalism. This liberalism became most apparent in the cross-denominational Social Gospel movement and its concern with ethics and solving urban problems. Some commentators, such as B. O. Flower, a Unitarian and editor of the *Arena*, became outspoken supporters of Christian Science ideals and methods of reform. Flower championed the Christian Science movement because he thought that rapid changes in society indicated the need for new social and religious institutions to keep abreast of the times.[6]

Competition and denominationalism among Protestant churches were attacked by many Protestant church reformers, including Josiah Strong, Samuel Loomis, and Washington Gladden, who all wanted a more unified evangelical Christian community in the city to face urban change. The Social Gospel supported by these ministers promoted the idea that a greater unity of purpose within churches was needed if they were to survive and attract new working members in the city.[7] Many believed that the church should embrace the community with a more "practical" form of Christianity and create new buildings to support the effort. As a result, settlement houses and new institutional churches were built and began attracting members.[8] In these new organizations, the traditional spiritual obligations of witnessing and proselytizing were supplemented (or even supplanted) by newer emphases on the physical needs of the workers and recent immigrants.[9] Examples of successful institutional churches were cited and applauded in the popular press.[10] By the 1890s, the Social Gospel had taken hold of a significant minority of Protestantism.[11]

There was no doubt that many people in the city had not been reached. There were those in need of moral and physical ministration—the Salvation Army targeted these.[12] But there were also many new young workers from the country whose moral virtues might be compromised in the city. The city was an especially lonely place for younger single people. An observer pointed out that people's close proximity to one another in the city did not necessarily produce a cohesive community: "It is for the want of inspirational and uplifting social environment that multitudes of young men and women, who come from the country to the great city, become in the city, first lonely, then desperate, then lost."[13] These displaced young working people were precisely those who were attracted to the Christian Science message. As a theology student at the Chicago Theological Seminary pointed out, Protestantism failed to attract new young city dwellers because it wasn't practical, and it separated the sacred from the secular. Christian Science, on the other hand, was attractive because it emphasized practicality and put the sacred and secular in a special proximity to one another. While the Social Gospel had addressed this somewhat, Christian Science addressed it consistently through its teachings and church services.[14]

The Christian Science vision was based firmly on individual democratic choice and American pragmatism.[15] Christian Science championed the idea that the individual could experience a radical relationship with God, and that this relationship was really a partnership. Each person possessed the power of God that could reform thinking, through "spiritual understanding," and affect the tangible reality of the human world of personal and business affairs. This gave younger urban dwellers the sense that they could demonstrate their potential for success in whatever activity they were engaged.

Christian Science theories of social change emphasized the freeing of the individual from materialism.[16] The impetus for reform in Christian Science was the conviction that humankind would be led to spiritual reality by the individual rejection of the belief that life and truth were material. Many of these spiritual verities resembled the practical conservative values of the Protestant middle class, particularly individualism, antiauthoritarianism, and temperance, within the broader ideological framework of freedom and equality. In 1902, a Tufts philosophy professor, Herbert Ernest Cushman, lecturing before the College Club in Boston, suggested that the emphasis on individualism was what made Christian Science so successful:

> In the first place, Christian Science is a reaction from the ecclesiasticism of the present period, and represents individualism in religion. . . . It is notorious that at the present time the denominations are complaining that the people do not go to church. . . . the church has grown more and more hide-bound and formal[,] . . . rigid in worship, and offers little scope for individual initiative. . . . Now, Christian Science represents a reaction against this church traditionalism. . . . New life was demanded, and the dead ecclesiastical shell could not be reanimated. The new wine could not be poured into [the] old bottle. A new church has been formed, in which every individual carries on the worship. No one can attend a Christian Science service without feeling how universal is the worship in the pew, nor can any one attend the usual Protestant church service without feeling how much of the worship is done by proxy. . . . Looked at from a social point of view, the Christian Science movement is a social reform. It represents the protest of the individual.[17]

Some Christian Science commentators viewed the emphasis on individualism as the point of departure for broader social reform. As a prominent New York follower put it: "[Christian Science] ought to regulate the masses and heal their differences. It will do this by regulating the individual. Most great and abiding reforms arise in just this way: and this is the only way. The moment you begin to deal with people in 'classes' and 'masses' you are in the best possible way to defeat the end you seek. Go after the individual, and make him satisfied. Individual happiness and prosperity make national and international peace."[18] Christian Science began to relate to the national religious environment, particularly in cities, by emphasizing a radical theology based in individualism.

In general, the new church had an increasingly adversarial relationship with Protestantism. The areas of challenge and conflict were mostly theological and medical. Christian Science was criticized as heresy and often viewed as a threat to public health.

It was thought of as an interloper or upstart religion. Criticisms of Christian Science increased into the first decade of the twentieth century. Most of organized religion's reproaches centered on Christian Science's relationship to the doctrines of historical Christianity and the status of Mrs. Eddy in the movement. The religion's morality, its relationship to general social ethics, and its implications for hygiene, sanitation, and the care of the sick were also roundly criticized.[19] Civic leaders often feared that health and sanitation laws would be undermined by a Christian Science influence.[20] While few people agreed with the Reverend William E. Blackstone of Chicago that the growth of Christian Science signaled that the end was near, many did note that the church was growing and acquiring property, in both big cities and villages, and building large temples that were filled with educated citizens.[21] In fact, most critical tracts of the movement began with statements such as Father V. H. Krull's: "At present Christian Science wields a wide influence in our country. Costly temples have been erected all over the United States by the Christian Scientists."[22]

What many ministers feared was the success of the new movement in converting some of their congregations' most active members. As the Reverend J. Winthrop Hegeman, a priest in the Protestant Episcopal Church, warned the readers of the *North American Review:*

> The church querulously wonders why so many thousands are leaving it for agnosticism, socialism, and material pleasure when it only has the words of life. To save itself it frantically resorts to every kind of attraction to interest people. It shifts its activities into social, civic, economic, and political reforms, institutes social commissions, urges the federation of national denominations, and proposes very pretty schemes for church unity, and some absurd plans of evangelizing the whole world. The church seems afraid to venture on the purely spiritual life which all people crave. It is as true of a church as of a man, "If one have not the spirit of Christ, he is none of His." Christian Scientists the world over testify that having the mind of Christ is the goal toward which they are daily striving and which they could not find as the aim of the churches they left. It seems clear that Protestantism must adopt this purpose as its reason of being if it would hold and attract individuals of the same disposition as those who have left its communions. It may be many years before our Church will grow into the spiritual conditions which make possible an adoption of the essential contents of Christianity which distinguish Christian Science. Thirty national denominations allied in federation, with twenty million communicants, refuse to recognize it, although it is working for the same end and in a better spirit.[23]

The main opposition to Christian Science came from the medical field, particularly during the first two decades of this century. Bills were introduced into state legislatures to ensure medical regulation, within the widest definition of medical practice, to force Christian Science practitioners to undergo state board tests in medicine, thereby eliminating them.[24] An 1897 editorial in *Harper's Weekly* stated that Christian Science was successful only because medicine was in its "experimental stage, the doctors of which are in pretty constant disagreement with one another." There was no doubt, to Christian Scientists, that the "drugging system" had the monopoly in the curative field.[25]

Though there were intense battles in the courts over the legality of hiring public practitioners of Christian Science to give prayerful "treatments" to their patients, Christian Scientists soon began winning suits, often based on their right to worship freely without government intervention.[26] Reaction by the medical establishment and attempts at legislation were sometimes extreme and restrictive. In 1899, an *Albany Morning Press* article reported that physicians in Philadelphia planned "a national war against the Christian Scientists" to convince Congress to censure the group.[27] As Mark Twain remarked in 1903 regarding some of the legal restrictions being proposed, "If the Second Advent should happen now, Jesus could not heal the sick in the State of New York. He could not do it lawfully; therefore he could not do it morally, therefore he could not do it at all."[28]

Some physicians recognized that Christian Science had the potential to heal stress-related syndromes, the "nervousness" endemic within the domestic sphere of dutiful women. Christian Scientists rejected this idea, arguing that Christian Science successfully healed organic diseases as well.[29] But Christian Scientists were instructed by Mrs. Eddy to submit to vaccinations and to report contagious diseases as dictated by law. Mrs. Eddy also suggested that "until the public thought becomes better acquainted with Christian Science, that Christian Scientists decline to doctor infectious or contagious diseases."[30] But this proviso was not always followed by Christian Scientists as the attention given to Christian Science in the popular press multiplied.

Aware of this growing public scrutiny, most Christian Scientists thought that the erection of church buildings would help to answer criticism and would fulfill the functions of their religion. Particularly in the area of lasting urban reform, charity began at home. As W. D. McCracken, representative of the New York COP, stated: "Their principal charity work is on lines which have never been fully carried out by any group of reformers since the days of primitive Christianity. . . . Christian Scientists are not only destroying the causes of poverty, but are also spending large sums in erecting what are virtually free dispensaries which are in keeping with their faith. They call them churches and reading-rooms, and the latter are open every day, and there those who are afflicted can find help in the most enduring way by learning to draw nearer to God, the source of all health, supply and holiness."[31]

Clearly, Christian Science methods did not fit in well with the Social Gospel. The Christian Science vehicles for social influence were really the *Christian Science Monitor* and the literature that the church published. Christian Scientists, as an organized body, rarely created organized charities but they did open readings rooms. These began as charitable dispensaries that provided free Christian Science healing to those in need and evolved into venues for the distribution of Christian Science literature and ideas.[32] Soon all Christian Science churches were responsible for opening and maintaining Christian Science reading rooms, as one of the more significant and specific adaptations to the conditions of urban society.

However, without quite realizing it, Christian Scientists in urban contexts found themselves sharing some of the same concerns about the city as Protestants, with whom they differed theologically and had little in common. They responded to these concerns with new methods of church work aimed at attracting the urban dweller and through metaphysical articles concerning the city in the Christian Science periodicals.

Many of the models of church work being introduced in the Christian Science church had already been called for by some commentators involved in the Protestant institutional church. The Reverend Andrew Mead, for example, was interested in the appropriate locale of the church; in unifying church interest through publishing; in efficient ushering, standardized services, and excellent music; in the provision of reading rooms, libraries, and temperance societies; and in new architectures suited to these purposes. Uniformity of architectural expression was also suggested as an ideal. While some attention to these new concerns gained support in Protestantism, the Christian Science church had already addressed many of them as part of its overall vision.[33]

The attention given to visitors was one area where the Christian Scientists excelled. Mead maintained that Protestant churches should take their cues for courteous welcoming from retail stores, where ushers were prompt and eager to help and fostered an esprit de corps.[34] Christian Scientists took ushering very seriously. It was, in fact, one of the most prestigious committees on which to serve. Ushers (usually males) were instructed to dress in semiformal attire.[35] In larger urban churches, up to twenty ushers were assigned specific places in the foyer and auditorium. They marched soundlessly into the auditorium as a corps and dispersed with great formality. They stood in rapt attention at assigned places and gestured with military precision to each individual until he or she was seated. The efficiency of the seating arrangements and ushering in early city churches was quite impressive, particularly to visitors to Christian Science services. To heighten the drama, readers were often brought solemnly onto their platform through doors that appeared to open on their own, or through curtains that seemed to part magically for their regal entrance. This growing formality of worship became dominant in the larger urban congregations.

The Christian Science organization emerged at a time when there were acute debates concerning traditional Protestantism's role in the city. It was also a period of civic-minded social movements supported within business arenas, which tried to solidify middle-class values that supported capitalist growth. The urban members of Christian Science, culled from traditional Protestantism, from displaced young working people, and from the world of business, believed that their institution would radically alter the urban environment for the better. The Protestant emphasis on city problems found its adherents in the Christian Science church as well, particularly regarding ideas of evangelizing within the city. Christian Scientists believed that their religion provided a spiritual leavening of science, theology, and medicine and would eventually spiritualize these disciplines.[36] Sometimes even the existing reform movements were construed as evidence of the general influence of Christian Science. The 1908 dedicatory address of Eighth Church, Chicago, took these into consideration:

> We are living in a wonderful age, eye witnesses to the greatest emancipation movement of all times, the delivery of mankind from all evil and untoward conditions. What signifies

the efforts of to-day toward social and moral reform; a wider suffrage, the elimination of unsanitary conditions, the campaign against disease, but the endeavor of a people in bondage, to fulfill their aspirations for a larger freedom? . . . No brighter, no more satisfying promise can be conceived than, that salvation from sin and disease is possible for man here and now. That this redemptive religion is fulfilling its promises, is evidenced by the beautiful Christian Science temples that are being erected throughout the world today, attended by multitudes who have been healed. . . . The church to-day, more than any other institution, is the force holding together the social structure.[37]

Christian Science was particularly successful in cities where citizens had begun to recognize urban problems and institute broad changes through civic federations. These people took as their task the improvement of city life through beautification and legislation concerning such things as zoning and public health.[38] Urban Christian Scientists were part of these reforms but viewed themselves as promoting a religion that would first reform and heal individuals.[39]

Christian Scientists shared in the utopianism of Protestantism, which was articulated as a distinctly metaphysical vision of the new Christian city, related to the New Jerusalem of the Apocalypse. The coming of this city depended on broad cultural and social reforms, including urban beautification schemes, accomplished by a return to a more individualistic form of Christian identity. Henry Drummond's *The City without a Church* of 1892, for example, recognized that the most remarkable feature of Christianity was its insistence that the final stage of redemption was located in the perfect city.[40] The progressive realization of the pure Christian city was to be accomplished daily through social reforms. But Drummond said that these reforms were considered secondary to the "deeper evangel of individual lives, and the philanthropy of quiet ways, and the slow work of leavening men one by one with the spirit of Jesus Christ."[41] With this leavening a new godly society would rise, recognizable in the very ideological and institutional fabric of the built environment.[42] Individual Christians, armed with the power of an ideal vision, could change the city.

This approach was well received by many Christian Scientists who followed Drummond's writings. They believed that the vision of the perfect city could be realized through a radical overturning of a material sense of the city by affirming what they believed to be the spiritual reality of the kingdom of God present here and now. Their church edifices were the very signs that the city was improving. An often grand vision for the possibility of the metropolis motivated the memberships. For example, First Church, New York, was for a time the center of a group that believed that New York City itself was from its early settlement the New Jerusalem. The group supported the idea that the "Harlem property rights" of the original English and Dutch settlers should be recovered. New York would become the property of the rightful "Anglo-Israelites."[43]

Christian Scientists also agreed with most Protestant Christians that the church should become the principal site for the inculcation of moral values that would change the city. They viewed their church edifices as places to hear the Word that would transform people into moral citizens, who would then practice their religion in the world. Armed with what they believed was the metaphysical foundation for healing the ills of humankind, the Christian Scientists created distinctive worship services and rituals within their inspired architectural styles, conceived their new society, and believed that they could transform the old one.

An Architecture of Urban Reform

Particularly significant in the relationship of Christian Scientists to urban reform were their new classical branch churches, whose emergence paralleled the view by architects and city planners that architecture was therapeutic. Urban Christian Science congregations soon entered, however peripherally, into the civic reform debates concerning the beautification of the city and the role of civic architectures in the creation of moral citizens. As the *Christian Science Journal* reported in 1903, where a Christian Science church was built, the community felt both the "blessing" and "rebuke" of its uplifted character and responded by becoming more honest and sincere. This also extended to the entire Christian Science community, who then had a "visible expression to the world of the power, might, majesty, and stability of [divine] Mind, and its applicability to human need."[44]

New civic federations that sought to improve the moral and physical structures of the city were established throughout the 1890s. Some of their leaders feared the increasing influence of Christian Science as a threat to public health. As Christian Science built its way into the urban environment, more often than not utilizing the rational classical style suggested by city reformers for public buildings, secular leaders of these reform groups felt it necessary to distance their concerns from those of the new religion. Charles Zueblin, founder of the Northwestern University settlement house (1891), one-time president of the American League for Civic Improvement (1901–2), and a popular "civic revival" speaker, believed that Christian Science was a new Epicureanism and, as such, focused too much attention on the physical welfare of the individual. In 1908 he wrote, "There are broad-minded people in the Christian Science churches; there are very kindly people, and socially disposed people; their positive contribution is found in the denial of the time-honored conception that virtue is inevitably associated with pain; but their complacent, personal satisfaction with health, physical or spiritual, interferes with social service and social organization."[45] He and other progressives believed that "the uplift of American cities" could be accomplished through broad social reforms that would create a heaven on earth.[46]

The Christian Science goal of improving the urban environment through the erection of churches was to be accomplished through reliance upon many of the same values that civic federations suggested—business efficiency, commitment to purpose, confidence of method, even patriotism. However, the Christian Science approach and justifications were theological rather than secular: the Scientists claimed that they would also produce the New Jerusalem, but through metaphysical means.

Nonetheless, the fact that Christian Science attracted numerous church members interested in civic reform undoubtedly confused many critics who thought the Christian Science approach was simplistic and nonsensical. For example, though Jane Addams's Hull-House usually avoided denominational affiliations, the settlement's Women's Club had as one of its first speakers a Christian Scientist, who at the close of a lengthy address declared, "When you are out at night, just as the sun is setting and you go down to the river and notice the odors which arise from it, you must think of the pine trees and how they smell and say to yourself, 'Oh! what a lovely evening; how sweet everything smells!'" As Ray Ginger commented concerning the scene: "An elderly German woman, well acquainted with the slimy stream, arose and remarked: 'Vell, all I can say is if dot woman say dot river smell good den dere must be somthing de matter with dot woman's nose.' The club members roared with approval."[47]

To Christian Scientists the church edifice most often stood as a reminder that Christian Science had healed them and offered a new method for spiritual growth. Church edifices were material signs of their spiritual conception of church. They were "lighthouses" guiding people away from materialism, "object-lessons" to the "weary and heavy-laden." As a *Christian Science Sentinel* author put it in 1902: "Their development marks an epoch of freedom from the world's bondage to sin and sorrow."[48] The church edifice itself, then, became a significant component of reform, a place for individual inspiration, and a beacon of social and civic enlightenment.

To Christian Science congregations, then, the building of an edifice was of utmost importance as it represented the metaphysical idea of "Church." As reported in an issue of the *Christian Science Journal,* "The church structure exists first as an idea, separate from any material environment, and is seen to be an offspring or product of Mind, protected and perfected by Mind in all its needs and requirements; and hence it becomes a harmonious demonstration,—a marvel to mortal sense, expressing beauty, symmetry, and substantiality,—an abiding place of comfort and peace for spiritual study and refreshment."[49]

This discussion of Christian Science architecture from within the movement was typical of much of the general architectural discourse concerning all churches of the period. The church edifice solidified the idea that Christian churches should raise both the aesthetic and moral values of the entire community. Speakers at Christian Science church dedication ceremonies often directed attention to the contribution made by the new edifice to the city as a whole, and the buildings were often located next to lovely parks and boulevards.[50] To Christian Scientists, the edifice was more than a symbol; it was believed to be effective in the moral as well as the aesthetic realm. They believed that the environmental beauty exemplified by their buildings could help heal social problems in the city through their order and uniformity. Such a claim was not unique to Christian Science architecture. It was similar to the fundamental precepts of the City Beautiful movement at that time, which profoundly influenced American discussion about the moral improvement of urban citizens through the creation of a new and unified physical fabric of the city.[51]

Generally, it was thought by City Beautiful proponents that civic and other public buildings that were stylistically unified and beautiful would constantly remind the individual urban citizen of the benevolence and democratic roots of political and social power. Similarly, Christian Science notions followed Charles Mulford Robinson's ideals that beautiful city spaces would "awaken" in urban dwellers their "high desires that had before been dormant," making better, more moral, even purer citizens.[52] As Zueblin put it, "If the architecture of the schoolhouse, its decorations and surroundings, impress the child mind with the meaning of the beautiful, he will demand as a citizen a fairer city. The modern community is burdened with the responsibility of great possessions, and may enrich itself both materially and spiritually by building stately mansions."[53] The classical forms that American architects were producing in that era suited this purpose because they were simple, grand, and not excessively ornamented. The classical style was also a "flexible" architecture that could be used for a number of public building types.[54] Sociologists agreed. Robert Park suggested that the classical style was an excellent urban style because it influenced positively the behavior of city dwellers.[55]

City Beautiful was Daniel Burnham's urban renewal movement based on the success of the 1893 World's Columbian Exposition in Chicago as a model for a civilized city. It promoted urban spaces defined by wide boulevards, lined with grand classical buildings flanked by gardens and open spaces. Christian Scientists aligned themselves with the projected unity of the public cityscape, believing that their churches would raise the moral and aesthetic standards of urban dwellers and contribute visually to the city as a whole—other City Beautiful ideals. Although City Beautiful was a secular movement, it grew out of some of the same religious tendencies from which Christian Science developed. Daniel Burnham's early membership in the Swedenborgian Church of the New Jerusalem and its relationship to his most prominent City Beautiful projects and ideals has yet to be fully addressed. Certainly Christian Science has sometimes been thought similar to Swedenborgianism.[56]

The origin of urban Christian Science building plans and the grandiose visions of Chicago theorized in Burnham and Bennett's 1909 *Plan of Chicago* arose from a common source—the World's Columbian Exposition (fig. 31). The Chicago Plan, a utopian projection of a new Chicago, promoted civic architectures similar to those in the ancient cities of Athens and Rome. Much like Burnham's ideals, the tenets of Christian Science suggested that spiritual order could be brought out of material chaos through the erection of church buildings. In the *Plan of Chicago,* Burnham suggested that churches were "visually not architecturally important" in larger city planning schemes, but he prophesied that "in the coming times, the spirit of unity will draw people together in religion as well as in business, and such a syndication of religious effort will prevail as shall find expression in permanent buildings devoted to the moral advancement of all people."[57] Christian Science periodicals of this era reveal that many Christian Scientists viewed their church as this new "syndication," and the diversity of the membership's earlier Protestant religious affiliations seemed to underpin this idea.

Christian Science buildings and their relationship to the unity of public architecture had an important relation to the renewed interest by business people, sociolo-

Figure 31. S. S. Beman, Mines and Mining Building on the Court of Honor at the World's Columbian Exposition, 1893 (Chicago Historical Society, ICHi-23166).

gists, and ministers alike in the status of the city in American society, where new institutional architectures were thought of as a means to improve public morality. The classical style endorsed by civic visionaries such as Daniel Burnham and Charles Zueblin symbolized the control of civic power by various governmental and social institutions. Christian Science churches in many cities were located so they would be part of larger ensembles of civic architecture.

The religious and social functions of urban church buildings as well as the religious values of style became increasingly debated in the architectural press during the Christian Science building boom. While many Christian Scientists believed their theology supported the ideals of civic reformers, other church members were skeptical about the use of a unified style to express a religion characterized by a self-reliant individualism, configured in Christian Science to mean "man governed by his Maker." To them, styles and designs of church architecture should be an individual congregational affair, though the success of certain styles in establishing Christian Science's differences from traditional churches was nonetheless attractive.

Christian Science and Protestant Church Architecture

Christian Science church architecture emerged during an identity crisis in religious architecture in general. This crisis concerned the changing function of the church in the city and the rise of non-Protestant religions. Many religious groups debated the religious and social values of architectural styles in establishing a religion's public identity. Many chose historical styles based on the ethnicity of its members. For instance, many of the first synagogues built in the United States were in the classical revival style popular in the 1820s and therefore not specifically identifiable as synagogues. However, by the 1870s, a Moorish revival style dominated many Jewish synagogue designs. By the 1890s, prominent Jewish congregations began to experiment with central-plan Byzantine and classical designs, also intended to recall the Middle Eastern origins of the Jewish people.[58]

By the 1850s, most American Catholic congregations chose segregated "ethnic" styles, based on conscious and specific stylistic reiterations from their histories in Ireland or continental Europe. However, by the 1890s, territorial parishes were established that privileged geography over ethnicity; Chicago classicism inspired by the World's Columbian Exposition became popular, and wealthier Catholic merchants began to suggest styles that accommodated to broader American stylistic tastes. In the early century, Catholic styles were also influenced by changing theology, liturgical reforms, and the power of individual priests and prelates. Urban Catholic churches became stylistically eclectic, and were usually Byzantine, Romanesque, or classical in style. Nonetheless, they all emphasized the Catholic continuity with historical Christendom.[59] On the interiors, axiality and hierarchy were important design elements due to the sequential nature of the liturgy of the Mass. Ornamentation also became quite complex and contributed to the mysticism and transcendence associated with Catholic worship. Firms such as the New York–based Rambusch craftsmen created rich didactic decorations for the more affluent congregations.[60]

Protestant church architecture in this "Gilded Age" was experiencing its own identity crisis. The cities filled with immigrants while the older, wealthier, and more prominent members of the Protestant community moved to the suburbs. Many churches faced a loss of authority and social influence. New church buildings were being built in these suburban areas, even though many of the older urban congregations were declining. The shift in location and the changing social functions of many Protestant churches demanded new buildings with room for an increasingly large number of educational and social activities. The creation of "tabernacles" and institutionalized churches was sometimes lamented by architects because it meant abandoning traditional or at least recognizable ecclesiastical forms.

Christian Scientists and traditional Protestants agreed that all community structures should relate directly to the needs of city dwellers. Many urban Protestant churches, particularly institutional churches, built new edifices or parish houses to accommodate their new methods of church work in the city. Because of space constraints, many of these congregations often built multiple-story buildings and chose styles that harmonized with the surrounding apartment blocks of the city. A striking aspect of late nineteenth-century United States church design was the increasingly civic nature of the buildings—some even resembled large theaters rather than traditional sanctuaries. Nelson and Van Wagenen's Bethany Memorial Chapel of the

Madison Avenue Reformed Church, New York, for example, had some ecclesiastical symbols on its Gothic brick facade but was described as "Plain in exterior and free from unnecessary interior decoration." It contained "ample assembly halls, airy rooms for clubs, classes, reading and social gatherings, a fine gymnasium with baths and all modern appliances, and provides unusually fine apartments for the large day nursery."[61]

There were increasing calls from the pulpit to create new religious buildings that provided better settings and ideals of worship. As Henry Potter told the readers of the *Forum Magazine,* the number of often inexpensive churches indicated a significant decline of interest in things spiritual:

> We have little reverence, because we have but a poor environment in which to learn it. The vast majority of church buildings in America are utterly unsuggestive of the idea of worship. There is nothing in them to hush speech, to uncover the head, to bend the knee. [But] we have been seeing a development of domestic, civic, and commercial architecture of the most costly and grandiose kind. I have been told that the costliest building in America is that which houses a life insurance company. . . . There is something, when we stop to think of it, in the relative cost and thought that men spend on the places in which they sleep, and eat, and lounge, and trade—on a club, a hotel, a theatre, a bank—on the one hand, and on a house for the worship of the Arbiter of one's eternal destiny on the other, which must strike an angel, if he is capable of such an emotion, with a sense of pathetic humor.[62]

One ecclesiastic observed that this was an age "not of cathedrals but of hospitals."[63] Office buildings were also overtaking churches in visual prominence. W. L. George exclaimed about "a big office building and a little church; what a change since the Middle Ages!"[64]

Due to denominationalism, there were more Protestant church buildings than were needed, and many of these were functionally outdated.[65] As Stephen Hasbrouck pointed out, frequently the older church architecture and technologies governing functions such as acoustics, ventilation, and heating were antiquated, and therefore less and less desirable. He suggested:

> Organized Christianity has thus been guilty of wasting or misplacing [an] enormous sum by reason of religious differences, divisions and sectarianism. . . . After the churches are built they must be supported. The needless duplication of church buildings involves a serious economic waste which amounts to the enormous sum of at least $100,000,000 per annum. Eliminate needless duplication, eliminate the spirit of competition which accounts in large measure for the erection of so many unnecessary churches, and robs many communions of that dominant influence which is imperatively needed.[66]

With the Protestant flight to the suburbs, a general competition of ideas about church architecture began to emerge. Howard Alan Bridgeman suggested in the *Andover Review* that the building of new suburban churches had actually begun to degenerate into an "unwholesome" and even "scandalous" contest for wealthy members, which prompted Josiah Strong to comment that the energies absorbed in church fairs and suppers caused church members to "lose sight of the real object of the church."[67]

Critics said that the new Christian Science edifices demonstrated that the religion enjoyed a measure of prosperity because its members voluntarily contributed all that was needed to their projects, without traditional church fairs and bazaars. By 1912, one account, probably inflated, claimed that the Christian Scientists had invested between twenty-five and twenty-eight million dollars in church property and buildings, without any public appeals for funds.[68] These churches were usually paid for in less than a decade after their erection. When asked "Why build more churches, when those [Protestant churches] already built are not full?" the *Christian Science Journal* replied, "Because each one represents the belief regarding the Supreme Being of those who occupy it. And as individuals rise to a higher conception of God, they must build and express what they believe and can prove to be true."[69]

Because of their many successes, Christian Scientists became somewhat captivated with reporting their own growth. By 1899, the *Christian Science Journal* and the *Christian Science Sentinel* began to publish descriptions of buildings and church dedications. Mrs. Eddy stopped this practice in 1903 with a *Manual* bylaw but by 1906 she allowed for the inclusion of descriptions of edifices excerpted from popular periodicals. By 1908 she forbade numbering the membership and publishing membership statistics.[70] She believed that "only by the modesty and distinguishing affection illustrated in Jesus' career, can Christian Scientists aid the establishment of Christ's kingdom on the earth."[71] However, the increased visibility of the religion caused Scientists to defend their building boom.

The *American Architect and Building News* reported on what some architects perceived as the bankruptcy of style in most new cross-denominational church architecture:

> To many, churchly traditions in architecture mean nothing, and the monstrosity that is part club-house, part town-hall, and a wee bit church is to them the nineteenth-century sanctuary in its most successful development. That every artistic and beautiful effect is lost in it, is a very secondary matter. It seems to be a widely accepted opinion that, if in the building of a church every accepted law of good taste is set at naught, every established canon of art is violated, then, on the mere face of it, that church must have broken away from the soul-fettering thoughts of past ages, and stand for advanced ideas and progress. A church can be well designed, its style can be pure and dignified and it can yet meet the requirements of the modern church life of to-day.[72]

The problem, evidently, was the ecclesiastical expression of concern over a crisis of secularization in late nineteenth-century American urban culture. In an illustrative denunciation, a *Chicago Interior* article in 1896 described a new church that resembled, in the author's view, a rather plain water-pumping station. The article suggested that some denominations had lost sight of their purpose and that this was reflected in the very "bricks and mortar": "What they don't know is so much more prominent in their preaching than what they do know that the church has no longer a font, an altar, or a spire. When the pulpit ceases to present heavenly themes, there is no reason why the building should be distinguished from secular markets, or banks, or cattlesheds. It will be needed for one or the other of these uses before long."[73]

Debates in professional journals on the appropriate architecture for churches were particularly acrimonious as a number of important ecclesiastical building commissions were being decided upon at this time. For example, in the 1890s several styles were suggested for the Episcopal Cathedral Church of St. John the Divine in New York City. Ralph Adams Cram's Gothic style was finally chosen, though not without controversy.[74] Examples of Christian Science churches were often considered in these debates on style.[75] In 1903, Montgomery Schuyler contributed to the *Architectural Record* a series of articles on the state of recent sacred architecture in New York, giving particular attention to Carrère and Hastings's First Church of Christ, Scientist, New York, as a new model for the metropolitan church. Although impressed by the new church, Schuyler quipped, "What is the right architectural expression of Christian Science we do not pretend to know. Neither, apparently, does the architect of this edifice."[76]

As more Christian Science edifices began to appear, pointed comments emanated from the traditional pulpits and the medical profession concerning the building boom. The Reverend Andrew Underhill, for example, recognized that Christian Science's acquisition of property indicated a response to the city that was different from that of voguish religions such as Spiritualism or Theosophy. Underhill warned that the Christian Scientists were "erecting temples of brick and stone—the permanent symbols of its determination to stay."[77] Some observers offered harsher criticism. One person asked, "Why do 'Christian Scientists'—carrying [their] principles to last results . . . build costly temples, splendidly elaborate in material substance,—brick, stone, mortar, and the rest,—in which to teach [the] renunciation of the thralldom of things?"[78] The Reverend Charles Locke charged that calling Christian Science edifices "churches" was a "gross impertinence." He said that they were "no more churches than are Buddhist temples or Chinese pagodas."[79]

One particularly severe criticism of the new buildings was leveled by the Reverend A. C. Dixon, who wrote: "Christian Scientists lavish their wealth upon buildings of stone and adorn them, that they may gratify their own aesthetic tastes. And why not? [They believe] the sickness, the pain, the impure atmosphere . . . are illusions."[80] However, even the most reactionary critics recognized that the new churches of the Christian Scientists were "some of the handsomest edifices of worship in the land."[81]

Whatever their views of Christian Science itself, architecture critics could not ignore the impact of so many impressive and conspicuous buildings around the nation, and they expressed a certain ambivalence about them. For example, an article in a 1906 issue of *American Architect and Building News* reported that a tour bus had overturned and injured several of the occupants, all Christian Scientists. The author suggested wryly that the injured Scientists would no doubt resort to an ordinary physician to set their bones. Nonetheless, he could not suppress his admiration for the extraordinary architecture of the newly completed Extension of the Mother Church. He concluded:

> Of all the religious cults that have waxed and waned in this country none has been so inexplicable as that of the Christian Scientists . . . because it has manifested its existence with such abundant architectural vehemence. It is only some twenty-five years, we believe, since "Mother Eddy" began to deliver her messages, and yet, scattered through the larger cities, there are already a score or more of church edifices erected to the glory of Christ, Scientist, with all the art their several designs could command and, seemingly, with a total disregard of economy and cost. . . . It is extraordinary; but it is the architect's duty to solve the problem his client brings him, even should it be to build an amphitheatre for the audience at a select suttee.[82]

Critical comments reached the pages of the popular press. For instance, the *Springfield Union* (Illinois) in 1907 told its readers that the old-fashioned church steeple was disappearing. As examples, the article mentioned several New York churches, such as McKim, Mead, and White's 1906 classical Madison Square Presbyterian Church, as well as the same Christian Science church on Central Park West and Ninety-sixth Street mentioned by Schuyler.[83]

Many conceded that the style and character of a church edifice revealed something about a denomination's position concerning modern life. As Stephen Hasbrouck wrote in 1912, comparing a traditional church with a newly built Christian Science edifice:

> On a broad avenue, in a choice residential section of one of our large cities, are two churches facing each other from opposite street corners. One of these churches was built years ago and is ivy covered; the other is a new church to which the finishing touches are being given. The facade of the one is of red brick, of the other Indiana limestone. The style of architecture of the red brick church is composite, with no particular order predominating, unless perhaps a suggestion of English Gothic; that of the other is Romanesque. The striking feature architecturally of the brick church is a massive square tower, broad and nearly one hundred feet high; the conspicuous feature of the other church is an immense dome. The dissimilarity in external appearance is paralleled by differences in the interior construction. The ceiling of the auditorium of the older church is supported by massive columns which obstruct the view. The roof of the newer church, is supported by a great framework of steel girders and trusses which free the auditorium from interior supports. The lobby of the tower church is small and barely sufficient for ingress and egress; the lobby of the other church extends the entire width of the avenue in front of the building and will allow more than half the audience to meet in social converse at the conclusion of the service. . . . On the one side of the avenue meetings are held, frequented by a fraction of the membership. Across the avenue the meetings, both Sunday and mid-week, tax the seating capacity of the edifice.[84]

Debates on the religious power of the style of new churches increased with the growing popularity of Ralph Adams Cram, who was not only an architect but a prolific writer and speaker of the day. James McBaker, in the foreword to Cram's 1915 *American Churches,* reiterated that the traditional church had become "apathetic in its indifference to its housing and its appointments"; the increased denomination-alism and lack of unity in the Christian church were among the factors responsible for the variety of church plans.[85]

Cram believed, in common with many architects, that religious architecture was the highest expression of public art. He thought that architecture also had the pow-er to transform people into responsible and spiritually informed citizens. Religious architecture, symbolizing spiritual relationships in solid architectural form, also could produce lasting healthful and spiritual effects in the public sphere. To Cram, the Gothic style represented the historical Christian spirituality that could create an at-mosphere of healing needed in modern society. He rejected many modern scientific insights as problematic and was increasingly attracted to "nonrational" ways of think-ing. For instance, one modern writer has noted that Cram "appreciated the fervent faith of Mrs. Mary Baker Eddy" even though "some of the particulars of her Chris-tian Science religion were repugnant to him."[86] Cram soon commended the Chris-tian Scientists' use of the "modern classic."[87]

Cram argued that the Gothic style would help unify Christians and enable them to create a rebirth of the true primitive Christian community. At first Cram declared that only the Catholics and Episcopalians should use the Gothic style, but later he stated that the style was "a kind of missionary force for the achievement of Chris-tian unity." To him, only the mysterious, subjective side of Christian Science was served by Gothic architecture. His book *American Churches* included Christian Sci-ence church designs by Edgar Mathews and Elmer Grey, both of whom promoted the use of traditional ecclesiastical styles.[88]

Other growing denominations, particularly Catholicism, were caught up in the building debates. Catholic prelates and congregations considered the social position their architecture would suggest. As Paula Kane points out, architectural style had an apologetic appeal and revealed the social function of the denomination. For ex-ample, both the traditionalism of the Gothic and the triumphalism of classicism were debated when architectural decisions were made in the archdiocese of Boston. The Gothic style most often won out because it was thought to provide a link between Catholicism and social conservatism.[89]

By the teens, Catholic ideals of architecture began to be publicized. For example, John T. Comes, a Pittsburgh architect and the most prominent American theorist of Catholic architecture, taught Catholic seminarians a course on church art and architecture that emphasized the modern requirements of liturgical worship and embraced the spirit of medieval styles. By 1920, Comes suggested that "unfamiliar-ity with the rudiments of art and architecture might make the new priest unwitting instruments of harm to the Catholic conscience, prestige, and influence, and a pos-sible money waster on bad art." Comes instructed that the "truth in architecture" was revealed through the honest use of materials with "no artificialities, shams, or insincerities of any kind." The church building should "function as perfectly as a steam engine or a living organism, like that of the human body." Harmony and unity between building and furnishings was tantamount to the creation of harmonious groups of churches, parochial schools, rectories, and convents. Comes applauded the new groupings of civic buildings in America, derived specifically from the Chicago World's Fair, suggesting that the successful styles in public building should also be taken up by Catholicism. The *Ecclesiastical Review* reported that past Gothic and Romanesque styles need not be slavishly reproduced; that new building materials and rituals might demand new methods of construction and interpretation. However, Comes believed that since the laws of order and harmony in architecture were as eternal as the institution of the Catholic Church was immutable, the architect's attention to Catholic liturgy demanded that the church remain a symbol of truth and beauty, not as a "meeting-house that may follow any style of beauty."[90]

Gothicists had long claimed that the moral position of churches set them apart in the city, and that a steepled architecture was the most honest expression of the highest goals of Christianity.[91] Mrs. Eddy seemed to concur. She preferred what Alfred Farlow, the COP official, called a "churchy church," that is, a building with "something pointing upward," similar to the one she had donated to the citizens of Concord. Her building was recognizable as a church. Bernard Maybeck picked up the idea and modernized it in his First Church of Christ, Scientist, Berkeley, completed in 1911 (figs. 12 and 32). The materials were simple and were selected with originality: poured concrete, fir and redwood, asbestos panels on the exteriors, medieval-looking glass placed in factory sashes, painted stenciled decorations—all exposed. The building was a radical departure from traditional styles, even though it seemed based in Victorian eclecticism. Maybeck's church has been written about at length as possibly the most noteworthy American church design of any denomination.[92] The design was developed in accordance with the ideals of the congregation:

> The church should be a perfect concept of mental architectural skill, manifesting *unity, harmony, beauty, light,* and *peace;* a structure denoting *progress* in all lines and strictly *individual in character,* designed to meet our present needs and to be in keeping with the artistic surroundings. . . . It should express *reverence,*—should look like a church. It should express *sincerity* and *honesty* exemplified in the use of genuine construction and materials which are what they claim to be and not imitations. . . . It should express welcome to all, exemplified in its entrance; . . . *comfort* . . . *quietness* and *peace,* exemplified in the plan of seating, the kind of seats, . . . the lighting . . . ventilation . . . and good acoustics. . . . and harmonious coloring . . . *joy,* exemplified in plenty of light . . . sunshine, color, etc.; . . . and *home-likeness,* exemplified in a surrounding garden, etc.[93]

The cornerstone of Maybeck's church was laid on December 26, 1910. The plan was a Greek cross. The interior walls were punctuated by gothicizing tracery, the roof supported by heavy Romanesque columns with unique narrative capitals. To some, the rough-hewn wood beams in the building and its setting evoked a Japanese garden shrine. Writing in 1921 to a Tacoma minister who had inquired about the "unique temple of Christian Science," Maybeck mused, "We sensed a need of permanence

Figure 32. Interior, First Church of Christ, Scientist, Berkeley (Ivey).

in religious monument rather as a symbol; therefore the floor was concrete and on the ground, and the walls are concrete to the seat of the trusses. . . . Sensually—the style was chosen to fit the congregation, i.e. we got the impression that they believed, as we think the earlier Christian did until 1100 A.D., in direct touch with an omniscient power in everything they did—perhaps a kind of partnership."[94]

Maybeck's church has been applauded as the first building that showed that new technologically advanced materials were not merely functional but could express, in Alan Temko's words, the "deep spiritual meanings for modern society." As Temko has affirmed, this was the most original Christian Science church and had successfully achieved what every building committee hoped for: it was "specifically intended for a radically new sect that was striving to meet the future while retaining the most precious associations with the past."[95]

At the time of the erection of First Church, Berkeley, the architectural rhetoric about classicism was acknowledging the style's simplicity and honesty.[96] Apologists and polemicists alike were beginning to identify the classical style with the Christian Science building movement. In the same year as Maybeck's innovative design, several congregations in southern California completed large classical buildings, for example, Second Church, Los Angeles, and First Church, Pasadena (figs. 33 and 34). They had requested of their architects the same qualities that the church members

Figure 33. Alfred F. Rosenheim, Second Church of Christ, Scientist, Los Angeles, 1910 (Van Horne).

at Berkeley had sought. Second Church, Los Angeles (1907–10), was designed by Alfred F. Rosenheim, an architect trained at MIT.[97] The engineer for the church was Albert Martin, who achieved widespread fame in the area for constructing for this church the largest poured-concrete dome of its time, a dome seventy feet in diameter constructed with a system of concrete girders and steel trusses. The church walls were masonry and glazed brick trimmed with terra-cotta. The building rose majestically above a manicured lawn with beautiful trees and shrubs. The portico was framed by six forty-foot Corinthian columns. The pediment above reached fifty feet. The dome was surmounted by a cupola and was sheathed in copper. As church historians put it, it was, "in all, an imposing heavenward building of classical beauty and spiritual harmony."[98] The congregation of First Church, Pasadena, chose the Los

Figure 34. Franklin P. Burnham, First Church of Christ, Scientist, Pasadena, California, 1910 (Church History, Division of the Church of Christ, Scientist, Boston).

Angeles architect Franklin P. Burnham's monumental classical design with an Ionic porch. This building was erected in 1909–10. The thick-walled edifice was built of reinforced concrete—with no girders or cross members. As a member stated, "The church building is . . . poured so as to make the building part as one solid rock."[99] The floor measured 120 feet square and the dome rose 80 feet above the auditorium floor. The seating capacity was over 1,400.

Christian Science congregations of the day were genuinely concerned with the rhetorical aspect of the architecture of their big-city churches, that is, what the buildings expressed. They thought the architecture should project the ideals of permanence, beauty, harmony, and unity and should create trouble-free environments. The churches should be comfortable and well-lit, with ample entrances and foyers, soft colors and cushioned pews or theater seating, and beautiful organs. Clearly, the needs of Christian Science congregations could be answered by several architectural styles that could all be described as pure, dignified, beautiful, and truthful.

Nonetheless, architectural style indicated a congregation's ideas of progress. The Gothic style was viewed as traditional and antimodernist; the classical style was generally defended as progressive. As the architect Russell Sturgis put it at the 1894 convention of the American Institute of Architects, modern architecture founded upon the Greek was plausible in the modern world. It was a "simple" and "autochthonous" architecture that was "as human as Romanesque, as direct and logical as Gothic." Its post-and-lintel construction technique was suited to the modern steel framework system. True classically inspired buildings had the ability to communicate tranquility, serenity, and repose, so needed in modern cities.[100]

Implementing new methods of church work and operating according to broadly contextualized ideals concerning the importance of individual and civic reform, Christian Science looked at architecture as a visible component of its method of influencing the urban environment and the city's citizens. As the religion was focused primarily in cities, the church entered into the cultural debates concerning the role of religion and architecture in American culture: How were churches going to be integrated in cityscapes increasingly defined by secular institutions, yet retain their theological sensibilities? How could the church both fit into the changing modern city and stand apart from tradition? What type of interior worship space would be functional for the reading of the lesson-sermon and also be comfortable and attractive? These were major questions during the first two decades of the century.

NOTES

1. See T. J. Jackson Lears, *No Place of Grace: Antimodernism and the Transformation of American Culture, 1880–1920* (New York: Pantheon, 1981), 1–58. See also Peter L. Berger, B. Berger, H. Kellner, *The Homeless Mind: Modernization and Consciousness* (New York: Random House, 1973), 206; Peter W. Williams, *Popular Religion in America: Symbolic Change and the Modernization Process in Historical Perspective* (Englewood Cliffs, N.J.: Prentice Hall, 1980); Robert Wiebe, *The Search for Order, 1877–1920* (New York: Hill and Wang, 1967).

2. Robert D. Cross, ed., *The Church and the City, 1865–1910* (Indianapolis: Bobbs Merrill, 1967),

xxxii–xxxiii. See also William Warren Sweet, *Story of Religion in America* (New York: Harper, 1939), 527.

3. For a discussion of this social change, see T. J. Jackson Lears, ed., *The Culture of Consumption: Critical Essays in American History 1880–1980* (New York: Pantheon, 1983), 3–37.

4. A writer for the *Methodist Review* ([Mar. 1894]: 225) told readers that Catholics outnumbered the members of all other communions in the ratio of nearly two to one. "Anti-Romanism" was also found in Christian Science. See William McAfee Goodwin, *The Christian Science Church* (Washington, D.C., 1916): 134–40.

5. See Josiah Strong, *Our Country: Its Possible Future and Its Present Crisis,* rev. ed. (New York: Baker and Taylor, 1891), ed. Jürgen Herbst (Cambridge, Mass.: Harvard, 1963); Josiah Strong, *The New Era, or The Coming Kingdom* (New York: Baker and Taylor, 1893). To bolster support for his theories of individualism in the city, Strong supported a loosely organized group of social reformers who addressed the problems of depopulating city churches and joined together for four interdenominational congresses in the 1880s. See also Washington Gladden, *Applied Christianity: Moral Aspects of Social Questions* (Boston: Houghton Mifflin, 1886); Samuel Lane Loomis, *Modern Cities and Their Religious Problems* (New York: Baker and Taylor, 1887); John R. Commons, *Social Reform and the Church* (New York: Crowell, 1894); Thomas Tiplady, *Social Christianity in the New Era* (New York: Fleming Revell, 1919).

6. Mary Baker Eddy, *Message to The First Church of Christ, Scientist, or Mother Church, June 15, 1902* (Boston: Christian Science Publishing Society, 1902), 2; B. O. Flower, *Civilization's Inferno, or Studies in the Social Cellar* (Boston, 1893), 60. Flower, a social reformer from Illinois, began to publish books and articles in which he agitated for social reforms. He converted to Unitarianism and moved to Boston, where he became an outspoken proponent of a utopian progressive vision of the unity and brotherhood of man. He founded the liberal magazine *Arena* in 1889 and was a member of the editorial staff off and on between 1889 and 1908. In 1909, he founded the *Twentieth Century Magazine* in Boston, which included discussions on politics, society, and education. He never converted to Christian Science, though he was its best defender in the secular press.

7. Some Protestants had been organizing group activities for quite a while. Many of these cross-denominational organizations, such as the YMCA, had a social or moralizing character. See Charles Howard Hopkins, *The Rise of the Social Gospel in American Protestantism, 1865–1915* (New Haven: Yale University Press, 1967), 303; H. Farnham May, *Protestant Churches and Industrial America* (New York: Harper, 1949).

8. See Rev. William Cross Merrill, "Spirituality and the Institutional Church," *Outlook* 49, no. 26 (June 30, 1894): 1191–92. Merrill emphasized that the new institutional church had been very effective in attracting new members, outpacing other city churches.

9. Settlements were based on the support for each individual's social assimilation and achievement. The settlement focused on specific immigrant populations, while the institutional church tried to attract the dispossessed in the city, immigrant or otherwise. Settlement houses were established in poor neighborhoods to tend to the physical, instructional, and social needs of their often immigrant populations. The best-known settlement house in the United States was Jane Addams's Hull-House, established in Chicago in 1889, whose mission was to inculcate middle-class values of social organization and work in the often transient immigrant population. Settlements advocated for the immigrant and impoverished, aided in their adjustment to work, and exposed them to middle-class social and cultural possibilities presented by the American city. This was accomplished primarily through the establishment of a charitable relationship between case worker and client that encouraged family cohesiveness and cultural integration into American activities of industry and leisure. Educational and vocational support was offered through in-house or college extension courses. Hull-House invested in the idea that it should become the center for social and political life of its entire local community, creating a space for equalization and mutual understanding among differing cultural groups and social classes while supporting cleaner, more hygienic neighborhood conditions, better health care, and improved housing. See Jane Addams, *A Centennial Reader* (New York: Macmillan, 1960), for excerpts from her most important writ-

ings on settlements and social reform. On settlements and institutional churches see Allen F. Davis, *Spearheads of Reform: Social Settlements and the Progressive Movement, 1890–1914* (New York: Oxford University Press, 1967); Paul Boyer, *Urban Masses and Moral Order in America, 1820–1920* (Cambridge, Mass.: Harvard University Press, 1978), 132–42; Aaron Ignatius Abell, *The Urban Impact on American Protestantism, 1865–1900* (Cambridge, Mass.: Harvard University Press, 1943), 137–65. The Protestant institutional church emphasized the "material environment through which [Christ's] spirit may be practically expressed." This environment would provide "educational, reformatory and philanthropic channels" to bring men back to Christ and back into the church. Abell, *Urban Impact*, 162. See also George Whitefield Mead, *Modern Methods in Church Work: The Gospel Renaissance* (New York: Dodd, Mead, 1897, 1909).

10. For examples see G. W. Cooke, "The Institutional Church," *New England Magazine* 14 (Aug. 1896): 645–60; Edward Judson, "The Institutional Church," *Sunday-School Times* 38, no. 48 (Nov. 28, 1896): 766.

11. See Hopkins, *The Rise of the Social Gospel*, 67. Other important books on the emergence of the influence of the city and the rise of the Social Gospel include Abell, *Urban Impact;* Paul Carter, *The Decline and Revival of the Social Gospel: Social and Political Liberalism in American Protestant Churches, 1920–1940* (Ithaca: Cornell University Press, 1954); Ronald C. White Jr. and C. Howard Hopkins, *The Social Gospel: Religion and Reform in Changing America* (Philadelphia: Temple University Press, 1976); Susan Curtis, *A Consuming Faith: The Social Gospel and Modern American Culture* (Baltimore: Johns Hopkins University Press, 1991); and Martin Marty, ed., *Protestantism and Social Christianity*, vol. 6 of *Modern American Protestantism and Its World* (New York: K. G. Saur, 1992).

12. The Salvation Army was founded in the late 1880s to deal with social problems in the city within a distinct quasimilitary religious corps structure. The American version of the original British group carried out its war on poverty by going door to door or saloon to saloon, in order to contact the "floating population," and to provide food and rescue services such as lodging. This direct effort, usually by women who called themselves "Slum Sisters," encouraged transients to attend religious services. The social vision of the group was to repopulate rural areas through the creation of agricultural colonies, rather than to reform the urban environment. See Maud Ballington Booth, "Salvation Army Work in the Slums," *Scribner's Magazine* 17 (Jan. 1895): 103, 110–12.

13. *Methodist Review* (Mar. 1894): 230–31.

14. See John Schwenke, "An Analysis of the Contributions of Christian Science to the Basic Human Needs of People Living in Modern Urban Society, with Special Emphasis on Evidence Collected in the Chicago Metropolitan Area" (B.D. thesis, Chicago Theological Seminary, 1948), 256–66.

15. As the philosopher Gerhardt Mars put it in 1908, Christian Science was one of the few religions that had developed the ideal in which the "individual freely accepts and understands the truth for himself." Gerhardt C. Mars, "Democracy and Religion," *Arena* (Aug. 1908): 287–92. See also his book *The Interpretation of Life* (New York: Appleton, 1908).

16. Even many Protestants thought that Christian Science was a forceful attack on gross materialism and a cry for renewed individualism. Some began to view Christian Science as an important phenomena against materialism regardless of its other claims of healing. Gladden, for example, even respected its attack on materialism. See Stuart E. Knee, *Christian Science in the Age of Mary Baker Eddy* (Westport, Conn.: Greenwood, 1994), 82. See also B. O. Flower, "The Rise and Onward March of Christian Science," *Twentieth Century Magazine* 4, no. 22 (July 1911): 310.

17. Herbert Ernest Cushman, *The Truth in Christian Science* (Boston: James H. West, 1902), 16–19. He also delivered the Russell Lecture of 1904 to the faculty and students of Tufts University, where he mentioned Christian Science. See his book *What Is Christianity?* (Boston: J. H. West, 1904), 22–23. For another viewpoint concerning Christian Science and individualism, see Walter I. Wardwell, "Christian Science and Spiritual Healing," in *Religious Systems and Psychotherapy*, ed. Richard Cox (Springfield, Ill.: Charles C. Thomas, 1973), 72–86.

18. William A. Johnston, "Christian Science in New York: History of the New York Organizations," *Broadway Magazine* 18, no. 2 (May 1907): 166.

19. A typical indictment was that of Rev. A. C. Dixon of Boston's Ruggles Street Baptist Church: "Boards of health are unnecessary, and are recognized by Christian Science only as a concession to public sentiment. A city, if the thought of Christian Science prevails, need pay no attention to sewerage or cleansing the streets. Filth would be as healthy as flowers. . . . Pay no attention to filth or microbes." A. C. Dixon, *The Christian Science Delusion* (Boston: Ruggles Street Baptist Church, 1904), 17. For an excellent overview, see Raymond J. Cunningham, "The Impact of Christian Science on the American Churches, 1880–1910," *American Historical Review* 72 (1967): 896. See also "Spiritual Healing, Report of a Clerical and Medical Committee," *Current Opinion* 57 (July 1914); L. Abbott, "Does a Christian Science Healer Practice Medicine?" *Outlook* 107 (1914–15): 835.

20. For example, see Charles M. Oughton, *Crazes, Credulities, and Christian Science* (Chicago: E. H. Colegrove, 1901), 87.

21. See William E. Blackstone, *Jesus Is Coming* (Chicago, 1908), 231; J. E. Roberts, "The Pulpit versus Christian Science," reprinted in *Christian Science Journal* 16 (Oct. 1898): 486. Alfred D. Kohn, *Christian Science from a Physician's Standpoint* (Chicago: Privately printed, 1906), noted that "in spite of all the palpable facts which go to make up our life, in spite of the great advances in medicine and kindred sciences, Christian Science temples, with thousands of converts, are springing up all over the country, and a new idealistic philosophy, which takes the scriptures literally, has arisen, numbering among its adherents many sober-minded and intelligent men and women" (1–2). See also John Slater in *Searchlights on Christian Science* (Chicago: Fleming H. Revell, 1899), 13; Judge Septimus J. Hanna, "The Growth of Christian Science," *Progress* (June 1898); Stephen Gottschalk, *The Emergence of Christian Science in American Religious Life* (Berkeley: University of California Press, 1973), 207–15.

22. V. H. Krull, *A Common-Sense View of Christian Science,* 5th ed. (Collegeville, Ind.: St. Joseph's Printing Office, 1914), 3; reprinted in *Christian Science, Controversial and Polemical Pamphlets,* ed. Gary Ward (New York: Garland Press, 1990), 117.

23. J. Winthrop Hegeman, "Must Protestantism Adopt Christian Science?" *North American Review* 198, no. 6 (Dec. 1913): 823. Hegeman also wrote "Must the Church Adopt Christian Science Healing," *North American Review* 200 (July 1914): 122.

24. Anson Phelps Stokes and Leo Pfeffer, *Church and State in the United States* (New York: Harper and Row, 1964), 310. For more information on the legal implications of Christian Science healing throughout the denomination's history, see Thomas Johnsen, "Christian Scientists and the Medical Profession: A Historical Perspective," *Medical Heritage* (Jan.–Feb. 1986): 70–78; Isadore Harold Rubenstein, *A Treatise on the Legal Aspects of Christian Science* (Chicago: Crandon Press, 1935); Edward Kimball, *Christian Science and Legislation* (Boston: Christian Science Publishing Society, 1906); "Physician's Impeachment of Christian Science Cures," *Current Opinion* 68 (Mar. 1920). In "Faith Healers Are Many," *Washington Times,* Aug. 2, 1897, it was claimed that the persecution was "winning recruits" to Christian Science.

25. *Harper's Weekly* (Dec. 25, 1897).

26. See the church's defensive articles: Alfred Farlow, "The Relation of Government to the Practice of Christian Science," *Government, a Magazine of Economics and Applied Politics* 1, no. 2 (May 1907): 1–20; Judge Clifford Smith, "Christian Science and Legislation," *Christian Science Journal* (Oct. 1905); Judge Septimus Hanna, "Civil Liberty and Religious Liberty," *Government, a Magazine of Economics and Applied Politics* 11, no. 5 (Feb. 1908). See also Clifford P. Smith, *Christian Science: Its Legal Status, A Defense of Human Rights* (Boston: Christian Science Publishing Society, 1914). See plea supporting Christian Science delivered on the Congress floor by U.S. Senator J. D. Weeks, *Congressional Record* 52 (1915): 1021–55. The Bird Stewart Scotland Collection (BSSC), CHD, contains several volumes of articles devoted specifically to legal questions and the status of Christian Science in civil law.

27. See "A Test for 'Christian Scientists,'" *Journal of the American Medical Association* 34 (1900): 759.

28. Mark Twain (Samuel Clemens), *Christian Science* (New York: Harper, 1899, 1907), 80.

29. See B. O. Flower, "Christian Science and Organic Disease," *Arena* 40 (1908): 442–53; idem, *Christian Science as a Religious Belief and a Therapeutic Agent* (Boston: Arena, 1909); "Outlaws Made through Class Legislation," *Arena* 24 (Nov. 1900): 548–50. See also the "Affidavit of Joseph Mann," reprinted in *We Knew Mary Baker Eddy, Vol. 3* (Boston: Christian Science Publishing Society, 1953), 29–35.

30. Mary Baker Eddy, *The First Church of Christ Scientist and Miscellany* (Boston: Christian Science Publishing Society, 1913), 226.

31. W. D. McCracken, "The Meaning of Christian Science," *Arena* 37 (Nov. 1907): 473.

32. The Chicago Dispensary, for example, was organized in 1899, after the Boston Dispensary's founding, and was endorsed by Mrs. Eddy. It was established "for the purpose of dispensing the Truth to the poor, both by visiting them and receiving them in these Rooms—with treatments for the healing of their infirmities and with conversation, to give them an idea of the gospel as taught by Christ and His faithful followers." "Executive Committee Report to the Mother Church, Christian Science Reading Rooms, Chicago," ms., 1931, CHD. Alfred Farlow was asked by Mrs. Eddy in 1909 to create a systematic free distribution system for Christian Science literature.

33. See Schwenke, "An Analysis of the Contributions of Christian Science": "Traditional Protestantism lacks the symbolization of the definiteness and stability of life that people in modern urban society seem to need and seek, and which we have found in the architecture of Christian Science, in the manner of its organization and control, and in its behavior pattern at group gatherings (worship services) . . . the element of consistency [in Protestantism]—from church to church—is missing. Thus, a Christian Scientist can always depend upon finding the same architecture, the same behavior patterns, the same order and content of service—no matter where he may be: in Massachusetts or in California" (267–68).

34. Mead, *Modern Methods in Church Work,* 68.

35. At Twelfth Church of Christ, Scientist, Chicago, in 1936, for example, a male usher at summer Sunday services would wear a blue or dark coat, white wool trousers, a dark blue polka-dot four-in-hand tie, white hose, and all-white shoes. For winter months he would wear a frock coat, striped trousers, a dress shirt, a standing wing collar, gray gloves, black shoes, and pearl gray spats. On Wednesday evenings he would wear a business suit. A female usher for summer Sunday services would wear a white dress with below-the-elbow sleeves, and white shoes. In the winter, she would wear a black or dark blue dress with below-the-elbow sleeves, and dark shoes. On Wednesdays, she was instructed to wear a dark dress, with no bold colors. Men also wore boutonnieres in their lapels. Ushers Committee Minutes, Twelfth Church of Christ, Scientist, Chicago, 1936, Corey Collection, Southern Methodist University.

36. See "An Allegory," *Christian Science Journal* 20 (1897): 127, which addresses the purification of society through Christian Science means: Would Christian Science simply do away with charitable institutions and hospitals? "No, only as they disappear in the natural order of events,—disappear as did the stage-coach before the railroad, or the cradle before the reaper."

37. "Report on the Dedication of Eighth Church of Christ, Scientist, Chicago," undated ms., CHD.

38. Kevin J. Christiano, *Religious Diversity and Social Change: American Cities, 1890–1906* (New York: Cambridge University Press, 1987), 192.

39. Harold W. Pfautz, "Christian Science: A Case Study of the Social Psychological Aspect of Secularization," *Social Forces* 34 (Mar. 1956): 246–51; Günther P. Barth, *City People: The Rise of Modern City Culture in Nineteenth-Century America* (New York: Oxford University Press, 1980).

40. *City without a Church* reprinted in Henry Drummond, *The Greatest Thing in the World and Other Addresses* (London: Hodder and Stoughton, 1904), 129. Drummond was an evangelical, educated in Scotland, and connected with Dwight Moody. An evolutionist, Drummond traveled to Africa to witness his notion that spiritual progress was compatible with natural selection, or "natural law." A popular college lecturer, Drummond published his most complete statement, *Ascent of Man,* in 1894 and became well known in Christian Science and New Thought circles through his book *The Greatest Thing in the World,* a commentary on First John's popular verses.

Drummond's *The City without a Church* (New York: Crowell, 1892) sold well over 55,000 copies by 1894.

41. Ibid., 150.

42. Washington Gladden, *Social Salvation* (Boston: Houghton Mifflin, 1902), 221–24, suggested that the idealized city must be kept before the citizen's eyes. He wrote: "Mr. Drummond tells us that as John saw in his vision the New Jerusalem, so we must see the New London, the New Boston, the New Chicago, the new New York; the city that ought to be; the regenerated, purified, redeemed city; we must see it, and believe in it, and be ready to work and suffer to bring it down to earth" (224).

43. See Henry Pennington Toler, *Arise! Take Thy Journey* (New York: Harlem Publishing Co., 1907); Charles Pease, *Exposé of Christian Science Methods and Teaching Prevailing in the First Church, C.S., New York City* (New York: Restoration Publishing Co., 1905), 114; *New York Herald,* Jan. 23, 1904.

44. Ella V. Fluno, "A Christian Science Edifice: The Result of Demonstration," *Christian Science Journal* 21 (1903–4): 158.

45. Charles Zueblin, *The Religion of a Democrat* (New York: B. W. Huebsch, 1908), 111. Later in his book he wrote: "Every extension of the intellectual horizon is fertile in new religious movements. The emotional temperaments are caught by soul-satisfying sects, like Methodism, Swedenborgianism, the Salvation Army, or Christian Science; while the exaggeration of rationalism produces secularism and new thought, of mysticism, theosophy and oriental cults. The sounder basis furnished by a knowledge of human needs, has produced positivism,—the worship of humanity; ethical culture,—the fellowship of humanity; and socialism,—the organization of humanity." He believed that Christian Science opposed "by its cheerful inertia the aggressive movements toward the unity of society" (150–51). Others agreed. Rev. George Bedell Vosbrugh, in *Christian Science Examined* (Denver: First Baptist Church, 1906), wrote: "This cult numbers some of our best citizens among its membership, not only in Denver, but wherever it has been established. I believe that as a class they are characterized by kindness, and like their founder lead kind and exemplary lives. It would not be far from the facts to say that as a class they are wanting in sympathy for the sorrows of the world, but this grows inevitably out of their conception of life and is not a personal matter" (4).

46. See the nine-part article he wrote called "The Civic Renascence," *The Chautauquan* 38, beginning in Sept. 1903.

47. Ray Ginger, *Altgeld's America, 1890–1905: The Lincoln Ideal versus Changing Realities* (New York: Funk and Wagnalls, 1958), 129.

48. A. K. Frain, "Christian Science Church Edifices," *Christian Science Sentinel* 5, no. 7 (Oct. 16, 1902): 106.

49. Fluno, "A Christian Science Edifice," 157–58.

50. For example, at the dedication of First Church, St. Louis, the audience heard that the church's "externalizing something of the beauty and grace of the spiritual idea which it represents, surrounded with ample grounds . . . is still a notable contribution to the architecture of the city." *Christian Science Journal* 30 (1912–13): 601.

51. See William H. Wilson, *The City Beautiful Movement* (Baltimore: Johns Hopkins University Press, 1989), 75–95.

52. See Charles Mulford Robinson, *Modern Civic Art: or The City Made Beautiful* (New York: Putnam, 1903), 35; and the discussion of the City Beautiful in Boyer, *Urban Masses and Moral Order,* 252–76.

53. Charles Zueblin, *American Municipal Progress: Chapters in Municipal Sociology* (New York: Macmillan, 1902), 240. See also Zueblin, *A Decade of Civic Development* (Chicago: University of Chicago Press, 1905).

54. See William H. Jordy, *American Buildings: Progressive and Academic Ideals at the Turn of the Twentieth Century* (Garden City, N.Y.: Doubleday, 1972).

55. Robert Park, "The City: Suggestions for the Study of Human Behavior in the City Envi-

ronment," *American Journal of Sociology* 20 (Mar. 1915): 577–612. See also Robert Park, Ernest Burgess, and Roderick McKenzie, *The City* (Chicago: University of Chicago Press, 1925); Boyer, *Urban Masses and Moral Order*.

56. See Sydney Ahlstrom, *A Religious History of the American People* (New Haven: Yale University Press, 1972), 1019–36. See Edward H. Bennett and Daniel H. Burnham, *Plan of Chicago,* ed. Charles Moore (Chicago: Commercial Club, 1909); Daniel Bluestone, *Constructing Chicago* (New Haven: Yale University Press, 1991). Emanuel Swedenborg's teachings were codified in the Church of the New Jerusalem. He taught that so-called material objects in reality reflected spiritual entities and qualities. This concept of correspondence could legitimize the practice of producing a "New Jerusalem" here on earth. Burnham's family members were devout Swedenborgians and, according to his biographer Thomas Hines, his upbringing was pervaded by those teachings, though he himself "was less interested in theology than in the practice of Christian ethics." See Thomas Hines, *Burnham of Chicago* (New York: Oxford University Press, 1974), xvii. According to *The New Church in Chicago, A History* (Chicago: Church of the New Jerusalem, 1906), 388, Burnham had been a member of the Chicago Society of the New Jerusalem since 1872 and was a man "prominent in affairs, whose achievements are distinguished, and whose reputation is national." On the influence of Swedenborg on Burnham's work, see Irving D. Fisher, "An Iconography of City Planning: The Chicago City Plan," in *Emanuel Swedenborg: A Continuing Vision,* ed. Robin Larsen (New York: Swedenborg Foundation, 1988), 245–62.

57. Bennett and Burnham, *Plan of Chicago,* 36.

58. On synagogue architecture, see Peter W. Williams, *Houses of God: Region, Religion, and Architecture in the United States* (Urbana: University of Illinois Press, 1997); idem, *America's Religions: Traditions and Cultures* (1990; Urbana: University of Illinois Press, 1998); *Recent American Synagogue Architecture* (New York: Jewish Museum, 1963); Rachel Bernstein Wischnitzer, *Synagogue Architecture in the United States: History and Interpretation* (Philadelphia: Jewish Publication Society of America, 1955).

59. Edward Joseph Weber, *Catholic Church Buildings: Their Planning and Furnishing* (New York: J. F. Wegner, 1927); M. T. Purdy, *Churches and Chapels: A Design and Development Guide* (Boston: Butterworth Architecture, 1991); John Theodore Comes, *Catholic Art and Architecture* (Pittsburgh: N.p., 1920); E. I. Watkins, *Catholic Art and Culture, an Essay on Catholic Culture* (London: Burns and Oates, 1942).

60. See Colleen McDannell, "Interpreting Things: Material Culture Studies and American Religion," *Religion* 21, no. 4 (Oct. 1991): 371; and idem, *Material Christianity* (New Haven: Yale University Press, 1995).

61. "Progress of the Institutional Church," *Review of Reviews* 15, no. 2 (Feb. 1897): 207–9.

62. Henry Potter, "The Significance of the American Cathedral," *Forum Magazine* (May 1892): 354.

63. Ibid., 352.

64. W. L. George, *Hail Columbia! Random Impressions of a Conservative English Radical* (New York: Harper, 1921): 153–55, 157–61.

65. Gladden, *Applied Christianity,* 203.

66. Stephen Hasbrouck, *Altar Fires Relighted: A Study from a Non-Partisan Standpoint of Movements and Tendencies at Work in the Religious Life of To-Day* (New York: Burnett, 1912), 333–34.

67. Howard Alan Bridgeman, "Have We Too Many Churches?" *Andover Review* 17, no. 101 (May 1892): 488–95; Strong, *The New Era,* 298.

68. Hasbrouck, *Altar Fires Relighted,* 59–60, 109. See also B. O. Flower, "The Recent Reckless and Irresponsible Attacks on Christian Science and Its Founder, with a Survey of the Christian-Science Movement," *Arena* 37 (Jan. 1907): 47–67.

69. *Christian Science Journal* 16 (1898–99): 307.

70. See Mary Baker Eddy, *Manual of the Mother Church, The First Church of Christ, Scientist, in Boston, Massachusetts,* 89th ed. (Boston: Christian Science Publishing Society, 1908), article 8, sec. 27 and sec. 28, 48.

71. Mary Baker Eddy, *Retrospection and Introspection* (Boston: Christian Science Publishing Society, 1892), 94.

72. *American Architect and Building News* 53, no. 1075 (Aug. 1, 1896): 37.

73. *American Architect and Building News* 89, no. 1590 (June 16, 1906): 197–98.

74. See discussion in James Marston Fitch, *Architecture and the Esthetics of Plenty* (New York: Columbia University Press, 1961), 203; "Cathedral of St. John the Divine," *Architectural Record* 2 (1892–93): 45–53; "St. John the Divine," *Scribner's Magazine* 41 (Apr. 1907): 385–401.

75. See, for example, Richard Franz Bach's five-part "Church Planning in the United States," *Architectural Record* (July–Dec. 1916). See also Joseph Dana Miller, "The Growth of Christian Science," *Era, a Philadelphia Magazine* 10 (1902): 14–33.

76. Montgomery Schuyler, "Recent Church Building in New York," *Architectural Record* 13 (June 1903): 527–30.

77. Rev. Andrew F. Underhill, *Valid Objections to So-Called Christian Science* (Yonkers, N.Y.: Arlington Chemical Co., 1902), 30–31.

78. Mrs. A. D. T. Whitney, *The Integrity of Christian Science* (Boston: Houghton Mifflin, 1900), 32–33.

79. Charles Edward Locke, D.D., *Eddyism: Is It Christian? Is It Scientific? How Long Will It Last?* (Los Angeles: Grafton Publishing Co., 1911), 24.

80. Dixon, *Christian Science Delusion*, 21.

81. Joseph Dunn Burrell, *A New Appraisal of Christian Science* (New York: Funk and Wagnalls, 1906), 5. See also Frank Podmore, *Mesmerism and Christian Science, A Short History of Mental Healing* (Philadelphia: G. W. Jacobs, 1909), 277.

82. *American Architect and Building News* 89, no. 1590 (June 16, 1906): 197–98.

83. Ibid.; quoted in the *Springfield Union* (Illinois), July 1, 1907.

84. Hasbrouck, *Altar Fires Relighted*, 325–27.

85. Ralph Adams Cram, *American Churches* (New York: American Architect, 1915), vol. 2, foreword.

86. Robert Muccigrosso, *American Gothic: The Mind and Art of Ralph Adams Cram* (Washington, D.C.: University Press of America, 1980), 29.

87. Cram, *American Churches,* vol. 1, preface.

88. Ibid., plates 49–55 and 113–18.

89. Paula M. Kane, *Separatism and Subculture: Boston Catholicism, 1900–1920* (Chapel Hill: University of North Carolina Press, 1994).

90. Comes, *Catholic Art and Architecture,* 8, 47, 50, 72–73, 76.

91. See, for instance, three books by A. W. N. Pugin: *Contrasts* (London: By the author, 1836); *The True Principles of Pointed or Christian Architecture* (London: J. Weale, 1841); and *An Apology for the Revival of Christian Architecture in England* (London: J. Weale, 1843). Pugin believed in a direct association between religious truth and architectural truth. See David Watkin, *Morality and Architecture: The Development of a Theme in Architectural History and Theory from the Gothic Revival to the Modern Movement* (Oxford: Clarendon Press, 1977); Kenneth Clark, *The Gothic Revival: An Essay in the History of Taste* (New York: Scribner, 1950); Phoebe Stanton, *The Gothic Revival and American Church Architecture: An Episode in Taste, 1840–1856* (Baltimore: Johns Hopkins University Press, 1968); *A. W. N. Pugin: Master of Gothic Revival,* ed. Paul Atterbury et al. (New Haven: Yale University Press, 1995).

92. Winthrop Sargeant, *Geniuses, Goddesses, and People* (New York: Dutton, 1949), 278. For descriptions see also Jordy, *American Buildings;* Sally Woodbridge and Richard Barnes, *Bernard Maybeck: Visionary Architect* (New York: Abbeville, 1992), 89–98; Richard Longstreth, *On the Edge of the World: Four Architects in San Francisco at the Turn of the Century* (Cambridge, Mass.: MIT Press, 1983); Edward R. Bosley, *First Church of Christ, Scientist, Berkeley* (London: Phaidon, 1994). See also "Maybeck's Magnificent Church," *Western Architect* (July 1959): 34–37. Both Jordy and Longstreth suggest that Maybeck's design was influenced by Viollet-le-Duc's conceptions of the massing of the Greek temple.

93. "Documents on the History of First Church, Berkeley," Field Collection, CHD.

94. Letter to Rev. Frank Dyer, Congregational Church, Tacoma, Washington, Nov. 14, 1921, CHD. Quoted in Kenneth H. Cardwell, *Bernard Maybeck: Artisan, Architect, Artist* (Santa Barbara, Calif.: Peregrine Smith, 1977), 129.

95. Alan Temko, *No Way to Build a Ballpark, and Other Irreverent Essays on Architecture* (San Francisco: Chronicle Press, 1993), 264. See also Sheldon Cheney, *The New World Architecture* (New York: Longmans, Green, 1930), 344.

96. On the rhetorical aspects of the work of Bernard Maybeck and Irving Gill, see Alan Gowans, "New Reality in Old Forms: Late Victorian Principles in Early Modern Architecture, c. 1885–c. 1920," in his *Images of American Living: Four Centuries of Architecture and Furniture as Cultural Expression* (New York: Harper and Row, 1976), 395–413.

97. S. Richey and H. Schick, "Second Church of Christ, Scientist, Los Angeles," undated ms., CHD. A member remarked, "May we not see in this natural harmony and symmetry, a hint of the spiritual qualities Christian Scientists are ever striving to manifest in their mental 'structure of Truth and Love?'" "Historical Sketch," undated ms., CHD. See also *Christian Science Journal* (Aug. 1913); *Brickbuilder* 19 (Apr. 1910); *Western Architect* 15 (Mar. 1910).

98. Richey and Schick, "Second Church of Christ, Scientist, Los Angeles."

99. Quoted in the *Pasadena Star-News,* Aug. 6, 1946, on the occasion of the fiftieth anniversary of the church's organization. See also *Western Architect* 17 (Feb. 1911); *Pasadena Daily,* Nov. 21, 1910. On Christian Science church building in California, see "The Scientists' New Churches," *Los Angeles Times,* July 25, 1909, 16–17.

100. Russell Sturgis, "Modern Style Founded on Ancient Greek Architecture," *Journal of the Proceedings of the Twenty-eighth Annual Convention of the American Institute of Architects* (Providence: E. A. Johnson, 1895), 88–90. See also A. D. F. Hamlin, "The Modern Architectural Problem Discussed from the Professional Point of View," *Craftsman* (June 1905): 331.

FRONT ELEVATIO
1/10 Scale

4 : To Build a Church

By the early twentieth century, many urban Christian Scientists believed that their new edifices could help shape society by enabling moral reform in the city. Church facades established the visibility and respectability of the denomination's social goals in the face of harsh criticism. But building an edifice in the first place was often fraught with many obstacles and there were debates behind the scenes. Erecting a church was often a first-time endeavor by Christian Scientists, who were investing significant amounts of their own money to create a public space for worship. An issue of the *Architect and Engineer of California* stated succinctly that a Christian Science church was, at its best, "an example of what a few earnest individuals can accomplish." Many decisions concerning construction took place in meetings with boards, trustees, building committees, and memberships. All participants agreed that branch churches should be respectable on the exterior and functional and comfortable on the interior. Exteriors attracted public comment because they existed in the public arena. However, the interiors elicited nearly as much comment. In fact, the new efficient interiors of branch churches were very important in drawing attention to Christian Science services. They were most often viewed as distinctive, comfortable, and modern. Also, technological innovations such as advanced acoustics, lighting, and state-of-the-art ventilation systems began to gain public attention.

Congregational Approaches

As branch church members prepared, mentally and physically, to build their own churches in the first decade of this century, projects surrounding the Mother Church in Boston continued. Appeals for financial support to erect the new buildings at headquarters frequently were issued from Boston to the Christian Science field. Congregations that had already collected money to erect local branch churches gave their entire funds for the construction in Boston. Most believed that this generous giving would be rewarded in increased "supply" for their own local efforts. The congregation in Bloomington, Illinois, for example, reiterated that "the completion of the Mother Church building fund did not bring poverty to Branch Churches . . . it was the greatest possible stimulus to church building activity throughout the Christian Science world."[1] Many congregations used an affirmative and assertive approach to gain the financial support they needed. The board of directors of the Colorado Springs congregation wrote to the membership, "We are told in *Science and Health* that 'giving does not impoverish us, neither does withholding enrich us.' . . . Believing that, no matter how much we have given to the Mother Church we are *each one* just as well able to give to our Building Fund. What has been done can be done; if we have given $8000 in two years to the Mother Church we can give $8000 in two years to our Church."[2]

Congregations of Christian Scientists were excited about building their church homes. While practical measures were needed to select architects and builders and to finance the projects, the metaphysical terminology of the church was used to unify the membership behind the goal of building. Building was viewed as only secondarily a physical and practical affair. It was chiefly another way for the congregations to give witness to Christian Science precepts.

Almost every member of the church was involved. The children in the Sunday schools were organized into groups such as the "Busy Bees" in Boston, the "Temple Builders" in Grand Rapids, or the "Beaver Band" in Portland. One issue of the *Christian Science Journal* boasted that a church with a "pure Greek front" in the lumber town of Schofield, Wisconsin, had been organized and built entirely by children.[3] These youthful groups had as their purpose "to bring out the true church in consciousness, while also serving as an incentive to greater work in saving pennies for the building fund."[4] In one instance a suggestion by a Sunday school student to use the money set aside for a picnic to erect a church was the impetus to start a building fund. This emphasized the precept that simple, childlike thought was needed to purify and prepare the congregations for their task.

Congregations thought of building as a spiritual activity, and the preparation for building always demanded "mental work" and prayer. Church building meant character building: "Any bright and intelligent man or woman could attend to the details of building a material edifice provided there is a faithfulness to detail and a willingness to give the necessary time. . . . Church building is an arduous task and requires humility and great self-denial, but its blessings are manifold and the reward comes in good measure pressed down and running over."[5]

Typically, the first ceremony celebrated by the branch church congregation, after an architect was selected and a design approved, was the laying of the cornerstone, which was thought of as paralleling the instilling of the divine Word in human consciousness. At the ceremony in Oakland in 1900, for instance, a reader spoke of the "implanting in consciousness [of] the foundation or cornerstone of our church, whose outward symbol" was the edifice.[6] Mrs. Eddy made provision for small cornerstone-laying ceremonies and these early cornerstones were often New Hampshire granite, an explicit reference to her home state. The Bible, *Science and Health* and other writings by Mrs. Eddy, as well as issues of the periodicals were laid in copper caskets within the cornerstones. The ceremony marked the beginning, but also foresaw the end, that is, the inevitable passing away of the congregation's material building. Church as spiritual structure, however, would endure. The importance of spiritualizing the conception of church was noted in periodical articles, in quotations from actual church dedication ceremonies, and in Mrs. Eddy's correspondence. The idea often expressed was succinctly stated by Mrs. Eddy at the dedication ceremony of her Concord church in July 1904: "Our proper reason for church edifices is, that in them Christians may worship God,—not that Christians may worship church edifices."[7]

Important to every building committee was the impact of prayer and metaphysical axioms on the "unfoldment" or "realization" of the ideal church. Unusually strong language was employed to strengthen the resolve of congregations to that end.[8] Behind the scenes, building committees often gave members detailed instructions on how to pray during the building process. Many committees requested that congregants read Joseph Armstrong's official account of the building of the Mother Church, which emphasized the overcoming of physical obstacles through spiritual means.[9] Membership and students' association meetings sometimes included emphatic directives for prayer. When Sue Harper Mims's Atlanta congregation was preparing to build its second and much grander classical edifice, one member recalled a students' meeting: "one broiling hot July day . . . duly impressed with the importance of demonstrating the building at once, Mrs. Mims bade us hold steadfastly to the thought that the infinite Mind is our builder, the infinite Mind is our architect, our artist, our attorney, our illimitable source of supply. As this enlarging, magnifying thought of the infinitude of Good was earnestly held, the very plans and specifications widened into larger dimensions and greater beauty."[10]

The Christian Science periodicals also focused on the potential for healing that the church edifice signaled. Writing in 1908, a *Sentinel* contributor summed up the metaphysical approach of Christian Science:

The Christian Science church rises out of the love, gratitude, and inspiration of hearts chastened and lives rescued. Our building appears when impersonal love opens the awakening heart. In Christian Science, building is healing. . . . Heaps of rubbish must be excavated from consciousness—love of money, improvidence, sloth, self-indulgence, extravagance, fear of poverty, business superstitions, rainy-day prudence, unintelligent management— all that makes for lack. Without a transformation in character, improved morals, better health through spiritual power, the Christian Science edifice could not appear. The visible structure stands in itself a testimonial of healing. The Christian Scientist knows that if he does not heal, he cannot build. . . . If men knew what a Christian Science church really is, they would rush to invest in it as they now rush to newly discovered goldfields. Our church building is our best investment; the task of erecting it, our pearl of good fortune. . . . Christian Science purges the temple, the inner mental building. As right thinking, it turns out of doors the inward money changers—worldly aims and fleshly desires. It opens the windows of consciousness, and heavenly lights of purity and spirituality, gleams of eternity, stream in. Then our mental building becomes a house of prayer, of Godward aspiration that heals every sick and sinful occupant of the building.[11]

On the practical matters of building, the Christian Science periodicals and Boston officials were generally silent. As branch churches prepared to build, church architects, engineers, builders, and the suppliers of pews, organs, heating, ventilation, and lighting systems were eager to sell their goods and services. Building committees were established and advice was eagerly sought from members of other branch churches in nearby cities who had already completed their own projects. Christian Scientists assured themselves that the appropriate architect for their building project would emerge through scientific prayer. After all, they believed that "[Christian Science] enables [the architect] to rapidly, surely, and correctly attain the ability to reproduce the great classical orders of the past, and acquire the religion, as well as the science and originality of art and architecture. . . . It brings the mind into harmonious relationship with the divine Mind,—the Principle of all beauty, symmetry, order, law, proportion, and design."[12] Members were confident that their chosen architect, knowledgeable about their religious beliefs, could only reflect the "Great Architect of the Universe."

The association of architectural forms with spiritual ideas, by congregations of lay people, undoubtedly had a great impact on the architects these congregations chose to work with. Many non-Science architects, such as Bernard Maybeck and Frank Lloyd Wright, were impressed by the keen sense of purpose exhibited by Christian Scientists.[13] During the building-boom years of the church, the unusual ideas of the Christian Scientists impelled many architects to form opinions about the teachings of the church and many were attracted to the idea of designing a branch church edifice.

Congregations first had to choose an architect within the context of an increasing professionalization of the field of architecture. This process began in earnest with Daniel Burnham's presidency of the American Institute of Architects (AIA) in 1893. The AIA no longer emphasized just the building "art," as the previous AIA president, Richard Morris Hunt, had done, but instead stressed architecture as a business or profession. The AIA set standards for competitions by 1910 and advocated for more prestigious commissions for its members.[14] Within this shift, however, the notion that the architect was an artist, capable of inspiration, intuition, and problem solving, with total control over the process of design, was still important. Although architecture was a business, its practice was meant to have radical social effects by influencing the built environment through the *art* of architecture.

The influence of the new professionalism on the architect selection process was illustrated when, as mentioned earlier, Solon Beman was asked to aid the board of directors in Boston in an associate's capacity in the building of the Extension of the Mother Church. Beman found himself in an awkward position. At first he cited AIA guidelines concerning professionalism and refused, but he soon recanted this position to go to Mrs. Eddy's aid. It was the right career move for Beman. Besides receiving a steady stream of branch church commissions, he became an unofficial "official" architect for the Boston church, completing the new Christian Science Publishing Society in 1907 (now razed), located across the street from the Mother Church Extension on Falmouth Street. In 1907 he also redesigned Mrs. Eddy's private quarters at her final home in Chestnut Hill.

By 1911, independent publishers had produced several books with photographs and descriptions of branch church edifices to help building committees. The most thorough, however, L. M. Holt's *Christian Science Church Architecture,* met with an unfortunate fate when most of the printed copies were lost in a fire. The book had been published to "show the material progress" and to "offer suggestions to architects and members of Church Building Committees."[15] Such texts were circulated among branch church members who were in the process of making building decisions and undoubtedly influenced their selection of styles and building designs, as well as their choice of architects.

In the first two decades of the twentieth century, competition intensified among Christian Science architects and others who were interested in obtaining branch church commissions. This competitive spirit often created problems for building committees, who were unaware of the new AIA guidelines that dealt with competitions. The guidelines stipulated that a "trained mind" was needed in order to conduct sanctioned competitions. This implied that only another architect could truly judge a colleague's work.[16] Christian Scientists were committed to capitalist ideals of honest competition and were sometimes confused by the refusal of many AIA members to enter into local competitions. But credentials were also important to Christian Scientists, and soon branch church building committees began to adhere to the requirements for competitions, though few followed the AIA guidelines to the letter.

Architects who were or claimed to be Christian Scientists had some advantage in negotiating commissions, whether or not they were prominent members of the architectural profession, though competition among church members increased as well after 1910. Even so, many architects who were Christian Scientists were awarded multiple commissions. Besides the credentialed architects, there were other building practitioners who called themselves architects who had not joined the AIA or accepted its professional mandates. These builders had little trouble soliciting entry into church building competitions. A well-financed branch church could have up to fifteen architects and builders competing for a commission, which would pay the winner over $6,000 for a $100,000 building.

As Christian Scientists became more familiar with the notion that buildings emerged gradually through a balancing of functional needs, site specifics, materials, styles, adjustments to the design, and other considerations, they tended to accept the AIA's idea that the good architect would work with the membership to create a unique work of art. Those branch churches who accepted this ideal tended to choose AIA architects. Some churches, due usually to economic necessities, chose church builders who had stock plans.

Many architects solicited interest from branch churches. For instance, G. Manning Gale, an architect from Buffalo, wrote to Second Church, Rochester, in 1921, soon after the congregation had been listed in the *Christian Science Journal*. His credentials were his architectural education at MIT, his eighteen-year practice, and his visits to "nearly every Christian Science Church of any consequence in this country." He also mentioned that he was a member of the Mother Church and a member of a students' association, which added a certain prestige to his proposal. He wrote that he trusted that the relationship established between the architect and the church would "prove that Christian Science enables one to express a keener sense of beauty in form and color."[17] L. B. Valk, a church architect with offices in New York and Los Angeles, also wrote to the Rochester congregation. He included an elevation drawing and plan of an ideal Christian Science church (fig. 35), with a form letter asserting that, based on his thirty years' experience in planning and building over nineteen hundred churches of all sizes, shapes, and costs, he could offer "features that produce the most striking effects for the exterior and remarkable effects in the interior, producing the best and perfect acoustic and churchly environment—from the $2000 country church to the great edifice costing over $100,000." In true advertising lingo he wrote, "No matter how small your church, have an ARCHITECT DO YOUR PLANNING, as has been repeatedly asked by the Boards of Church Erection of the Methodist, Baptist, Presbyterian, Christian and Christian Science Churches. . . . Good taste in building a church is intellectual consciousness, it means refinement in architecture—no matter how small the church."[18] He also listed his Christian Science commissions, claiming to have designed over thirty churches, mostly in smaller upstate New York towns, in New York City, and in California.

Charles Draper Faulkner (1893–1979), a Chicago architect who began his career in Solon Beman's office around 1912, was an early competitor with Beman's son, Spencer Beman (1887–1952). Both Faulkner and Spencer Beman built Christian Science churches over four decades and both were members of the AIA. Both architects also wrote to the Rochester church. Faulkner's theme was economics: he claimed to have "found a solution which would go a long way toward reducing the cost of church edifice erection" and cited the five Christian Science churches he was currently building.[19]

Christian Science congregations faced, sometimes naively, the increasingly complex practices of architectural competition. The competitive environment they encountered often focused the need for community spirit as members from many walks of life made their spiritual and financial investments in their new buildings. Church building was a chief form of community building in Christian Science. The strong argumentative methods of Christian Science prayer provided congregations with a solid sense that they could prove the truth of their religious teaching as a community through the erection of a branch edifice of the Mother Church. During the build-

L. B. Valk, Architect

L. B. Valk, Church Architect
ESTABLISHED SINCE 1858, OVER 1900 CHURCHES BUILT SINCE THEN

Office, 420 Stimson Block
Los Angeles, Cal.

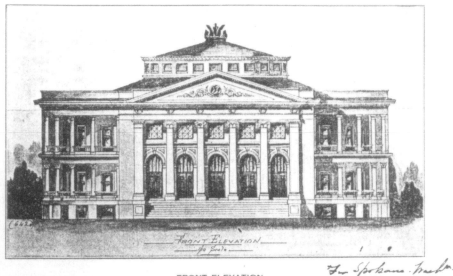

FRONT ELEVATION
CHRISTIAN SCIENCE CHURCH
THE NEW PLAN THAT SEATS EVERYONE CLOSE TO
THE READERS

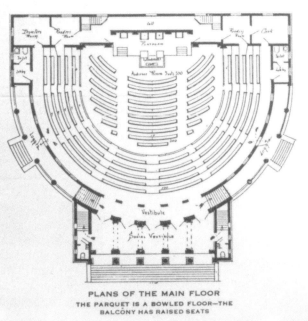

No. 642

Note:

The lot for this Church is 100x117 to alley in rear.

This plan brings the audience all equal distance from the Rostrum so that all can hear the Readers and Testimonies for the mid-week services—there is no plan equal to it.

It is what is required for Science Churches that all should be in close touch with the readers.

The Vestibule is large for social greetings.

The windows are all shaded from the sun and open out on to a Loggia around the audience room and gallery.

For sight, for hearing the half circle plan is perfection, it is on the order of the theatre, and get no appearance of a theatre is shown inside.

Its cost was $70,000 this size seating 782 to 800.

PLANS OF THE MAIN FLOOR
THE PARQUET IS A BOWLED FLOOR—THE
BALCONY HAS RAISED SEATS

Figure 35. A "New Plan" for a Christian Science Church by L. B. Valk of Los Angeles (Church History, Division of the Church of Christ, Scientist, Boston).

ing boom, church congregations merged their spiritual concepts with the practical and often arduous tasks of erecting public, denominational meeting places. This was not an easy task, particularly financially.

To Christian Science congregations, the building of a church edifice was positive proof of the spiritual growth of the membership. In turn, the edifice itself was thought to help spiritualize the larger community. As one member put it: "Multiplied millions are expended in the construction of universities, colleges, schools, and libraries, yet the most important study which can engage the attention of man is that of Christian Science. For the proper exposition of this Science, so essential to the happiness of all, buildings are erected to meet its demands which, completed without sacrifice, free from debt, beautiful, and harmonious,—are not yet commensurate with their supreme need as focal points for the instruction of mankind."[20]

Members believed that the edifices were evidence of the new institutionalization of God's healing and regenerative power revealed through Christian Science. The realities of architectural competitions and the expenses of building challenged many branch churches, whose congregations approached the problems of building with what appeared to be unstoppable zeal and determination. However, the new Christian Science congregations had to complete often difficult negotiations with the architecture and building professions, as well as with financial institutions, in order to accomplish the consolidation of their religious, social, and urban ideals.

The Christian Science building boom intersected with the period of the professionalization of architecture. Both Christian Scientists and architects had to learn from this. Architects who were Christian Scientists easily understood the spiritual ideas of Christian Science building. Others accommodated Christian Science visions for the buildings or tried to translate Christian Science ideals into architectural reality, as this was their mission in architecture as "artists." Christian Scientists educated themselves in the architectural profession and, depending on the size of the congregation, each group did it differently. The prominence of a commission was undoubtedly a major factor in the design of church buildings and perhaps influenced whether non-Science architects were willing to associate themselves with the Christian Science building boom.

Interiors of Churches

The increasing use of classical architecture, inspired by Solon Beman's First Church of Christ, Scientist, Chicago, and demonstrated in the style of the Mother Church Extension, revealed that the exterior of the branch church was of great importance in representing Christian Science to the public. No matter what the exterior style, however, branch churches in many cities had functional, efficient, and innovative interiors. Often plain and unornamented, these interiors also attracted public comment.

Under the influence of women, who offered numerous suggestions in the planning phase of branch churches, the church interiors, reading rooms, and practitioners' offices were designed and maintained as refined, comfortable, and efficient environments. Christian Science women often served on church building committees and usually believed that church interiors should be homelike. This homely atmosphere was undoubtedly easier to achieve in the smaller churches of the early building boom. Nonetheless, the desire for a comfortable interior was the motivation to redefine church spaces of all sizes and to demonstrate a new model for femininity derived from reports about Mrs. Eddy's practical—some would say fastidious—concern with her own well-run household. The use of innovative technological features that, although often unseen, contributed to worshipers' comfort also led to the perception that the Christian Science church represented modern building sensibilities.

Increasingly the interiors of the churches were influenced by so-called feminine values.[21] Artfulness, cleanliness, and comfort were of utmost importance, and the inclusion of plants and flowers instead of established ecclesiastical symbols created an environment of domesticity and gave the interiors the look of an upper-middle-class parlor.[22] Church music was traditional but also somewhat "highbrow" in the use of English and continental compositions, representing a refined femininity. This same refinement was represented in the eloquent speech of the female readers.[23]

Efficiency was a hallmark of the interiors. Well-lighted and inviting foyers, convenient coat and hat checking facilities, proficient ushers, standardized formats of worship—all contributed to an economical use of space. A healthful environment was also a goal, and church building committees and architects attended to ventilation and the circulation of fresh air within the auditoriums. The Christian Scientists "spiritualized" their ideas of cleanliness and sanitation, and the comfort of their church interiors did not go unnoticed in the popular press.

A comfortable interior was viewed positively as it provided the churchgoer with a restful atmosphere.[24] Christian Science reading rooms were constructed as traditional and comfortable parlors, often decorated with Arts and Crafts furnishings and with potted ferns. They provided church members with quiet places to read and pray and to purchase authorized church literature (fig. 36). These spaces, which were sometimes like small bookshops, expressed a homelike femininity. They were much more intimate spaces than were public libraries, although like libraries they were staffed mainly by women. The comfort and restfulness of Christian Science services and reading rooms were often noted by outsiders:

> On entering a Christian Science church one is quickly impressed with the air of quietness and reverence in the place. The people enter noiselessly and sit in silence, and late comers, entering while some exercise is going on, are shown to a rear seat until there is a proper place in the service for them to go forward. The Christian Scientists emphasize the value of silence and meditation and practice these exercises more than most other people. At their headquarters in each city they have a "Silent Room" where anyone can enter it in silence and read Christian Science literature or engage in meditation. We are in danger of losing these fine means of grace in this noisy, hurrying age, and the followers of this faith set us a good example in this respect.[25]

Figure 36. Reading Room of First Church of Christ, Scientist, Grand Rapids, Michigan (Holt).

Christian Scientists were aware that the innovative features of their church and reading room interiors contrasted with the elements of traditional Protestant interiors. As one wrote, with the usual grandiloquence,

> Well-built churches are appearing in many places, and a beauty, even greater than has been manifest in those of other denominations, characterizes their building. And so it should be, for the world is rising to cognize the beauty of Truth, Life, and Love,—the creative Principle. God is being understood more as Love instead of an avenging Judge, and as this conception of God is more fully realized, the gloom which once hung over and in the churches will disappear; and in its stead we will find beauty and life. No longer should we congregate there to pour out to God a woful [*sic*] tale of sin committed, but rather to find in the church a sweet, restful place, to which we may flee from the bustle of the senses for sweeter and closer communion with God.[26]

Even critics of Christian Science viewed these feminine interiors as innovations in church architecture. Charles Sellers remarked on the good common psychology of the warmth and comfort of the Christian Science church, with its individual seats positioned so that all could see. He suggested that if churches were to stay in business they should remember that "wooden benches and cold churches have been the butt of jokes since Jonathan Edwards," and he advised that they should refit their interiors following the Christian Science example.[27] There also was a spiritual component to the idea of comfort. COP manager Alfred Farlow, in suggesting that proper beauty, convenience, and comfort were needed to comply with the demands of Christian Science, said that "an ideal church will be convenient, comfortable and suitably adorned, for, from the standpoint of Christian Science, an unnecessarily unpleasant picture, or an avoidable discomfort which needlessly fasten one's attention upon material things, interferes in so far with the contemplation of spiritual things, and is therefore objectionable."[28]

Another feminine facet of Christian Science churches was expressed in the entry foyer. Spacious and homelike, the foyer encouraged social interactions and enabled Christian Scientists to relate to each other in small family-like groupings. With the erection of First Church, Chicago, in 1897, the large foyer began to be codified. Many branch churches had several fireplaces located strategically throughout their foyers. Aside from their obvious purpose for heating, these fireplaces became focal points for social interactions and allowed for personal groupings and attachments to be formed that were officially sanctioned by the church, although this socialization

Figure 37. Foyer of Fifth Church of Christ, Scientist, Chicago (Church History, Division of the Church of Christ, Scientist, Boston).

sometimes produced rivalries and friction among members. Nonetheless, the architecture of the foyers allowed for easy circulation within an open and comfortable social environment. Within the Christian Science church, individual members could associate with a specific professional practitioner and/or with an authorized teacher of Christian Science, often a woman, and develop closer affiliations. Authorized teachers were those who successfully completed a Normal class, governed by the *Manual.* After completing the class, teachers were given permission to hold a yearly class and their students then gathered together to form a students' association. Many foyer plans accommodated this social system (fig. 37).

The notion of comfort and sociability extended beyond the configuration and decoration of interiors to the consideration of technological innovations, including the use of theater seats; state-of-the-art ventilation, vacuum, and lighting systems; and the acoustic properties of the buildings. Pews were often regarded as old fashioned, and some branch churches turned to theater seating, which advertisements from seating

Figure 38. Interior, Eleventh Church of Christ, Scientist, Chicago, showing popular cove-lighting system (Church History, Division of the Church of Christ, Scientist, Boston).

manufacturers described as modern. Theater seats were thought to be more individualistic, more homelike and comfortable than pews.[29] The use of uniformly diffuse, distinctly white lighting from concealed sources in the interiors was another innovation found in Christian Science churches. "Eye Comfort Fixtures," equipped with silver reflectors, provided such an effect and were featured by the Chicago-based National X-Ray Reflector Company. These fixtures became very popular in Christian Science churches throughout the United States and were subsequently represented in the firm's advertisements in architectural magazines (fig. 38).[30]

Good acoustics also contributed to the comfort of those attending Christian Science services. Since the auditoriums were for listening and speaking, proper acoustics were of utmost importance, and many architects sold branch churches on their acoustical designs. Some architects even pointed out that the design of the Christian Science church was primarily an acoustical problem. Since speaking from any point in the church was part of the Wednesday evening meetings, the church needed to be well insulated from outside noise and shaped to complement this aspect of the service. A large portion of the Sunday service consisted of readings from a dual pulpit, in fixed positions, another aspect that church designers had to take into consideration.[31] One architect suggested that the octagonal shape was the best for Christian Science's acoustical needs, but others disagreed. All architects understood the importance of acoustics to Christian Science worship.[32]

The various technological innovations in the buildings had no apparent religious significance to some critics. The English physician Stephen Paget criticized these innovations as an "aversion of Christian Science from Christian art and the Christian Church . . . [particularly] displayed in architecture." He discussed First Church, London, a refurbished Jewish synagogue near Sloane Street that was occupied by the Scientists in 1898, as combining "the features of a Synagogue with those of the New Gaiety Theatre." He considered it like a concert hall and "the most luxurious lounge in London." Paget quoted at length from a commentary on the branch churches in Chicago, where he read that they were "as beautiful and chaste in architecture and construction as that of First Church [Chicago], which would have been an ornament to Greece itself in its palmiest days. Like the religion out of which it sprung, they are light, cheerful, beautiful, homelike, inviting. There is nothing of the austerity that still clings to the most modern of the churches of other denominations. The entrances are like those to some beautiful temple of art, and within is a wide, high-arched reception hall." Paget commented that the Christian Scientists represented a religion of comfort; it was "Down with the Cross," and "Let us be cheerful and light, like Greece in her palmiest days: let us have none of that austerity."[33]

Female Christian Science members were often asked for recommendations concerning the exteriors and interiors of new branch churches being built, but they tended to address the interiors. For example, the building committee for Second Church, Portland, wrote to the congregation that recommendations from all members about the interior and exterior of the church were welcomed because it was the church home for everyone. Most of the replies about the interiors were from female members. One female member summed up the sentiment of many, writing that so long as the building committee followed the teachings of Christian Science, the appearance of the building would bring to thought "nothing but the idea of stability, simplicity, harmony and purity."[34] Other women who had visited newly opened churches in the Northwest were more direct in their advice. One female member, who had visited First Church, Seattle, suggested that the Seattle church's cove lighting system, which created the effect of sunlight, should be used in the Portland church as well. Another female member thought that the church should follow the "simple artistic lines" of Beman's First Church, Portland. She suggested pews and a pipe organ and thought that "cream walls with ivory white woodwork and brown carpets" would please the majority of members, though her own preference was for walls tinted a very pale lavender, violet carpets, and ivory white woodwork.[35] As many have joked in Christian Science circles, Christian Scientists agree on theology, but division emerges in discussions concerning the right color for the carpets.

Through compromise and democratic consensus, the interiors were often plain and painted white. Even this drew some critics' attention: there was no mystery, no room for wonder or awe. Frank Podmore wrote that "Here are no 'long-drawn aisles and fretted vault.' The Scientists' outlook on the spiritual world is as plain and bare as the walls of her temple, shining white under the abundance of electric lamps."[36]

An example of the importance of interiors, particularly feminized ones, comes from the annals of First Church, New York. At the church's peak of popularity, Mrs. Stetson had a bustling group of twenty-five practitioners with offices in the building. She had absolute control over them and fifteen other healers associated with her church. The church's 1908 annual report recorded that 52,555 visitors had been received at the reading room and over 3,000 visitors treated.[37] A reporter for the *Metropolitan Magazine* was impressed with the idea that the fashionable salonlike, feminine atmosphere of the practitioners' offices somehow elevated the minds of patients in the healing process (figs. 39 and 40):

> The healer's rooms were, to me, the most interesting parts of the church. Mrs. Eddy teaches that one's environment reflects one's thoughts, and the scheme of decoration in each room is created and carried out by the practitioner to evidence strikingly his or her distinctive mentality. There is a prevailing color scheme in each room, a light gray, a wine red, a pale yellow, a dark green, carried out in rugs, portraits, paintings, etchings, crayons, pastels, with the very refinement of exquisite taste and conscientious delineation. It is a fact that each of these rooms breathes irresistibly a living presence. . . . And so in each of the healers' rooms the very atmosphere helps to elevate the patient above the sense of physical and mental suffering into a condition of—well, what shall we call it? Thousands of patients call it health and peace of mind.[38]

Sunday schools provided another important forum for women in Christian Science. The Sunday schools were staffed mostly by women and were an effective setting for the rather methodical instruction provided for children and young people up to the age of twenty years. Many of the early Christian Science Sunday school

Figure 39. Practitioner's office in First Church of Christ, Scientist, New York City (*Broadway Magazine* 18, no. 2 [1907]).

Figure 40. Interior of Mrs. Stetson's office in First Church of Christ, Scientist, New York City (Church History, Division of the Church of Christ, Scientist, Boston).

designs followed the radial Akron plan, a panoptic structure whose prototype was constructed by the Reverend Lewis Miller and the architect Jacob Snyder for use in the Methodist Episcopal Church at Akron, Ohio, around 1866.[39] At First Church, Rochester (fig. 41), students would register to become part of a standardized Sunday school routine and curriculum. During the opening and closing exercises, pupils faced the Sunday school superintendent, usually a woman, who stood on a raised platform. Students then moved to smaller radiating alcoves around the perimeter of the room to receive instruction, which consisted of Bible stories and expositions on their implications for the young, as well as lessons from the weekly lesson-sermon for youth. The students reassembled in the center of the main room at the end of the teaching period. Many Christian Science churches had large one-room Sunday schools, often located beneath the auditorium. Individual classes were assigned a particular table in the room by age group. This arrangement paralleled the organization of children's reading rooms in the new Carnegie libraries.[40] In fact, the Sunday school lending library was the centerpiece of most Sunday schools. Students were

Figure 41. An example of an Akron-plan Sunday school, First Church of Christ, Scientist, Rochester, New York (*Architectural Record* 41, no. 3 [1917]).

encouraged to read authorized children's books and were able to check them out to take home. In addition, popular Christian Science children's novels featuring young female protagonists, such as those in Clara Louise Burnham's *Jewel* series, began to be published through several mainstream presses.[41]

Conventional ideals of masculinity and femininity were important in the establishment of the Christian Science congregational identity and architectural style. The classical exterior associated the religion with enlightened ideals of business and commerce while the interiors expressed the cleanliness and order of the modern Christian home. The new interior spaces, such as the practitioners' offices, reading rooms, and Sunday schools, were institutional arenas where feminine conceptions of the home could be introduced and could influence the public business domain. Most important, through architectural style and interior arrangements, the church emphasized its relationship to modernity. This was achieved not only in the use of advanced steel frame construction and technological innovations, but through the creation of spaces and interiors that denoted the spiritual influence of femininity. Christian Science could thus balance the male and female spheres and contribute an effective religious architecture representative of all members.

After the erection of the Mother Church Extension, questions within the church about the cultural and social meanings of architectural style emerged with greater urgency as the building boom gained momentum. Undoubtedly, many members were aware of the growing use of the classical style by Christian Science congregations, particularly those in Chicago and other parts of the Midwest. With classical influences apparent in the Mother Church Extension, many members must have been convinced that this was the appropriate style. Certainly the social and civic connotations of the classical style were understood by larger urban congregations. The most important challenges, however, remained: How could architecture be utilized to unify and strengthen the public expression of this new vision of Christianity? Was the classical style an appropriate architectural idiom for the Christian Science church? Was there a place for other architectural forms of expression?

NOTES

1. "History of First Church of Christ, Scientist, Bloomington, Illinois," undated ms., CHD.

2. Board of Directors' letter, Jan. 5, 1907, Church Records, First Church of Christ, Scientist, Colorado Springs.

3. See Henrietta Williams, "Among the Christian Science Churches," *Granite Monthly* 28, no. 5 (May 1900): 264–78; *Christian Science Journal* 16 (1898–99): 810–12.

4. Church Records, First Church of Christ, Scientist, Portland, CHD: "The name Beaver Band has been chosen because of the characteristics of the beaver, it being an incessant worker, industrious and careful in its building. Then too, the name seemed fitting for a band in Oregon, the Beaver state."

5. Letter to the Fresno Church from the Long Beach congregation, Apr. 1915, Church Records, First Church of Christ, Scientist, Fresno, CHD; the letter concerned the steps the Long Beach congregation took in finding a suitable architect.

6. *Christian Science Sentinel* 2, no. 46 (July 19, 1900).

7. Mary Baker Eddy, *The First Church of Christ, Scientist, and Miscellany* (Boston: Christian Science Publishing Society, 1913), 162. See the account of Mrs. Eddy's statement in Robert Peel, *Mary Baker Eddy: The Years of Authority* (New York: Holt, Rinehart, and Winston, 1977), 224. On spiritualizing the concept of church, see Anne May Lilly, "The Church Triumphant," *Christian Science Journal* 30 (1912–13): 31–32; Linscott, "Universal Church Militant," *Christian Science Journal* 11 (1893–94): 49; Lida Stone, "The True Church," *Christian Science Journal* 11 (1893–94): 220–21; George Delano, "The Universal Church," *Christian Science Journal* 12 (1894–95): 11; Robert Ziller, "The Church," *Christian Science Journal* 20 (1902–3): 278–86; Arthur E. Blainey, "The Church of Christ, Scientist," *Christian Science Journal* 29 (1911–12): 559–62, and idem, *Christian Science Journal* 30 (1912–13): 665.

8. For an example of this language, see "The Report of Conference Committee, To a Meeting of Members and Congregation of First Church of Christ, Scientist, Chicago," Aug. 6, 1896, CHD:

> The operative effect of Christian Science in human behalf is manifested only in visible and constant progression. As Christian Scientists who seek salvation from sin, disease and death, we are either progressing or stagnating, and the ultimate of stagnation is disease and obliteration. As members of this Church it is impossible for us to progress, individually or collectively, if we fail to perceive the steps that should be taken, or fail to walk therein when the steps are made known to us. In common with all the other Christian Science Churches, it has been given us to know that it is in accord with the divine order that Christian Scientists should possess their own church edifices; and that the time for a response to this revelation is at hand. A failure to perceive this and act accordingly, would be a lapse in the course of progressive salvation, and for us to stagnate under the plea that we are situated well enough as we are, and can afford to "let well enough alone," would be extremely dangerous. Your committee is urgently impressed with the necessity for persevering without cessation in the endeavor to obtain a building, and until that object shall have been accomplished.

9. See Joseph Armstrong, *The Mother Church* (Boston: Christian Science Publishing Society, 1897). Second Church, Portland, reminded its members that progress in building would be made "when we think of a Church membership that is thoroughly *alive,* progressive, possessed of indomitable courage and perseverance, happy—all imbued with the idea that nothing is impossible, and that which ought to be done *can be done.*" Church Records, Second Church of Christ, Scientist, Portland, Oregon, CHD.

10. "How It All Began," ms., 1963, CHD.

11. Anna Friendlich, "Church Building in Christian Science," *Christian Science Sentinel* 11, no. 12 (Nov. 21, 1908): 224–25. Reprinted as pamphlet by Christian Science Publishing Society in 1966.

12. Carol Norton, *The Christian Science Movement* (Boston: Christian Science Publishing Society, 1899), 23.

13. See Joseph M. Siry, *Unity Temple: Frank Lloyd Wright and Architecture for Liberal Religion* (New York: Cambridge University Press, 1996), 96.

14. See Henry Saylor, *The A.I.A.'s First Hundred Years* (Washington, D.C., 1957), 98–100.

15. L. M. Holt, *Christian Science Architecture* (Los Angeles: Press of Times-Mirror, 1908), 4. For other photo books, see Herbert Dunbar, *Illustrated Historical Sketches Portraying the Advancement in Christian Science from Its Inception to the Present Time, Including Some of Its Church Edifices* (Boston: Herbert Dunbar, 1898); E. S. Van Horne, *Some Christian Science Churches* (Columbus, Ohio: Privately printed, 1911).

16. See, for example, the *AIA Circular on Architectural Competitions* (1914), 3, 7: "In order to insure the best results in an equitable competition there should be a clear program, competent competitors, a business agreement and a fair judgment, based on the merits of the design as indicated by a trained mind." The circular suggested nineteen distinct steps in providing the program, which included rules for competitive conduct, instructions for competitors and jury, model agreements between owner and competitors, the need for uniform conditions, and payment schedules.

17. Letter, G. Manning Gale to Board of Directors, July 18, 1921, Church Records, Second Church of Christ, Scientist, Rochester, CHD.

18. Letter, L. B. Valk to Otto Reed, Sept. 30, 1919, Church Records, Second Church of Christ, Scientist, Rochester, CHD.

19. Letter, Charles Draper Faulkner to Board of Trustees, Oct. 15, 1925, Church Records, Second Church of Christ, Scientist, Rochester, N.Y., CHD.

20. A. K. Frain, "Our Church Edifices," *Christian Science Sentinel* 5, no. 7 (Oct. 16, 1902): 106.

21. As Jeanne Halgren Kilde put it: "Auditorium churches of the 1890s borrowed a religious language, a set of material codes, well established in the middle class home since the 1840s. The sacred meanings of the auditorium sanctuary lay precisely in its ability to provide worshippers with a pleasant and comfortable 'church home.'" Jeanne Halgren Kilde, "Creating Sacred Meaning within Secular Space: Auditorium Churches in the 1890s," paper delivered at Sacred Space Conference, Miami University, Oxford, Ohio, Mar. 5, 1993, 10. See also Gwendolyn Wright, *Moralism and the Modern Home: Domestic Architecture and Cultural Conflict in Chicago, 1873–1913* (Chicago: University of Chicago Press, 1980); Witold Rybczynski, *Home: A Short History of an Idea* (New York: Viking Penguin, 1986); Maxine Van de Wetering, "The Popular Conception of 'Home' in Nineteenth-Century America," *Journal of American Studies* 18 (1984): 12–16; Colleen McDannell, *The Christian Home in Victorian America, 1840–1900* (Bloomington: Indiana University Press, 1986).

22. See Martha Crabill McClaugherty, "Household Art: Creating the Artistic Home, 1868–1893," *Winterthur Portfolio* 18 (Spring 1983): 10–15.

23. See Jean A. McDonald, "Mary Baker Eddy and the Nineteenth-Century 'Public' Woman: A Feminist Reappraisal," *Journal of Feminist Studies in Religion* 2, no. 1 (Spring 1986): 89–111; Lawrence Levine, *Highbrow/Lowbrow: The Emergence of Cultural Hierarchy in America* (Cambridge, Mass.: Harvard University Press, 1988).

24. See B. O. Flower, "Reckless and Irresponsible Attacks on Christian Science and Its Founder, with a Survey of the Christian-Science Movement," *Arena* 37, no. 206 (Jan. 1907): 63.

25. James H. Snowden, *The Truth about Christian Science* (Philadelphia: Westminster Press, 1921), 210.

26. See *Christian Science Journal* 16 (1898–99): 309.

27. Charles Sellers, *The Private Life of Mary Baker Eddy* (Detroit: Privately printed, 1935), 38.

28. Alfred Farlow, "Christian Science Church Architecture," *New England Magazine* 32 (Mar. 1905): 47.

29. Kilde gives the new use of theater seats in Protestant auditorium churches a class significance. Congregations that were more highbrow and used to theater and music hall entertainments began to demand for their churches the comfort that theater seats provided. See Kilde, "Creating Sacred Meaning," 7. Some Christian Science churches did have singers and pianists give special concerts on rare occasions, particularly in the Bay Area. See various church files for programs, CHD. Among several prominent national manufacturers of church and school furniture, Heywood Brothers and Wakefield Company approached many Christian Science churches. The company's letters and flyers often mentioned other church commissions. Writing to the Fresno congregation in 1916, for instance, a company representative said: "If you have visited [First Church, Los Angeles] you will without a doubt have noticed the very 'Home Like' appearance of the auditorium." Company literature reiterated:

A pew end will take up more room than an end on an opera chair. . . . the seat on the pew is stationary while the seats on opera chairs can be released and permit very much more room for entrances and exits,—thus a chair will require less room than a pew. You will also realize the fact that each person will obtain an individual seat where opera chairs are used and no one will annoy his neighbor. . . . While the older church of most denominations have used pews, yet the modern church takes advantage of the comfortable seats that are now manufacturered [*sic*] and the fact is that all the larger sized churches of all denominations with the exception of the Roman Catholic and Episcopalian's perfer [*sic*] opera or assembly chairs.

Letter, Heywood Brothers and Wakefield Co. to Mr. Henry Gindelfinger, Aug. 30, 1916, and company flyer, Church Records, First Church of Christ, Scientist, Fresno, CHD.

30. For example, an undated 1911 issue of *Illinois Illustrated Review* (p. 12) featured Leon Stanhope's Christian Science Church at Oak Park. See also Kenneth Curtis, "Artificial Lighting in Churches," *American Architect* 126 (1924): 610. A representative of the National X-Ray Reflector Company wrote to Fresno Church in August 1916, listing sixteen of the churches that utilized the Eye Comfort System. Many of them were edifices designed by Solon Beman and Leon Stanhope. In another letter, a company spokesman wrote: "An illumination from the Eye Comfort Fixtures is very cheerful, restful, and harmonious and especially fitting for Science Churches." Church Records, First Church of Christ, Scientist, Fresno, CHD.

31. On Christian Science buildings and acoustics, see Hope Bagenal, *Practical Acoustics and Planning Against Noise* (London: Methuen, 1942), 62; idem, "The Church Form and Christian Science," *Architect's Journal* (May 25, 1927), 727–28; Vern O. Knudsen and Cyril M. Harris, *Acoustical Designing in Architecture* (New York: John Wiley), 374–75, 383–86. For a more general discussion about church acoustics of the period see A. E. Kidder, *Churches and Chapels* (New York: William T. Comstock, 1900).

32. F. R. Watson, "The Influence of Shape and Materials on the Acoustics of Church Auditoriums, Part Two," *Architectural Engineering and Business* (Mar. 1929): 441–46.

33. Stephen Paget, *The Faith and Works of Christian Science* (London: Macmillan, 1909), 210. Also see Anne Harwood, *An English View of Christian Science: An Exposure* (New York: Fleming H. Revell, 1899), where the exterior style of the church was compared to other Nonconformist churches. She writes that the "spacious and sunny" interior with its bright flowers and its upholstery in "cream color and pale green" gave her the impression that the members, who "seemed to belong entirely to the richer classes," had chosen "the aspect of a pretty and cheerful drawing-room or ballroom" (17).

34. Letter, Miss Ethel Arnold to Building Committee, Feb. 7, 1914, Church Records, Second Church of Christ, Scientist, Portland, CHD.

35. Letters, Mrs. M. J. Barry to Building Committee, Mar. 5, 1914, and Anna Morrell to Building Committee, Mar. 7, 1914, Church Records, Second Church of Christ, Scientist, Portland, CHD.

36. Frank Podmore, *Mesmerism and Christian Science: A Short History of Mental Healing* (Philadelphia: G. W. Jacobs, 1909), 283.

37. Sibyl Marvin Huse, *Twelve Baskets Full* (New York: Knickerbocker Press, 1922), 627–28. Also quoted in Altman K. Swihart, *Since Mrs. Eddy* (New York: Henry Holt, 1931), 39. For Mrs. Stetson's account see Augusta Stetson, *Vital Issues in Christian Science: A Record* (New York: Putnam, 1914), 118.

38. William A. Johnston, "Christian Science in New York: History of the New York Organizations," *Broadway Magazine* 18, no. 2 (May 1907): 162.

39. On the Christian Science Sunday school, see Clara E. Choate's reminiscence in *Miscellaneous Documents Relating to Christian Science and Its Discoverer Mary Baker Eddy* (Providence, R.I.: Privately published, 1934), 27–33; Mary Baker Eddy, *Manual of the Mother Church* (Boston: Christian Science Publishing Society, 1895, 1908), 62–63, 127; Robert Peel, *Christian Science: Its Encounter with American Culture* (New York: Holt, Rinehart, and Winston, 1958). On the Akron plan see Marion Lawrence, "The Akron Plan—Its Genesis, History and Development," *Thirty-Second Annual Report of the Board of Church Extension of the Methodist Episcopal Church, South* (1914), 270–71: "The strong point of this building—and this is the essential test of any building—is its utility in the highest sense. . . . Such completeness and comprehensiveness is almost without parallel among the inventions of man." Quoted in James F. White, *Protestant Worship and Church Architecture* (New York: Oxford University Press, 1964), 128. See Kidder, *Churches and Chapels,*

38–44, for a discussion of Sunday school arrangements. Concerning Sunday school planning, see Richard Franz Bach, "Church Planning in the United States," parts 3 and 4, *Architectural Record* (Sept. 1916): 223–43 and (Nov. 1916): 449–77. The Sunday school building of the Christian Science Center in Boston (1971) was a monumentalization of the Akron plan.

40. See Abigail A. Van Slyck, *Free to All: Carnegie Libraries and American Culture, 1890–1920* (Chicago: University of Chicago Press, 1995), and idem, "The Lady and the Library Loafer: Gender and Public Space in Victorian America," *Winterthur Portfolio* 31, no. 4 (1996): 221–42.

41. See Clara Louise Burnham, *Jewel; a Chapter in Her Life* (Boston: Houghton Mifflin, 1903); idem, *The Right Princess* (Boston: Houghton Mifflin, 1904); Gertrude Smith, *Delight, the Story of a Little Christian Scientist* (Philadelphia: H. A. Hemus, 1907). See also books by William W. Walter such as *The Pastor's Son* and *The Doctor's Daughter* (Aurora, Ill.: Privately printed, 1908).

5 : Chicago and the Triumph of the Classical Style

I n the 1880s Chicago was, in the words of one of the first Christian Science teachers to locate there, "the advanced guard in the West" of Christian Science.[1] By 1893, Chicago stood at the geographic and demographic center of the Christian Science movement. Christian Science in Chicago grew rapidly. One newspaper account from 1900 reported that in thirteen years it had attracted fifty thousand new adherents, primarily business people and professionals. Between 1893 and 1910 eight church edifices were built, each seating between 1,000 and 1,500 people.[2] These were all classical buildings, constructed of stone and inspired by the example of the "White City" of the World's Columbian Exposition of 1893. In this short time, Chicago built more Christian Science churches than any other city. Did this prominence mean that the Chicago Christian Scientists would influence the style of branch churches beyond their city's borders?

This begs the question: why did the classical style become so identified with Christian Science, for Scientists and for the public alike? First, the popularity of Christian Science in Chicago and the influence of the World's Columbian Exposition on concepts of progressive architecture and religion were dominant reasons for the move toward the classical style. Second, if church architecture represented religious ideals and associations, then the classical style harmonized well with law and the authority of government, a concept conveyed by the progressive designs of proponents of city beautification movements such as City Beautiful. The classical style reiterated an important relationship that the Christian Science branch church wanted to maintain with law and concepts of civic responsibility, areas in which the movement was criticized. Third, the classical style was often discussed using the metaphysical language of Christian Science and could also be justified through its theological ramifications.

Christian Scientists undoubtedly presumed that the growth of their religion in the rapidly expanding commercial city of Chicago indicated that their message of healing and success, eloquently stated in a session at the World's Parliament of Religions Auxiliary Congress in 1893 at the Columbian Exposition, was having a profound influence on the urban population. The exposition launched Christian Science into the limelight and also provided a model for the architectural style of new edifices.

The World's Columbian Exposition

After the Great Fire of 1871, Chicago was quickly rebuilt as the center of the railroad industry and a hub for food distribution. The growth was haphazard, with no orderly plan of development. The Chicago commercial elite worked diligently to change the image of Chicago as a dirty, dark, industrial wasteland. They fought hard for congressional support for a World's Fair to be held in Chicago to mark the quatercentenary of Columbus's "discovery" of the New World. The Columbian Exposition confronted the tough American metropolis with a vision of an ideal city of gleaming white faux-marble staff in a style that was derived from historical European models. The contrast between the city and the exposition was overwhelming. As an observer put it, "The city had the reputation for slaughter, elevators, and coal smoke. As if she felt this sadly for the nonce, she went to the utter length of Athenian art to gain a social distinction in the scornful world."[3] Inspired by the 1893 fair, new civic federations and the capitalist business elite, working in a spirit of reform, resolved that new planning and urban design principles should be employed to change the image of Chicago. As Harry Thurston Peck argued, "The importance of the Columbian Exposition lay in the fact that it revealed to millions of Americans whose lives were necessarily colourless and narrow, the splendid possibilities of art, and the compelling power of the beautiful."[4]

The fair became best known for its White City, a visionary stage-set urbanscape that consolidated the appeal of classicism as the official style for monumental building in the United States. In its Woman's Building it also provided an arena for the celebration of traditional femininity. The exhibits of faraway nations gave the crowds who thronged to the fair from the North American heartland a taste of the exotic that was far from their daily experience, and yet not more striking than the White City itself. All these aspects of the fair were significant for the history of Christian Science, which emphasized progress, the enfranchisement of women, and the glories of progressive spiritual enlightenment.

The impact of the Columbian Exposition on urban design and development in the United States has been extensively discussed by architectural historians. A neglected but crucial part of this history, however, is the role of Christian Science, which used the fair as a convenient stage from which to attract the attention of the nation and quickly began to utilize the architectural forms displayed in the White City. There were resonances between the new faith and the ideology of progress in society, commerce, and religion promoted by the fair. The Christian Science belief in the present spiritual perfection of God's creation, and its denial of the diseased, the divisive, or the unpleasant, coalesced marvelously with the image of a city that applauded capitalist development, that was devoid of disease and poverty, where women had a new and much more powerful role in the future, and whose architecture, though built of temporary materials, spoke a language of permanence and authority.

The fair concealed or at least temporarily disguised the symptoms of the nation's slide into an economic depression of unprecedented severity. The depression of 1893 sharpened the debate about the values symbolized and promoted by the fair, especially in the field of architecture and urban design. Louis Sullivan's bitter criticisms are well known in this matter. His own Transportation Building for the fair was the exception to the fair's pervasive monumental classicism, which he denounced as a contagion that would infect American architecture for fifty years. However, he could not hide his admiration for the success of the fair, though he attributed this triumph to a kind of "dementia."[5] He recognized that the fair, with its spacious and interesting grounds and its cultures on display, was a laboratory in which the curious crowds learned the pleasures of spectacle alone. The spectacle value also implied a moral potential for the fair architecture.[6]

The architecture critic A. D. F. Hamlin disagreed with Sullivan's views and believed that the success of the fair's architecture lay in its ensemble of buildings and their possibilities for monumentalizing and unifying city architecture. Concepts of harmony and order were implicit in the fair's classical style. Daniel Burnham, in attempting to design the Chicago civic center as a permanent architecture based on the fair, suggested that the buildings and their harmonious relationships "would be what the Acropolis was to Athens, or the Forum to Rome, and what St. Mark's Square is to Venice,—the very embodiment of civic life."[7] Solon Beman, who at Burnham's request had contributed a classical building, the Mines and Mining Building, to the White City, soon converted to classicism and to Christian Science for their respective architectural and religious ideals.

Solon Spencer Beman: Models and Prototypes

The impact of the Columbian Exposition on Christian Science architecture was immediate. Soon after the fair, Solon Spencer Beman (fig. 42), a relative latecomer to architectural classicism, became an important apologist for the classical style of Christian Science edifice. After completing First Church and Second Church in Chicago in 1897 and 1901, respectively, he converted from Episcopalianism to Christian Science, replacing what the historian Thomas Schlereth called the "emotionalism of the gothic" with the "rationalism of the classic."[8] Early in his career Beman specialized in private, largely residential commissions in the Romanesque or Queen Anne style. His earliest classical designs were in 1893, namely the Mines and Mining

Building and the Merchant Tailors Building for the World's Columbian Exposition and a Blackstone Library in Branford, Connecticut.[9] Schlereth considers that Beman's "personal journey and bifurcated career, involving both . . . the high-church tradition of Episcopalianism and the simple self-reliance of Christian Science, help us understand the artistic and aesthetic, spiritual and moral complexity of the latter half of nineteenth-century America."[10]

Beman was born in Brooklyn in 1853. He was inspired by his father to enter the practice of architecture and in 1870, at the age of seventeen, he began his training in the office of Richard Upjohn, the leading architectural ecclesiologist of the nineteenth century. To Upjohn, the building of a church was a distinctly serious calling. According to him, a church was a "temple of solemnities" that should "fix the attention of persons, and make them respond in heart and spirit to the opening service— The Lord is in his Holy Temple—let all the earth keep silence."[11] He believed that the Episcopal church was the "legitimate" church for the Gothic style. The moral aspect of architecture, so well developed in Upjohn's writings, influenced Beman's own attitudes toward building churches.

After working his way up in Upjohn's firm and achieving the rank of associate designer, Beman left the firm in 1877 to establish himself independently, and by 1879 he had won a prestigious commission from George Pullman, the famous railroad magnate. He had already designed Pullman's mansion in Chicago, and, at Pullman's request, he and Nathan Barrett, a landscape architect, were put in charge of developing Pullman's company town on the shores of Lake Calumet, south of Chicago.

Figure 42. Portrait of Solon Spencer Beman, painted in 1911 by Oliver Denton Grover for the Illinois chapter of the American Institute of Architects (Chicago Historical Society, ICHi-09501).

Beman moved his office to Chicago and between 1879 and 1884 spent much of his time overseeing the development of the town of Pullman, complete with rail and water facilities, a shopping arcade, a church, a theater, a hotel, schools, parks, and eighteen hundred houses, as well as factories and workshops. Beman created the town as a moral statement—a utopia established to ensure the morality and efficiency of its residents. His design of the "noble experiment" at Pullman made him famous. Stewart Woodford, a New Yorker who lectured at the opening of the Pullman arcade, wrote of Beman's design, "Everywhere is order, cleanliness, and beauty. These are the silent teachers to eye, to heart, to brain. They must make men live more cleanly lives, within as without; they must help children, women and men to grow into sweeter, whiter, nobler and more productive manhood!"[12] The moral order that Pullman demanded, however, clashed with the realities of the worker's lives. In June 1894, Eugene Debs, head of the American Railway Union, ordered a boycott of Pullman cars and goods. This led to a general strike and demonstrated to some observers that the Pullman experiment was essentially a failure.[13]

During the 1880s and the 1890s Beman built a number of office buildings in Milwaukee and Chicago before designing the Mines and Mining Building for the World's Columbian Exposition. But, more important, Beman's commission to design the small Merchant Tailors Building for the fair was a major factor in his conversion to classicism in the 1890s (see fig. 22).[14] It was this building that became the prototype for Beman's First Church of Christ, Scientist, of 1897.

The next phase of Beman's career was intimately bound with the use of classicism as the appropriate style for a series of conspicuous edifices, including Christian Science churches. He continued to develop his own concepts of morality and beauty as solutions to urban blight. He promoted his notions of the ethical city into a citywide and even nationwide church-building movement by erecting classical revival Christian Science churches that he believed expressed the spiritual yearnings of the people. It was not merely his ideals or skill as a designer that brought him commissions, however. He benefited from an intertwining, typical of Christian Science, between business and commercial interests and those of the church. For example, in the project to build the second edifice for the congregation of First Church, Minneapolis, bankers supporting the bonds being sold by the church suggested that Beman would be a more appropriate architect than the original choice of the congregation. Beman worked out practical solutions to Christian Science building problems at the lowest cost. This was another advantage to classical revival architecture. Its facades and fenestration could readily disguise modern steel-frame construction. Beman's designs became industry standards throughout the Midwest.[15]

Beman was interested in maintaining an upright, "moral" practice. It was this theme that underpinned the relationship between his business and Christian Science. It is, therefore, not entirely paradoxical that Louis Sullivan, the great enemy of monumental classicism or formalist historicism of any kind, was amicably disposed toward Beman. Sullivan had worked for Beman. Beman's own innovative architectural ideas had already informed some of Sullivan's own.[16] To Sullivan, Beman "was always in advance of his time, always very willing and always in accord with spirited movements of the day."[17] His positive assessment of Beman's classicism was clearly based on the latter's flexible handling of classical architecture as a moral and even modern style.

Sullivan's own encounter with Christian Science is not well known. He produced architectural sketches that fulfilled the requirements for the first Christian Science church in Chicago (fig. 43), although this subject was confirmed only in the 1950s when William Gray Purcell, Sullivan's former associate, recognized the drawings as a Christian Science project.[18] The drawings resemble Sullivan's famous Transportation Building for the Columbian Exposition, but one bears the notation "Readers," an apparent reference to that Christian Science convention. Sullivan mentioned Christian Science in a lecture delivered on February 13, 1905, before the Chicago Architectural Club and asserted that "its so-called philosophy is mostly rubbish" but that its use of what he called "Infinite Energy" as the source of all health for mind, body and soul, translated into "give nature a chance"; and, he said, "its dictum: 'disease and evil are errors of mortal mind' is sound to the core."[19]

Beman, on the other hand, rarely wrote didactically about architecture or Christian Science. Upon the completion of his U.S. Trust Company Building in Terre Haute, Indiana, in 1902, he suggested that buildings could project moral values and

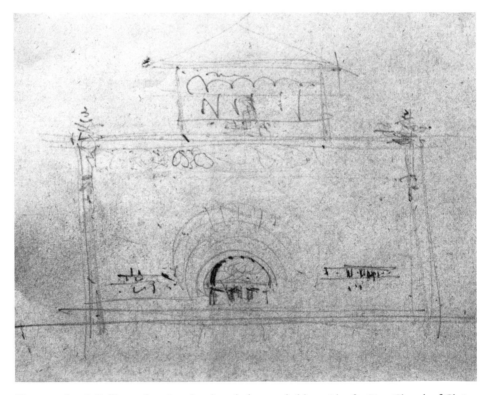

Figure 43. Louis Sullivan, elevation sketch and plan, probably an idea for First Church of Christ, Scientist, Chicago, c. 1896 (Collection Tim Samuelson).

thus help create moral citizens. He believed his building spoke for the "commercial values of beauty": "Beauty is a good thing to invest in. Its dividends are both physical and metaphysical. Beauty always pays in the long run. . . . Beauty has not only commercial value—it has more—a moral value. Under its influence there is nearer approach to right living and honesty and incentive to nobler aims in life: more respect for law and order, its influence ramifying through all activities of life, making for better citizenship, more refined home life and general uplift."[20]

Although Beman was reticent about expressing his own ideas on architecture, he broke his silence in 1907. He published a sweeping defense of classical revival church architecture in *The World To-day,* and his essay became central to the debates on church styles that characterized the first two decades of the new century, a subject explored in the next chapter.

Through Beman's Chicago churches, his published statement on architecture, his involvement with Boston Christian Science officials, and his ready-to-order plans, his church designs assumed a major significance in Christian Science visions of self-representation. Many of his designs superseded Romanesque- and Gothic-style models that were used by branch churches, such as First Church, Buffalo.[21] His influence was greater than his actual output would suggest. Beman designed fewer than forty churches, and these were generally from three templates that he varied for each commission. The three standardized designs were of a basilica with classical porch, a large central-plan domed church with classical porch, and a smaller, library-type edifice.

These ready-to-order plans were attractive to some congregations. For example, in 1906, when the members of First Church, Colorado Springs, were ready to build, the building committee approached a local architectural firm to produce sketches, and they also contacted Solon Beman. The committee received plans from Beman but were unimpressed. However, one person on the building committee wrote that "Mr. Beeman [*sic*] [is] building so many Churches right along—it was decided to make an effort to get something more satisfactory from him." Beman was contacted and he replied that the cost of changing his plans would be expensive, and so the building committee decided to revisit his "Design no. III." He called this design his "little village church" but it could easily have been a design for a new Carnegie library. The group had heard from the Boston church spokesman Judge Hanna of a "very artistic and harmonious church at Highland Park" (fig. 44), and they asked Beman if this plan was similar to that one. Beman replied that it was similar to the Illinois building as well as to the Northampton, Massachusetts, branch church. After a few modifications were agreed upon, the congregation chose Beman.[22]

Solon Beman's son Spencer took over the completion and design of many branch churches after his father's death in 1914.[23] Spencer Beman also became an experienced architect of Christian Science churches due to his policy of soliciting interest from branch churches listed in the *Christian Science Journal.* For example, he sent an informational form letter to the congregation of Second Church, Rochester, in 1921, two years after it organized. He wrote, in part:

Figure 44. S. S. Beman, First Church of Christ, Scientist, Highland Park, Illinois, 1904 (Church History, Division of the Church of Christ, Scientist, Boston).

For many years I have specialized in the design and construction of Churches of Christ, Scientist, and it has been the privilege of this office to have guided in the aggregate an expenditure of over $6,000,000. in this work alone. Accommodations for over 47000 persons exclusive of Sunday School children, have been provided in a total of some seventy-five church edifices, distributed throughout the United States and Canada including the Extension of the Mother Church in Boston. This work embraces some twenty-two million cubic feet of structure and has entailed the careful study and development of almost every conceivable structural and aesthetic phase peculiar to a Christian Science church edifice.[24]

He assured the membership that he could deliver "a maximum result at a minimum cost," with close attention to each phase of the work. Spencer Beman championed the Georgian and colonial style, which eclipsed the classical style by the mid-1930s.

The Bemans together designed at least ninety Christian Science churches.[25] Upon Solon Beman's death, Louis Sullivan remembered his friend as "a religious man," noting that Beman "lived his religion seven days a week. The Golden Rule and the Beatitudes in the Sermon on the Mount were his daily guides. It was an inspiration to come into his presence. He radiated goodness. I always felt better after meeting and talking with him."[26]

Solon Beman's impact was partly due to the Christian Science movement's enthusiastic response to an architecture that church members believed embodied progressive ideals consonant with their social and metaphysical values. Awareness of these characteristics gathered momentum once Christian Science was introduced at the

World's Parliament of Religions. This international meeting, which was held at the Columbian Exposition's Palace of Fine Arts, provided the opportunity to introduce Christian Science to the leaders of world religions.

Christian Science and the Fair

Mrs. Eddy's attitude toward the fair, including the World's Parliament of Religions, was ambivalent.[27] She was concerned that merely human means of publicity and the successes from this publicity would lull her students into a false sense of security, a focus on material gains instead of arduous individual spiritual practice. She also feared that Christian Science might be associated with Eastern mysticism rather than Christianity. Mrs. Eddy's Chicago supporters did not share her qualms about the exposition. They felt that exposure at the parliament and at an additional exhibit space was enough to ensure Christian Science a more respectable national profile.

First Church, Chicago, founded in 1886, decided that Christian Science should be represented at the exposition by an exhibit. At first refused by fair organizers, the Christian Scientists were finally given a place to sell books and pamphlets on Christian Science. Their exhibit centered on Mrs. Eddy's books and, according to her biographer Robert Peel, was well-designed, attracting "a flood of interested visitors, and compliments from all concerned."[28]

The greatest exposure for Christian Science, however, was at the World's Parliament of Religions, hailed by one commentator to be the "most wonderful event since the time of Christ." The official watchwords of the congress, "NOT THINGS BUT MEN! NOT MATTER BUT MIND!" would set the tone for the meetings and dovetailed perfectly with Christian Science precepts and rhetoric. While "secularists and freethinkers" and the Mormons were excluded from participating in the meetings, the Christian Scientists were invited to present a talk at a plenary session and to hold a congress of their own.[29] As a result of this congress, many influential exposition organizers were converted to Christian Science. These included several members of the immediate family of Charles Bonney, the president of the World's Congress Auxiliary.[30] Mrs. Eddy's own address was presented by Judge Hanna in her name, at a well-attended plenary session.

President Bonney himself inaugurated the Christian Science congress with great aplomb, saying, "No more striking manifestation of the interposition of divine Providence in human affairs has come in recent years, than that shown in the raising up of the body of people which you represent, known as Christian Scientists."[31]

The *Inter-Ocean* reported, "One of the best congresses yet held in connection with the Parliament of Religions, judged by number and interest, was that of the Christian Scientists which took place yesterday afternoon in Washington Hall. For two hours before the hall opened crowds besieged the doors eager to gain admission. At two o'clock, the time set for opening the proceedings, the house was filled to the roof, no seats being available for love or money."[32]

Christian Scientists embraced a central tenet of the parliament: there was, or could be, a universal unity of religions. The organizers of the parliament believed that the congresses would contribute to the unity of religions and help produce a "true, universal" religion—one that would ameliorate all social differences and class-based problems.[33] Christian Scientists claimed that their religion was this universal religion, a panacea that would bring all people to an understanding of their spiritual relationship and unity with God. This compelling message was all the more plausible in conjunction with the model White City, which represented cooperation, idealism, and social responsibility.

Ironically—in light of Mrs. Eddy's initial concern—the World's Parliament of Religions is now remembered mostly for its role in introducing Eastern religions into America. It was not known for its contributions to American Christian movements, aside from many Protestant leaders' recognition of a need to move toward church unity. However, it gave the young Christian Science church an opportunity to establish and promote its religious identity among a profusion of theologies within Protestantism.[34]

The Classical Style: Civic and Metaphysical Associations

A few years after the fair, in 1897, the congregation of First Church built its edifice and Solon Beman was the architect. Subsequently, Beman also was commissioned for a Second Church, completed in 1901. Both of these buildings reflected his embracing of the classical idiom. Solon Beman was now established as the leading Christian Science architect in the grandest and most successful city for the new religion, and his designs for these first two Chicago edifices were soon imitated by other architects. Although Hugh Garden received the commission for Third Church, the Conference Committee turned to Beman for the designs of Fourth (1904), Fifth (1904), Sixth (1910), and Seventh (1907) churches. These other Chicago churches by Beman departed somewhat from the Greek "purity" of his First and Second Chicago churches. One of the most impressive was Fifth Church, a monumental temple with a large Doric porch, without a pediment but including a large entablature supported by six massive columns (fig. 45).

In the first decade of the new century, Beman's work for Christian Science spread to the more affluent suburbs of Chicago such as Highland Park (1904), LaGrange (1906), and Evanston (1912). Beman continued to build churches around the nation, in Wisconsin, Iowa, New York, Oregon, Michigan, Nebraska, Pennsylvania, and Colorado. In Chicago his style was taken up by other architects, such as Carl Barkhausen, N. Max Dunning, Leon Stanhope, and Charles Hodgdon, the latter of whom was well known for his University of Chicago buildings.

In 1910, the congregation of Eighth Church, Chicago, hired Stanhope, a Christian Scientist, as its architect (fig. 46). He also designed a church for the congregation in Oak Park, which, in its interior simplicity, retained a quality not unlike that of Frank Lloyd Wright's Unity Temple, located only two blocks away. In fact, Unity Temple had been used briefly by the Oak Park Christian Science congregation.[35] By

Figure 45. S. S. Beman, Fifth Church of Christ, Scientist, Chicago, 1904 (Church History, Division of the Church of Christ, Scientist, Boston).

1918 Stanhope's Eleventh Church, Chicago (fig. 47), caught the attention of both the *Architectural Record* and the *Western Architect*. Robert Moulton wrote in the *Architectural Record,* "Prominent officials in the Christian Science movement have pronounced Eleventh Church, Chicago, to be the most solidly constructed, the most complete in equipment and furnishings, the most harmonious in detail and decoration, and the most perfect in the matter of lighting, heating, ventilation and acoustics of any of the branch churches. In these respects it is possibly only surpassed by the Mother Church in Boston."[36]

The classical style related directly to new civic architectures being built in Chicago and other cities. Courts of law, in particular, had a special meaning for Christian Scientists. First, it was through litigation in the courts that they were enabled to practice their religion—and court cases were many. Second, to the Christian Scientists, the religion represented a higher order of authoritative spiritual law. Many Christian Science congregations wanted to make this association tangible. It was exemplified by the style and siting of First Church, Providence, Rhode Island, designed by Hoppin and Field and erected between 1906 and 1913 (fig. 48). This grand domed building overlooked the city and, more pointedly, McKim, Mead, and White's state capitol, completed in 1904 (fig. 49).[37] The dome of the church, rising within a respectable residential area, echoed the larger dome of the state house.

Associations with civic architecture were expressed in other contexts as well. In late 1900, the *Denver Sunday Post* wrote that the Christian Scientists had tried to get the lot "right opposite the Capitol" but that they had to be content with a parcel of

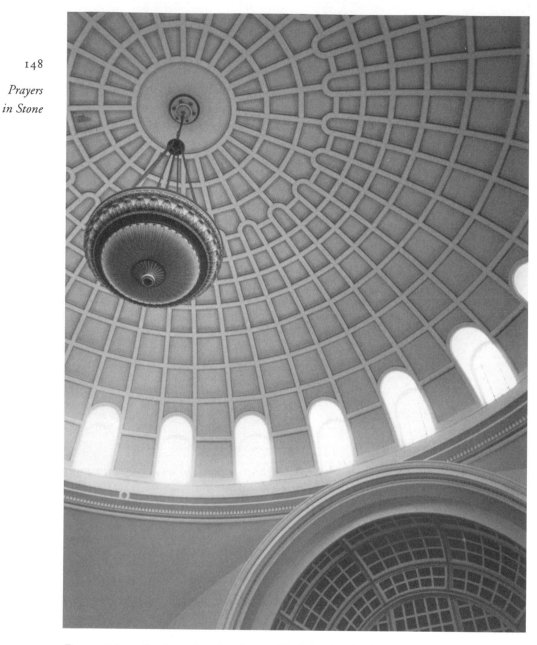

Figure 46. Leon Stanhope, interior, dome of Eighth Church of Christ, Scientist, Chicago, 1911 (Photo by Timothy Wittman, Commission on Chicago Landmarks).

land a block away, although still in proximity to the new government complex. The church was designed by Varian and Sterner and modeled "wholly on the old Greek temple of justice style" (figs. 50 and 51). It was built of lava stone and completed in 1903. The edifice was the largest Christian Science church at the time except for the Mother Church in Boston and was the largest church in the West with the exception of the Mormons' temple in Salt Lake City. Seating capacity was eighteen hundred and the church was usually filled.[38] While the membership of First Church, San

Figure 47. Leon Stanhope, Eleventh Church of Christ, Scientist, Chicago, 1918 (*Architectural Record* 51, no. 5 [1918]).

Jose, wanted only a "quaint California mission style of architecture,"[39] the architect Willis Polk designed a classical church to fit in with new civic structures in a large-scale building campaign in San Jose (fig. 52). Possibly he was developing City Beautiful design concepts in preparation for his work with Daniel Burnham on the San Francisco Civic Center. The 1905 San Jose church structure harmonized perfectly with the county buildings in the vicinity—the Court House, the Hall of Records, and the new Hall of Justice. A newspaper at the time reported that the building was "chaste and exquisite" and that with these qualities came "the conviction of its solidity and permanence."[40] Tom Barnett's classical First Church, University City, Missouri (1925), prominently featured in an article on the rise of the steel-segmented dome in America, was also located in a prominent City Beautiful context, announced by a Lion's Gate, flanked by the City Hall, a Masonic Temple, and later by an important synagogue.[41] These examples indicate that Christian Science architecture in many cities harmonized with a range of large government buildings.

The classical style became predominant in Christian Science not just for its civic association but also because this architectural style predated the rise of ecclesiasticism and therefore could be said to represent primitive Christianity. According to the Christian Scientists, not since Jesus' time and the time of the early Christian

Figure 48. Howard Hoppin and Frederick E. Field, First Church of Christ, Scientist, Providence, 1906–13 (Ivey).

church had healings been accomplished in the manner of Jesus. The Scientists theorized that the teachings of their church, as the new/old church of a new/old dispensation, actually predated ecclesiastical histories. The Christian Science classical style was clearly historical, but its historicity could be mitigated by the incorporation of up-to-date technological innovations and standards that ensured comfort, peace, and shelter from disorder and pain. Though the underlying technologies were modern, Christian Scientists knew that the classical style predated the rise of the Gothic style and so they believed it represented a return to the unfettered and pure time of primitive Christianity. The classical style itself could be configured as "new/old."

Discussions about the theological ramifications of the classical style as an articulated language—reflecting the prevalence of reading that characterized the church services—also explain the classical style's popularity. The edifices provided a community setting for the reading of the Bible and *Science and Health.* To many, this reading was a simple, rational articulation. The architecture promoted this simplicity and rationality. Some Christian Science apologists and architecture critics thought a rapport existed between Mrs. Eddy's teachings and the classical building. Others suggested that the style embodied a more tangible notion, found in Mrs. Eddy's own writings, about God as the center and circumference of Being, or about the sphere as the symbol of Mind.[42] Christian Science writers, not specifically versed in architecture, saw in the concepts of symmetry, purity, and unity an affinity with the clas-

Figure 49. McKim, Mead, and White, Rhode Island Statehouse, Providence, 1904, with the dome of First Church of Christ, Scientist, in the distance (Ivey).

Figure 50. Varian and Sterner, First Church of Christ, Scientist, Denver, 1903 (Van Horne).

Figure 51. Interior, First Church of Christ, Scientist, Denver (Holt).

sical style. These concepts were viewed as therapeutic to a "neurasthenic" population. The new religion was also generally nonsymbolic: the congregations eschewed the use of overt ecclesiastical symbols, preferring a simplicity of surroundings, though stained glass windows and restrained ornamentation were sometimes symbolic.[43]

To many people, the classical style embodied the abstract and idealistic qualities of the Christian Science vision and discourse, which emphasized rationality and logic as science. Solon Beman, the staunch supporter of the classical style, stated that Christian Science was "scientifically true, rational, and natural." Unlike the Gothic style, he said, the classical, "with its sense of calm proportion, its sincerity and refinement, and . . . its rationalism, seems to represent the faith of those who employ it in their houses of worship."[44] Decades later, architectural historians such as Donald Drew Egbert agreed that the "rationally clear form" of the Mother Church edifices was comparable to the Christian Science idea that "mind is the fundamental principle of the universe."[45]

However, some contemporary critics pointed out that Christian Science churches looked like banks. Fiscal responsibility was certainly important to the new movement, and the solid style associated with bank buildings was often translated into Christian Science edifices. Several congregations, such as those at New Albany, Indiana, and Natchez, Mississippi, actually bought mid-nineteenth-century bank build-

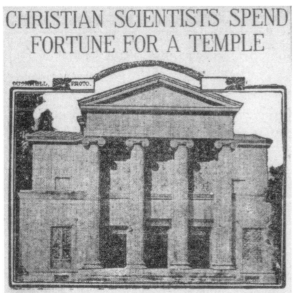

Figure 52. Typical newspaper announcement of church dedication (*San Jose Post,* January 2, 1906).

ings and refitted them to produce what one journalist called the "usual Greek type" prevalent in the architecture of the church.[46]

As if to underscore the acceptance of the classical style by Christian Scientists, in 1917 the Mother Church board of directors memorialized Mrs. Eddy with a classical monument at her gravesite at Mount Auburn Cemetery, Cambridge, Massachusetts. The board held a competition, following the AIA rules, and chose the classical design of the New York architect Egerton Swartwout, well known for civic designs (fig. 53). The board of directors set the cost at a little over $100,000 and established the lot as a square, one hundred feet on a side, but otherwise it made no restrictions except that sculpture should not be used. Models were produced, and the directors asked that ornament be confined to conventional urn and floral motifs, particularly the wild rose—Mrs. Eddy's favorite. A review of the monument in the *Architectural Record* reported on its "great strength and beauty, fittingly austere and reverent, yet relieved by rare grace of vigorous outlines." The granite was felt to enrich the "feminine character of the monument." Writing about the memorial, John Taylor Boyd Jr. remarked that it faintly resembled the Tower of the Winds at Athens.[47]

Inspired by the classical revival architecture of the World's Columbian Exposition, Christian Scientists embarked on a monumental church building campaign in Chicago. Many architects involved in the building movement, in Chicago and elsewhere, were inspired by the debates concerning the important place classical architecture might inhabit in the urban civic centers of the United States. What became apparent in the discussions by architects in popular and architectural publications was the substantial nature of the buildings being erected by the Christian Science church and their similar styling as a means of self-representation in America. This solidarity of church architecture was a way to unify the church itself as well as to exemplify the more rational influences within its theology. The experiences of large congregations with monumental church architecture in the Chicago area advanced a strong rational and civic-minded sensibility throughout the Christian Science movement in the early part of this century, one imbued with the idea that the classical style represented the social, moral, and religious values of Christian Science in the United States.

Although the classical revival architecture characteristic of Christian Science continued to gain adherents, especially between 1905 and 1915, church officials maintained that there was no "official" style, and indeed many suburban and rural churches seemed closer to the small meetinghouses of New England than the temples of Rome (although many featured classical porches). William B. Johnson, clerk of the Mother Church, wrote to the clerk of the branch church in Laurel, Mississippi, in 1902:

> I will state that I know of no prescribed style of architecture for constructing churches of the Christian Science denomination, but this thought has been expressed—that the church edifices of our denomination should have the appearance of a *church* to the degree that they will not be taken for a city building, library, school or a hall.
>
> No special architect has been appointed or authorized by our denomination to draw plans for Christian Science Church edifices. It is the privilege of each church to employ any architect it thinks proper.[48]

Figure 53. Egerton Swartwout, Mary Baker Eddy Memorial, Mount Auburn Cemetery, Cambridge, Massachusetts, 1917 (Ivey).

Statements like this set the stage for increasingly heated debates between architects concerned with Christian Science institutional representation. But the influence of Chicago Christian Scientists and architecture and the urban reform movements that began in Chicago clearly influenced subsequent Christian Science church commissions.

Many Christian Scientists looked to the grand spectacle of the Extension of the Mother Church in Boston as their architectural model, but few realized the influences of the Columbian Exposition and of Solon Beman on the design of that model.

Because of the religion's success in Chicago, the influence of the Midwest metropolis during the early building boom was paramount in associating the successful exposition architecture with Christian Science. Chicago classicism significantly marked the movement's early buildings and even came to symbolize what was, after all, the New England faith of Mary Baker Eddy and her followers. In this sense, Louis Sullivan was right: the influence of the classical idiom was pervasive, and during the early century it outstripped regional architectural styles. The Christian Science building boom is a striking example of this. However, the influence of the classical style, though dominant, proved somewhat unstable. Debates in architecture, spearheaded by Burnham and Sullivan, among others, were heard within Christian Science circles.

NOTES

1. Bradford Sherman, *Historical Sketch of the Introduction of Christian Science in Chicago and the West* (Chicago: F. M. Leyda, 1915), 1.

2. These were First Church (1897), Second Church (1901), Third Church (1901), Fourth Church (1904), Fifth Church (1904), Sixth Church (1910), Seventh Church (1907), and Eighth Church (1910).

3. Quoted from an article on Chicago in *Halligan's Illustrated World's Fair,* ed. John McGovern, part 24 (Chicago: Illustrated World's Fair Publishing Co., 1893), 709.

4. Harry Thurston Peck, *Twenty Years of the Republic, 1885–1905* (New York: Dodd and Mead, 1906), 352.

5. Louis H. Sullivan, *The Autobiography of an Idea* (New York: Norton, 1926), 324–25.

6. Reid Badger, *The Great American Fair: The World's Columbian Exposition and American Culture* (Chicago: Nelson, Hall, 1979), 97. As the architecture critic Mrs. M. G. Van Rensselaer put it, the "mind-hungry, beauty-starved, ignorant, but eagerly ambitious masses" could best make use of the "civilizing and uplifting ministrations" of the fairground's unity, beauty, and harmony. *A Week at the Fair* (Chicago: Rand McNally, 1893), 78. For another voice proclaiming the fair's moral imperatives, see Henry C. Kinney, *Why the Columbian Exposition Should Be Open on Sunday: A Religio-Social Study* (Chicago: Rand McNally, 1892).

7. Edward H. Bennett and Daniel H. Burnham, *Plan of Chicago,* ed. Charles Moore (Chicago: Commercial Club, 1909), 117.

8. Thomas J. Schlereth, "A High-Victorian Gothicist as Beaux-Arts Classicist: The Architectural Odyssey of Solon Spencer Beman," *Studies in Medievalism* 3, no. 2 (Fall 1990): 144.

9. Beman's Architectural Scrapbook, Burnham and Ryerson Library, Art Institute of Chicago, includes the statement that the Blackstone Library "is an elaboration of the design for the Merchant Tailors Building at the World's Fair, which was also planned by Mr. Beman, and from which Mr. Blackstone received the first impression of the design [of] his gift" (73). The most complete biographical summary of Beman is Charles E. Jenkins, "Solon Spencer Beman," *Architectural Reviewer* (Chicago) 1, no. 1 (Feb. 1897): 47–101. The *American Architect,* no. 1471 (Mar. 5, 1904), includes an illustration of the 1901 Blackstone Library in Chicago's Kenwood district.

10. Schlereth, "A High Victorian Gothicist," 144. On Beman, see also Schlereth, "Solon Spencer Beman, 1853–1914: The Social History of a Midwest Architect," *Chicago Architectural Journal* 5 (Dec. 1985): 8–31; idem, "Solon Spencer Beman, Pullman, and the European Influence on and Interest in His Chicago Architecture," in *Chicago Architecture, 1872–1922: Birth of a Metropolis,* ed. John Zukowsky (Munich: Prestel, 1987), 173–88; A. T. Andreas, "Solon Spencer Beman," *History of Chicago* 3 (1884–86): 72. On Beman's Christian Science designs, see Lawrence Schlack, "Solon Spencer Beman," *Quarterly News, Mary Baker Eddy Museum* 16, no. 1 (Spring 1979): 241–43.

11. Everhard M. Upjohn, *Richard Upjohn: Architect and Churchman* (New York: Columbia University Press, 1939), 71.

12. Quoted from the *Chicago Inter-Ocean,* date unknown.

13. Debs later went to prison on conspiracy charges. Debs, who often contributed to Flower's *Arena* magazine, particularly articles on Socialism, had been healed through Christian Science. See Robert Peel, *Mary Baker Eddy: The Years of Authority* (New York: Holt, Rinehart, and Winston, 1977), 442 n. 60.

14. By 1892, the Chicago Exchange subcommittee of the Merchant Tailors National Exchange proposed to erect a Greek-style building at the exposition consisting of an exhibition space with reception rooms and toilets for the subscribers to the building fund. A circular was distributed on September 1, 1892, describing the building as a reproduction of the Erechtheion at Athens. See *A Week at the Fair,* 167–68. In the *Monthly Bulletin of the Illinois Society of Architects* 18–19, no. 12 (June–July 1934): 1, the architect Irving Pond noted that "it was really through Mr. Pullman and his sartorial connection that Beman designed . . . the Merchant Tailor's display building which became the inspiration for and prototype of the myriad classical Christian Science churches which embellish the landscape in the United States and foreign countries."

15. For examples of Beman's works, see Paul Eli Ivey, *Tabernacle to Temple, The Christian Science Building Boom, 1895–1925: The Triumph of the Classical Style* (Ann Arbor, Mich.: UMI, 1992), 261–305.

16. Sullivan, working as a draftsman in Beman's office, designed elevator grilles in the Pullman Building, though some scholars dispute Sullivan's role in Beman's office. Certainly Sullivan and Beman had numerous professional connections. See Hugh Morrison, *Louis Sullivan: Prophet of Modern Architecture* (New York: Peter Smith, 1935), 59. When Sullivan and Adler's Auditorium Building was constructed in 1886–89, many of the more innovative massing ideas had already appeared in Beman's 1885 Studebaker Building, its next-door neighbor.

17. "Address by Mr. Louis H. Sullivan," June 8, 1915, quoted in Louis Sullivan, *The Public Papers,* ed. Robert Twombly (Chicago: University of Chicago Press, 1988), 209–10.

18. In the late 1950s, the preservationist Richard Nickel, who then owned the drawings, contacted Purcell, who identified them as a Christian Science project. Personal communication, Timothy Samuelson, 1998.

19. Louis Sullivan, "Natural Thinking, a Study in Democracy, an Address Delivered Before the Chicago Architectural Club," ms., Burnham and Ryerson Library, Art Institute of Chicago, quoted in Maurice English, ed., *The Testament of Stone: Themes of Idealism and Indignation from the Writings of Louis Sullivan* (Evanston: Northwestern University Press, 1963), 105–23. See also Louis Sullivan, *Kindergarten Chats and Other Writings* (New York: Wittenborn and Schult, 1947), 99; Robert Twombly, *Louis Sullivan: His Life and Work* (New York: Viking, 1986).

20. Beman's Architectural Scrapbook, unidentified clipping, 18.

21. For illustrations of some of these earlier church facades see Herbert L. Dunbar, *Illustrated Historical Sketches Portraying the Advancement in Christian Science from Its Inception to the Present Time, Including Some of Its Church Edifices* (Boston: Herbert Dunbar, 1898).

22. Building Committee Report, April 21, 1907, Church Records, First Church of Christ, Scientist, Colorado Springs, Colorado.

23. Solon Beman was working on Fourth Church, New York, at the time of his death. See *Architecture and Building* 50 (July 1918).

24. Letter, Spencer Beman to Board of Directors, Aug. 25, 1921, Church Records, Second Church of Christ, Scientist, Rochester, CHD.

25. This number comes from a list entitled "Christian Science Churches Designed in the Office of S. S. Beman, Architect, Chicago, Illinois," prepared by Solon Beman's grandson, Jeremy Beman, c. 1975, CHD. According to *Chicago Architects Design: A Century of Architectural Drawings from the Art Institute of Chicago* (Chicago: Chicago Art Institute, 1982), 91, Spencer Beman alone executed nearly one hundred designs in twenty states before his death in 1952. See, for example, First Church, Birmingham, Michigan (1926); First Church, Winnetka, Illinois (1933); Twentieth

Church, Chicago (1948); Twenty-first Church, Chicago (1950); First Church, Hinsdale, Illinois (1951).

26. Quoted in Schlack, "Solon Spencer Beman," 243.

27. There are many indications, however, that Mrs. Eddy was interested in participating in the fair, if only to gain more exposure for her books. She had already started thinking about a book she hoped would be ready for the exposition. In March 1893, Mrs. Eddy employed James F. Gilman, of Concord, to illustrate the book-length poem she had written, *Christ and Christmas.* See accounts in James F. Gilman, *Reminiscences of James F. Gilman* (Privately printed, 1917), 17, and *Church History, Painting a Poem: Mary Baker Eddy and James F. Gilman Illustrate* Christ and Christmas (Boston: Christian Science Publishing Society, 1998). For a more complete account of Mrs. Eddy's attitudes toward the Columbian Exposition, see Peel, *Mary Baker Eddy: The Years of Authority,* 47–50.

28. Peel, *Mary Baker Eddy: The Years of Authority,* 48. For other sources that address the Christian Science presence at the fair, see Moses P. Handy, *The Official Directory of the World's Columbian Exposition, May 1st to October 30th, 1893: A Reference Book* (Chicago: W. B. Conkey, 1893), 371, 381; "Caroline D. Noyes, C.S.D.," ms., 1936, Chicago Historical Society, 3.

29. Hubert H. Bancroft, *The Book of the Fair, an Historical and Descriptive Presentation of the World's Science, Art, and Industry, as Viewed Through the Columbian Exposition at Chicago in 1893,* 3 vols. (Chicago: Bancroft Co., 1893), 3:943. On the auxiliary congresses, see also James W. Shepp and Daniel B. Shepp, *Shepp's World's Fair Photographed* (Chicago and Philadelphia: Globe Bible Publishing Co., 1893); Handy, *Official Directory;* David F. Burg, *Chicago's White City of 1893* (Lexington: University Press of Kentucky, 1976), 267; Walter R. Houghton, *Neely's History of the Parliament of Religions and Religious Congresses at the World's Columbian Exposition* (Chicago: F. T. Neely, 1893).

30. "History of First Church of Christ, Scientist, Chicago," 1939, CHD.

31. Quoted in the *Christian Science Journal* 11, no. 8 (Nov. 1893): 388.

32. *Chicago Inter-Ocean,* Sept. 21, 1893.

33. Badger, *Great American Fair,* 126.

34. For example, Charles Little told the readers of the *Methodist Review* (Mar. 1894): "The display of Protestant Christianity . . . lacked unity and coherence. It was abundant in variety and abundant, too, in power. One thing, however, was painfully and conspicuously absent, namely, a clear, definite, and powerful statement of the fundamental positions of Protestantism" (216).

35. "Will Share Unity," *Oak Leaves* (Aug. 21, 1909): 3. Quoted in Joseph Siry, *Unity Temple: Frank Lloyd Wright and Architecture for Liberal Religion* (New York: Cambridge University Press, 1996), 96, 291.

36. Robert H. Moulton, "Eleventh Church of Christ, Scientist," *Architectural Record* 51 (1918): 428. For another account of Eleventh Church, see Robert Craig K. McLain, "The Eleventh Church of Christ, Scientist, at Chicago," *Western Architect* (Jan. 1918).

37. See Edward Carpenter Jr., "Foundation of Christian Science Church in Providence Nearly Thirty Years Ago," *Newport County Sentinel,* June 9, 1932; John S. Gilkeson Jr., *Middle-Class Providence, 1820–1930* (Princeton: Princeton University Press, 1986), 265. According to *The Book of Rhode Island* (Providence: City of Providence, 1930), "The most recent [denomination] is the First Church of Christ, Scientist, the dome of whose stately church on Prospect Hill is the most conspicuous feature of the eastern skyline of Providence" (54).

38. *Denver Sunday Post* quoted in the *Christian Science Sentinel* 3 (Dec. 13, 1900): 233. The building cost over $165,000 to build and furnish. See *Denver Daily News,* Oct. 13, 1907; *Inland Architect* (Apr. 1903). It was reported in the *Architectural Review* 10, no. 5 (May 1903), that the "Christian Science Tabernacle in Denver is quite properly civic, rather than ecclesiastical in its style" (59).

39. *San Jose Daily Mercury,* quoted in the *Christian Science Sentinel* 2 (Mar. 29, 1900): 480. The members were inclined to have the church built in the mission style because they were impressed with the buildings at Stanford University.

40. *San Jose Daily Mercury,* Dec. 18, 1905.

41. See "A Domed Roof Construction," *American Architect* 76, no. 2462 (Dec. 31, 1924): 635–40; "First Church of Christ, Scientist, University City, Missouri," *American Architect* 81 (May 20, 1927): 667–68. The church is also mentioned in John Albury Bryan, *Missouri's Contribution to American Architecture* (St. Louis: St. Louis Architectural Club, 1928).

42. For example see Mary Baker Eddy, *Science and Health with Key to the Scriptures,* final revision, 1906 (Boston: Christian Science Publishing Society, 1971), 203–4, 240, 262.

43. Solon Beman, for example, often included seven-branched candelabra on readers' platforms, for instance in First Church, Chicago, and First Church, Grand Rapids. Bliss Knapp, a Christian Science teacher known for his prophetic sensibilities, wrote that John of the Apocalypse had seen seven candlesticks that represented the seven Christian churches and in the midst of them "one like unto the Son of man," whom Peter had acknowledged as the Christ. According to Knapp, the number seven symbolized the "full and complete illumination which Christ bestows upon his Church." See *Christian Science Sentinel* (Jan. 26, 1924). Mary Baker Eddy had also defined God using seven synonyms. Images of bundles of wheat and seven-pointed stars were sometimes used in church windows, for example, in First Church, Coronado, California (with the seven synonyms listed in the seven-pointed star) or as exterior pediment decorations, as at First Church, Long Beach. Some branch churches also placed large lanterns on the readers' platform, echoing the ones in the Extension of the Mother Church that projected hymn numbers on the large pilasters. A perusal of early books of photographs of Christian Science churches, such as L. M. Holt's *Christian Science Church Architecture* (Los Angeles: Press of Times-Mirror, 1908), reveals a much more defined symbolic orientation than contemporary Christian Scientists recognize. Stained glass windows with cross-and-crown and burning-lamp motifs were common. Some churches even hung reproductions of paintings of Jesus over the readers' platform. Other reproductions of paintings of biblical scenes, such as Daniel in the lion's den, were also customary. Plants, particularly ferns and palms, were very popular, and cut flowers were also placed on many platforms. Bible texts and citations from Mrs. Eddy's writings were commonly displayed on the walls, so much so that she restrained their use. See Mary Baker Eddy, *The First Church of Christ Scientist and Miscellany* (Boston: Christian Science Publishing Society, 1913), 213–14.

44. Solon S. Beman, "The Architecture of the Christian Science Church," *The World To-day Magazine* 12, no. 6 (June 1907): 586–88.

45. Donald Drew Egbert and Charles W. Moore, "Religious Expression in American Architecture," in *Religious Perspectives in American Culture,* ed. James Ward Smith and A. Leland Jamison (Princeton: Princeton University Press, 1961), 387. John R. Scotford wrote in *The Church Beautiful: A Practical Discussion of Church Architecture* (Chicago: Pilgrim Press, 1945): "The Christian Scientists have chosen a style of building which is in harmony with their attitude of philosophical detachment from the here and now" (150). See also Willard B. Robinson, *Reflections of Faith: Houses of Worship in the Lone Star State* (Waco: Baylor University Press, 1994), 173. Robinson suggests that the Palladian motifs of many Texas Christian Science churches emphasized the abstract qualities of Christian Science.

46. See Holt, *Christian Science Church Architecture,* 102. The New Albany congregation bought an 1850s brick and sandstone bank building in 1907 and redecorated it. First Church, Natchez, Mississippi, bought one of the oldest buildings (1809–11) in Natchez and remodeled it in 1945. See "Christian Science Church Here Opens," *Natchez Democrat,* Jan. 20, 1946, and "First Church of Christ, Scientist, Will Be Dedicated in Services Today, *Natchez Democrat,* June 8, 1947.

47. John Taylor Boyd Jr., "The Mary Baker Eddy Memorial," *Architectural Record* 21, no. 5 (May 1917): 449–50. For other discussion of the monument, see Egerton Swartwout, "The Memorial to Mary Baker Eddy," *Architecture* 35, no. 4 (Oct. 1917): 185–89.

48. Letter, William B. Johnson to clerk of Laurel, Mississippi, church, Nov. 4, 1902, CHD.

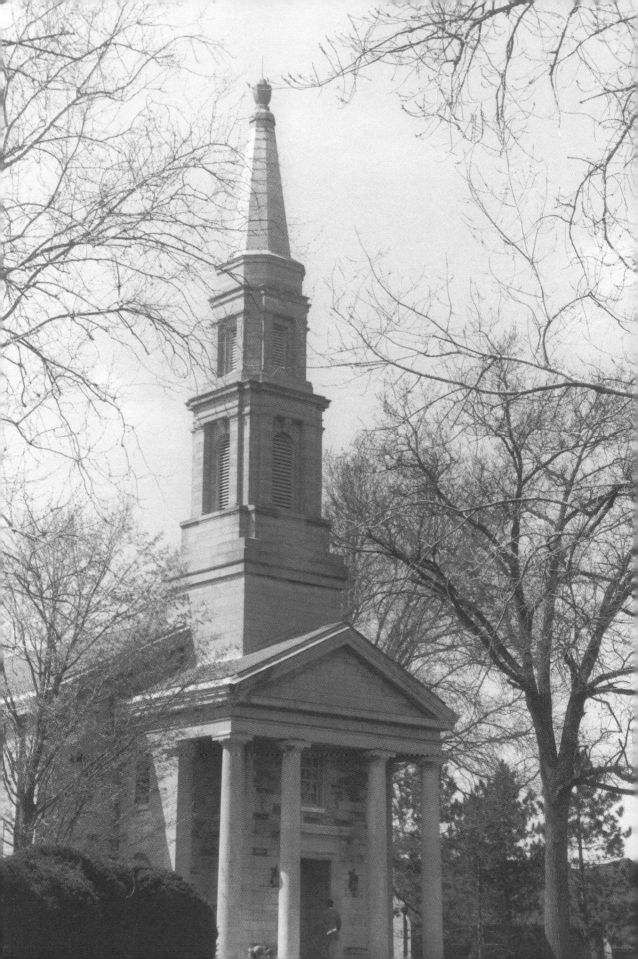

6 : Debates on the Significance of Style

Although the classical idiom was increasingly associated with the Christian Science denomination through the second decade of this century, acute debates over style took place within the church. After all, the original Mother Church building and its Extension contrasted sharply with one another and suggested that the choice of architectural style was not clear cut for Christian Science. Which edifice should branch churches emulate?

The debates, which were carried out in the popular press as well as in professional architecture journals, concerned two competing ideas about the status of Christian Science within historical Christendom. Some people believed the church should pronounce itself the modern dispensation of the original primitive Gospel, which included physical healing as well as moral and spiritual reformation. To them, classical architecture was the appropriate idiom because it represented a restoration of a perfected architecture associated with the time of primitive Christianity and it was also aligned with broader modern reform movements. The style also could accommodate modern building technologies. Other people, however, believed that Christian Science was the culminating moment of the history of Christianity. They thought that Christian Science derived from the theology of the suffering savior a message that emphasized the resurrection of the human condition from matter to Spirit: it was a progressive unfolding from suffering to Science. The religion's self-representation, therefore, should underscore this continuous relationship with ecclesiastical Christendom. In this view, new church architectures should emphasize the transformative power of Christian Science as a completion of historical and traditional Christianity: a church should be recognizable as a church, that is, Romanesque or Gothic in style.

Many architects and church members were unsure what the appropriate architectural expression for Christian Science should be. However, they agreed that there should be a "Christian Science architecture." That is, the exterior style of the Christian Science church should be indicative of a congregation's ideals of religious association, social appeal, and public reform. Different styles would be associated with different values. Gothic architecture seemed to orient the church toward social conservatism and ecclesiastical Christianity—the very tradition that reacted so strongly against Christian Science. On the other hand, models of business and civic reform were being redefined in the architectural and design professions. Within these professions, supported by the new business elite, classical architecture was often presented as part of the progressive modern solution to configuring urban space. Classical architecture introduced the ideals of rationality, moral order, and efficiency into the city and dominated the building boom, despite Mrs. Eddy's tendency to favor more traditional church architecture. The classical style separated the church from traditional Protestant denominations and also associated the new institution with public authority, respectability, and permanence.

Church officials maintained the democratic standards that Mrs. Eddy had established in the *Manual* concerning branch church government. However, they did have opinions about church architecture and published them with Mrs. Eddy's support. Alfred Farlow, as the manager of the Committee on Publication, published the first major article on the architecture of the church in *New England Magazine* in March 1905. He claimed that new church buildings demonstrated a conviction and liberalism on the part of congregations that believed that "church edifices will redound to the welfare of mankind." He suggested that the requirements of Christian Science worship dictated that the auditorium be "a simple class-room with furnishings suitable to its purpose, and decorations in harmony with Christian Science ideas." His article was illustrated with photos of new prominent branch churches, mainly in the classical style. However, he suggested that styles such as the Romanesque and the Gothic were more specifically Christian, and that a classical edifice might be confused with other civic buildings. Farlow thought the classical style had lost its religious connotations. He advocated, instead, a recognizable but "distinctive style of church architecture . . . such as will enable the passerby to distinguish it from a city hall or library, such as by its very appearance suggests its grand and lofty purpose."[1]

In the same month that Farlow's article appeared, the *Craftsman* published an article on Christian Science architecture. This magazine was published by Gustav Stickley, founder of United Crafts and a disciple of William Morris and John Ruskin. By 1904 the magazine had begun to publish articles on subjects beyond the Arts and Crafts furniture designs that made the company well known. The March 1905 article was polemical in tone; indeed, it is the first coherent critique of Christian Science architecture. The article criticized Farlow's position, stating that the "simple class-room" that Farlow suggested would be falsified, not defined by, a "churchly exterior."[2]

Whereas Farlow believed that the creation of the classical church edifice indicated that architects sought to depart as widely as possible from the ordinary church design in order to express the newness of the religion, the *Craftsman* editor suggested that the Christian Scientists, "professedly a philosophic body, have reverted to classic models . . . because architecture was the highest and most complete art of the people who developed philosophy from crude beginnings to a perfect science." Moreover, according to the editorial, the classical models were the most interesting, and were evidence that "much refinement and taste, supplemented by no small originality, characterize that body of our people of which these churches are intended to be the highest aesthetic and spiritual expression." This assessment of Christian Science architecture outside the pages of the official church periodicals was soon echoed in numerous articles on the subject in a wide range of journals.[3]

Solon Beman and Elmer Grey

Two Christian Science architects were central to the debates on how to represent the new religion architecturally. They were Solon Beman, of Chicago, and Elmer Grey, a Milwaukean who settled in California. In 1907 Beman published his defense of the classical style he was popularizing. In his article, which appeared in the *World To-day Magazine,* one of the most popular Chicago periodicals,[4] Beman suggested, "No modern architectural development, not even that of the great office building, is more striking than that seen in the churches of the Church of Christ, Scientist. It is something more than a matter of technic. It is a matter of social psychology."[5] Beman believed that the religious architecture of the church would, in fact, "influence architectural art generally" and that Christian Science was poised to have a central role in the formation of a new American culture. The article was replete with photographs of new Christian Science edifices, many of them designed by Beman himself. Beman developed the idea, similar to Cram's, that architecture made visible an inner conviction that summarized the social life of the people: Beman wrote, "Architecture finds in religion its most powerful incentive. Religion creates a nation's ideals, and in its architecture we must trace their record." Church architecture, therefore, should express "the faith and spirit of its builders."[6]

Beman believed that the new churches needed to be of "practical, straightforward, utilitarian character . . . clothed in the most artistic and consistent architectural form within the reach of the building committee." According to Beman, the classical style of church was not that of a "pagan temple" but a "vital force" of the "first principles of truth." The classical style had been the guide and inspiration for great architecture throughout history. This style was, therefore, appropriate and logical for a religion that concerned itself with the well-being of the individual and the welfare of society—a religion devoted to the public welfare. Because of religion's central place in the creation of national ideals, as well as the exalted public nature of church architecture, Beman thought that the Christian Scientists should choose a "straightforward" and "enduring" architectural style.[7]

The predominance of the classical in Christian Science churches, moreover, indicated to Beman that the church was progressive. Gothic architecture represented the religious ritualism of the past: "The Gothic style has been interwoven in warp and woof with everything ecclesiastical and the emotional ceremony and forms of what is called the Orthodox Church. In fact, the Gothic style is the very outgrowth and development of such ritualisms, and is quite the essential artistic frame and background of ecclesiastical rites and ceremonies. It is, then, hardly to be expected that Christian Science should find its expression through its churches to any great extent in Gothic architecture."[8] Beman also turned to practical considerations such as acoustics, lighting, comfortable banked opera seating, clear sight lines, and the need for unusually large foyers for socializing after services. Steel trusses, which allowed for modern open auditorium spaces, and the use of state-of-the-art ventilation and lighting also could be accommodated in Beman's classical buildings, which were quite responsive to newer modern building materials and engineering practices.

Beman's article elicited many responses. Some pundits felt that Christian Science architecture was setting "an example that every denomination should follow. . . . if Christian Science does no more than reform church architecture, it will assuredly not have lived in vain."[9] A *Minneapolis Tribune* writer told his audience, "Sufficient credit has not been given to the builders of Christian Science churches for the rather remarkable growth of Italian church architecture in the United States. Before the older church began to design beautiful Renaissance temples like the cathedral buildings in St. Paul and Minneapolis . . . the Christian Scientists had exhibited several modest examples of the classical style. . . . It has not been generally understood how universal this type is in the architecture of the new church."[10]

Many architects rallied around Beman's position. The Chicago architect Leon Stanhope believed that the classical style of church edifice was very important in spreading the church's teachings. When in 1915 the congregation at South Bend, Indiana, had outgrown a quaint little gray stucco frame church that Beman had built for them in 1905, they turned to Stanhope for a more suitable and monumental building of Bedford stone (fig. 54). Stanhope wrote to the local board of directors: "I do not use the Gothic or Romanesque architecture, which expresses human thought which developed after the third century and continued on through the dark ages down to the present date, but rather I go back to that period of the first century and draw my motifs from the early Greek architecture, which is pure and inspiring."[11]

Beman and Stanhope were reiterating a sensibility supported by many architects at the time. For example, the important architect Henry Van Brunt recognized in the modern classical style a sign of "the highest result of pure creation in the history of mankind, [which] brings receptive and intelligent minds into immediate and sympathetic contact with the operations of the most subtle and most fastidious intellects ever devoted to the development of form in art."[12] Van Brunt appreciated Beman's Mines and Mining Building for the World's Columbian Exposition, noting that it was a modern building animated by the classical spirit. Frank Howe, Van Brunt's architectural partner, commented that their adopted homebase of Kansas City

Figure 54. Leon Stanhope, First Church of Christ, Scientist, South Bend, Indiana, 1918 (Church History, Division of the Church of Christ, Scientist, Boston).

had few standouts in ecclesiastical architecture, but two of them were Christian Science churches. First Church of Christ, Scientist (figs. 55, 56), a church in the English Gothic style where Farlow was an important member, was "interesting yet modest" with an "excellent interior." Howe characterized the costly new Second Church of Christ, Scientist (fig. 57), together with his firm's own Prospect Avenue Christian Church, as "purely academic"—in other words, classical.[13]

Kansas City, then, had two fine examples of Christian Science architecture, but like the Mother Church and Extension, they were quite distinct from one another. First Church, Kansas City, was a Gothic edifice of Missouri limestone and had a 75-foot tower. The church seated 1,500 people in its pews. The interior decorations were Craftsman inspired. It was designed by George Mathews and built and dedicated in 1898. Second Church, a 1902–3 classical design by Frederick Comstock, built at the highest point in Jackson County, was a Roman Doric structure of Phoenix stone, with a dome of metal and glass that rose 102 feet above the street. The two-story vestibule of the church included murals by Edward J. Holslag of Chicago, who had contributed decorations to the Congressional Library. The auditorium seated 1,050 people on leather-upholstered opera chairs and was illuminated by modern indirect lighting. The amber dome, 48 feet in diameter, rose 62 feet above the auditorium floor. As John Wheeler told the readers of the *Illustrated Review,* Second Church,

Figure 55. George Mathews, First Church of Christ, Scientist, Kansas City, Missouri, 1898 (Church History, Division of the Church of Christ, Scientist, Boston).

Figure 56. Interior, First Church of Christ, Scientist, Kansas City (Holt).

Figure 57. Frederick Comstock, Second Church of Christ, Scientist, Kansas City, Missouri, 1903 (Church History, Division of the Church of Christ, Scientist, Boston).

Kansas City, was "the handsomest and most complete church edifice west of New York City."[14]

Several California architects also utilized the classical style made popular by the Columbian Exposition. The first classical church edifice built by the Scientists in California was First Church, Los Angeles, whose congregation began meeting in 1892.[15] In 1902 they erected a small classical church, designed by M. Paul Martin (fig. 58). Most of the Christian Science churches in the Bay Area were also built in the classical style. Carl Werner, an Oakland architect, was responsible for several Masonic temples and Christian Science churches in the area, including First Church, Alameda; Fourth and Fifth Churches in San Francisco; and Fourth Church, Oakland (razed in the late 1980s, provoking public outcry).[16] Fourth Church (1922, fig. 59) fit elegantly within the newly emerging civic center in Oakland, which had as its focus the Oakland Auditorium (1913–15). Werner believed that the classical style represented a pure, timeless spirituality. In defense of his prominent classical Masonic Temple design for Oakland, which was to be located directly across Lake Merritt from Fourth Church, Werner wrote to the board of directors for the Masonic Cathedral Association in 1924: "I adopted the Classic because it is the true type of ar-

chitecture which purely and truthfully spells 'Temple.' It is possible to design our
building either in Italian, Spanish, or Gothic, which may have artistic charm, but it
will not possess that spiritual quality—it will lack that crystal-like character and the
calm stately dignity, all so necessary in a Temple."[17] The Masonic Temple for Oakland, which included large banquet halls and lodge rooms, featured a tremendous
Roman classical meeting chamber sixty-five feet in height from the base of the dome,
with walls and columns in travertine.

Designs for the Christian Scientists by Werner were also characteristically classical and introduced City Beautiful ideals and orientations into several urban neighborhoods. For example, Werner's Fourth Church, San Francisco (1913), a large marble church fronted by Corinthian columns with Latrobe-inspired tobacco leaf
capitals, and a well-detailed entablature topped by urns, was located near the Presidio on an important parkway (fig. 60). A 1985 account said that the gleaming white
exterior provided a "note of sober dignity in its urban and residential setting."[18] A
church for Alameda, completed in 1922, was also classical in form and was echoed
by the large classical-style high school building, designed by Werner in 1925, located
across the street from the church. The pairing comprised his first version of a civic
center.[19]

Figure 58. M. Paul Martin, First Church of Christ, Scientist, Los Angeles, 1902 (Holt).

Figure 59. Carl Werner, Fourth Church of Christ, Scientist, Oakland, 1922 (Church History, Division of the Church of Christ, Scientist, Boston).

Figure 60. Carl Werner, Fourth Church of Christ, Scientist, San Francisco, 1913 (Ivey).

Other architects and commentators modified the debates about Christian Science church styles by suggesting that the centrality of New England to Christian Science should dictate the style of the edifices nationwide, even though many New England churches were also being built in the classical style.[20] For example, Omen Washburn believed that the appropriate Christian Science model was "something synonymous, if not identical, with the Protestant Congregational meeting-house." He noted, however, that the new "spirit of faith" also required an "utterance more explicit than a mere reiteration of a Baptist or Presbyterian building to express a creed that apparently concerns itself so immediately with the terrestrial welfare of man."[21]

According to Washburn, the Gothic style associated with the Catholic faith was "not within the range of contemplation" for a Christian Science church. Writing about First Church, New York, by Carrère and Hastings, he asserted that the building was "a model of modern ideas in church building."[22] In fact, First Church, New York, was a truly American church, with modern elevators, reading room, and practitioners' offices. Thomas Hastings, the primary architect of the church, defended his use of a renewed classical style in ecclesiastical architecture.[23]

Impassioned responses to Beman and the supporters of the classical style were published in 1907 and 1908. The most deeply felt and fervently argued position was taken by Elmer Grey. As early as 1900 Grey had lectured on "Indigenous and Inventive Architecture for America" at the second annual convention of the Architectural League of America, held in Chicago. Grey said on that occasion: "For all architectural beauty which is natural and vital to the best American life will contribute to the growth of an indigenous and inventive American architecture. To further the growth of such an architecture in every possible manner should be our ambition; our methods should correspond with the noblest methods of men who are working for the benefit of mankind in other walks of life; and our hope of success should lie in a consciousness of our relation to the divine Source of all life, of all growth, and of all accomplishment."[24] Following Grey's talk, Louis Sullivan commented on the necessity for an American architecture based on freedom: "As Mr. Grey has truly said . . . style is the evolution, if there be nothing other than the expression of its personality. . . . what is final and of consequence is the individual."[25] Grey had referred to Sullivan as the mentor who had stimulated young architects "by the most vital thought on architectural expression."[26]

Grey derived his architectural theories from Sullivan's ideas and transformed them into the basis for a successful architectural practice in California in the teens. By this time, California was challenging Chicago as the most fertile ground for Christian Science. Grey believed that the classical style was mechanical and static and it was therefore opposed to the organic growth that characterized the true spiritual growth of the people. According to Grey, architecture should blend into and emerge from nature, not be distinct from it.

Grey asserted that Christian Science had added to Christianity, therefore it should not "exclude from its architecture anything worthy in the Christian architecture of the past."[27] He fervently supported a regionally informed approach to his designs and believed in what he called a liberated "new-world" architectural form.[28] Grey agreed with Beman that church edifices should be "conveniently planned" to express the "practical efficacy of the religion they stand for."[29] He agreed that the foyers should be large, and that the auditoriums should not be overornamented. In an article published in the *Arena* in 1908, however, Grey rejected the classical style outright and aligned it with pagan beliefs. He supported Farlow's arguments and reiterated that Mrs. Eddy wanted Christian Science churches to be recognizable as churches. Grey also rejected the New England meetinghouse as model.[30] The illustrations for his articles showed buildings of Gothic and mission types, and many of his own designs.

As a follower of Sullivan, Grey believed that the classical style enjoyed popularity due only to its association with the Columbian Exposition. He argued that American architects should turn their attention to "indigenous" architectural solutions as expressions of national identity. Architecture should emerge from the freedom and individualism of the American community as it grew spiritually, not solely from an historical epoch. Grey thought that the main interest of the architect should be the spiritual growth of the people; without this emphasis no new spirit would animate or inspire architectural forms. His ideas echoed the Anglican socialist Edward Carpenter's notions that an architecture built upon natural principles for free men and women would arise in its own beauty by a "law unfolding from within."[31]

Grey's architectural solutions rested on the ideals of site specificity, emerging from the organic relationship between the site and the building. *The Brickbuilder* noted this emphasis in Grey's work: "[It seems] to grow out of our soil, [and] offer just the right mass against the sky, or find position among the eucalyptus and oak in such a way that one has no doubt they have always been there."[32]

The idea that architecture should harmonize with its surroundings did not address only the notion of style. Grey's approach also used the "unseen laws" of nature in building, laws that grew out of and were reflected by the natural setting. The moral idealism of Grey's approach was applauded in many periodicals of the time. For example, B. O. Flower, writing in the *Arena,* commended Grey and his one-time partner Myron Hunt as "architects of the first rank who have original ideas and the courage to strike out from the beaten path of imitative conventionalism."[33] Grey himself wrote three articles on Christian Science architecture by 1916, which were reprinted in pamphlet form complete with advertisements from firms specializing in church furnishings.[34] He had also contributed to the Christian Science periodicals as early as 1909, though he never joined the church.[35] He claimed that the built material world of art and architecture arose from the world of eternal thought. Linking Christian Science ideals with the expression of one of America's greatest sculptors, for example, Grey wrote: "[The Christian Scientist] realizes that what underlies outward manifestation and makes Chicago's greatest statue great, is not its stone, but St. Gauden's comprehension of the nobility of thought, the strength of purpose, the simple grandeur of Lincoln, and the wonderful skill with which he has conveyed that comprehension to us. [The Christian Scientist] applies to literature, to music, to architecture, to all the arts, this same idea that the real is 'that which is eternal and incapable of discord and decay' (*Science and Health,* p. 468), and thus religion enters every vital experience of his life."[36]

According to Grey, Christian Science architecture would be better, by evolutionary necessity, than most "current Orthodox church work, as is its system of metaphysics . . . above current theological dogma."[37] Rather than support Beman's model, which suggested that pure architectural forms applied to the city would compel moral and spiritual change in society, Grey believed that spiritual growth would occur when people heeded the evolutionary and organic laws of nature, as manifested in his buildings and revealed in the individual Christian Scientist's spiritual growth.

Grey's architectural ideas were tangibly expressed when he was hired in 1911 by the congregation of First Church, Los Angeles, to design a building (fig. 61) to replace its earlier small, classical church. The *Christian Science Journal* announced that "the edifice will be Italian Romanesque in style, expressing utility, simplicity, cordiality."[38] Grey took on the commission as an opportunity to plan an edifice as "the logical outcome of the peculiar conditions which happen to pertain to any particular architectural problem, rather than merely a compilation of some historic style mechanically adjusted to a plan, but having little organic relation to it."[39] The style of the building and its plan were carefully defended in a series of articles by Grey that were meant to establish the prominence of his architectural theories. His other California commissions included a large mission-style church for the Scientists in Palo Alto (1916, fig. 62) and First Church, Long Beach (1914), a classically styled building that resembled a Beman church.[40] An earlier edifice by Grey for a Christian Science Society in Milwaukee was definitely Gothic (c. 1908).[41]

Figure 61. Elmer Grey, First Church of Christ, Scientist, Los Angeles, second edifice, 1911 (Church History, Division of the Church of Christ, Scientist, Boston).

Figure 62. Elmer Grey, First Church of Christ, Scientist, Palo Alto, 1916 (Church History, Division of the Church of Christ, Scientist, Boston).

While Grey clearly made his stylistic choices on a building-by-building basis, he claimed Christian Science no longer needed to establish its difference from other denominations and had, by 1916, progressed to the point where it could be truly innovative and responsive to regional possibilities and local building traditions in its architecture. By rejecting a unified adoption of the classical style, Grey suggested that Christian Scientists follow the dictates of their individual congregations, a position that had been the "official" policy all along.

Interested Christian Scientists and architectural critics commented on the new edifices in the press. Willard Mattox, in a 1909 *Illinois Illustrated Review,* suggested that the state of church architecture in Christian Science was "uncertain and confused," without any "distinct modern religious type of architecture."[42] According to Mattox, this was due to the individualism of Christian Science, which mandated a diversity of styles. George Wharton James, editor of the Los Angeles–based *Out West* magazine, also supported the theories of Grey and of Irving Gill, who had just completed a church for the congregation in San Diego. James asserted that even though many people believed that the classical ideal was "essentially characteristic of Christian Science," they were simply in error.[43] He argued that in order to "typify aspiration," a church edifice needed a steeple: "A church should also be a commanding enough edifice, if possible, to demand interest and attention. In this world of rush and hurry, commercialism and absorption in business, it is well that upon man's physical sense something shall constantly be before him as a reminder that these things are not all there is to life, and that in and through them all he must not forget that he is a spiritual being, seeking spiritual expression." According to James, freedom of expression was essential in the representation of Christian Science as different from other churches, as "a departure rather than an evolution" of historical Christianity. Christian Science was "free to develop an architecture all its own, equally free from tradition and old standards." Christian Science edifices were successful when they attracted attention "by their strength, power and simplicity," and invited citizens to contemplate thoughts "over and above the material and commercial."[44]

Other Models Introduced

There were many new stylistic experiments evident in the Christian Science church commissions in California that contributed to the debates. Several churches were hybrid mission-style designs. Arthur B. Benton's First Church, Riverside (1900), mixed classical with Spanish colonial revival and mission-style elements, such as roof tiles, arcades, and twin towers (fig. 63).[45] The most innovative early mission-style church was designed and executed in San Diego by Irving Gill, who had worked for Louis Sullivan. Gill designed two buildings for the congregation of First Church and one for the congregation in Coronado (1927).

Figure 63. Arthur B. Benton, First Church of Christ, Scientist, Riverside, California, 1900 (Van Horne).

The first building for First Church, San Diego, was designed by Gill in 1905 (fig. 64). Newspapers published a description of the church that had been provided by the COP representative Fannie M. McKoon: "Some say that the style of the building is old English; some that it is old Mission, but it is not old English, neither is it old Mission, but it has an individualism all its own. The departure from the stereotyped form of church building, after much study, seemed to be an inspiration of Hebbard and Gill, the architects . . . [who] realized that this unusual service must have an original design for its church home . . . to meet the needs and wants of the new/old simplicity of the teachings of Christ by the wayside." The church was reminiscent of an oversized cottage, its porch a rustic arched gateway leading into a small

Figure 64. Irving Gill, First Church of Christ, Scientist, San Diego, 1905 (Holt).

Figure 65. Irving Gill, First Church of Christ, Scientist, San Diego, second edifice, 1909 (Van Horne).

English-style garden. The auditorium was replete with half-timbered walls and large iron-clasped braces. McKoon called the church a "reconstruction of the temple" or the "house beautiful."[46]

First Church, San Diego, continued to grow, and in 1909 Gill designed another building for the congregation. The members were excited by the innovative design of their new 950-seat auditorium (fig. 65). The edifice was of masonry construction with abstracted Italian Romanesque features. Gill's truss system supported a splendid dome of art glass illuminated through an outer translucent copper dome.[47] The building's style was a stripped-down geometric classicism. The church was Gill's largest commission to date. Wharton James thought that the edifice evoked the Franciscan mission style, but a completely modernized rendition.[48]

In Chicago, examples of the Prairie style were evident, promoted by Frank Lloyd Wright and others who were inspired by Louis Sullivan's ideals. Hugh Garden's Third Church, Chicago, of 1899–1901 reveals the impact of Prairie School ideas, which are particularly recognizable in the organic ornamental motifs in terra-cotta and in the stained-glass details (figs. 66, 67, 68). Garden, a lifelong Episcopalian, had apprenticed in Minneapolis in the office of the Harvard-educated William Channing Whitney.[49] He was a draftsman for several major firms in Chicago, including Shepley, Rutan, and Coolidge, who designed Second Church, Boston (1916), and he also freelanced and made renderings for Louis Sullivan and Frank Lloyd Wright.[50]

Hugh Garden's structural design for Third Church followed the classical proto-

Figure 66. Hugh Garden, Third Church of Christ, Scientist, Chicago, 1901 (Van Horne).

Figure 67. Terra-cotta relief medallion on the frieze of the main facade of Third Church, Chicago (Photo by Elaine S. Batson, Commission on Chicago Landmarks).

Figure 68. Terra-cotta capital from Third Church, Chicago (Photo by Elaine S. Batson, Commission on Chicago Landmarks).

types of Beman. But his facade contained decorative elements. Nevertheless, in overall effect, the massing was classical. A press release noted that the architecture followed "slightly classic lines in its general form," but that it departed from the classic in every other respect and was not designed in a historical style.[51] The gleaming white exterior walls were of glazed brick, and the window and door frames, capitals, and cornices were made of terra-cotta. The two freestanding columns at the entrance were carved granite.[52] Garden also produced a series of low-relief medallions for the frieze on the main facade. Architectural drawings indicate that the motifs were originally meant to be organic and geometrical, showing the influence of Sullivan. However, three symbolic designs consonant with Christian Science teachings were executed instead.[53]

The interior design of Garden's church also resembled Beman's interiors. The auditorium was on the second floor, its individual theater seats arranged on a floor surface that sloped down toward the pulpit. As in Beman's designs, no interior pillars cluttered the seating area. A central stairway led up into the auditorium from the large vestibule, another Beman feature. But as the architectural preservationist Timothy Wittman has pointed out, there were radical innovations in the interior and exterior details of the church. The vestibule contained biomorphic mosaic fireplaces without mantels, around which were grouped Gustav Stickley furnishings from his Craftsman Studios of Eastwood, New York. The floral designs on the iron supports of the theater seats in the auditorium were reproductions of the Sullivan design that was first utilized in the Auditorium Building. The large readers' desk was Craftsman inspired.[54]

Garden also designed the Christian Science church in Marshalltown, Iowa, in 1902–3 (fig. 69).[55] It was a much less pretentious example of Prairie School architecture. The Marshalltown church was "honest" in its materials and function, and not historical in its stylistic references. A newspaper account reported that the small edifice was patterned on Garden's Third Church. It was another cruciform plan, and the roof was formed by four steep gables that intersected at the crossing. Under the gables were large stained-glass windows of opalescent greenish-yellow glass. The building's structural elements were undisguised and purposefully exposed. The architectural historian Wesley Shank, commenting on Garden's designs, suggested that the architectural principles of the Prairie School could be considered architecturally correct for a Christian Science church. As the Marshalltown *Evening Times-Republican* put it, "Christian Scientists look upon their church buildings as a concrete manifestation of the spiritual truths of Christian Science, and consequently in the present structure the architect has given the building the qualities of simplicity, steadfastness, and truth embodied in a quiet . . . structure with simple gables, strong and enduring construction that it is believed are not out of harmony with the truths of Christianity. No effect has been made to make the building showy or important, indeed the contrary is true."[56]

Architects of Christian Science churches, in short, were sensitive to urban settings and the utopian visions projected onto them by architects and city planners who were inspired by the classical style. But they were also aware of the often distinctive, more recent and intimate suburban landscapes. Even so, they rarely used the Prairie School idiom. The Prairie style did not become the appropriate suburban style in opposition to an urban classicism: the simple unadorned meetinghouse and the colonial building became the suburban models. However, there were exceptions to this, notably Howard Cheney's First Church, Riverside, Illinois (1920), built in the Prairie style as a result of a particular patronage situation (fig. 70). Avery Coonley, one of Frank Lloyd Wright's clients, was head of the Riverside church's original building committee that in 1914 purchased a lot directly across the street from Wright's 1907 Tomek House.[57] At the time there were only four churches in Riverside.[58] By January 1917, the building committee, after thirty-four meetings and interviews with five architects, "determined that the building should be of a character adapted to our village, notable for its openness, long vistas, spacious lots, ample parking and beautiful trees. This would naturally suggest a building of a less formal type than that suitable to the restricted space and straight lines of a city."[59] The First World War delayed the acceptance of building plans, but in 1919 the committee was reactivated and Howard Cheney of Chicago was chosen as architect. The church was completed in 1921.[60]

Cheney designed a building that on the exterior fit well into the Riverside neigh-

Figure 69. Hugh Garden, First Church of Christ, Scientist, Marshalltown, Iowa, 1903 (Church History, Division of the Church of Christ, Scientist).

Figure 70. Howard Cheney, First Church of Christ, Scientist, Riverside, Illinois, 1921 (Ivey).

borhood and with Wright's Tomek House. The interior space, however, was completely classical in character. Members believed that the "balance and proportion of inner space express[ed] a sense of well-being."[61] The congregation had expressed their belief that it was important for their church building to complement the suburban environment of Riverside, and yet they chose the classical style, with its rational characteristics, for the interior of the church.

Increasingly, the democratic and individualistic ideals of Christian Science emerged as an effective justification for the denomination's increasingly eclectic architectural styles. Several prominent branch churches were featured in the architectural press in 1917, providing the occasion for comment on the changes in architects' perceptions of Christian Science commissions. I. T. Frary, writing on Gordon, Madden, and Kaelber's superb First Church, Rochester, New York (1914–16, figs. 71, 72), believed that the most interesting feature of the growth of Christian Science, architecturally, was still the dominant classical style of its edifices. He felt that not only did the exterior classical style reflect the nonritualistic orientation of the faith, but that the interior seating arrangements were very democratic because each seat was placed so the occupant could see and hear the "interchange of ideas and thoughts" that made up the services.[62]

Figure 71. Gordon, Madden, and Kaelber, First Church of Christ, Scientist, Rochester, New York, 1916 (Church History, Division of the Church of Christ, Scientist, Boston).

Figure 72. Gordon, Madden, and Kaelber, interior, First Church of Christ, Scientist, Rochester (*Architectural Record* 41, no. 3 [1917]).

Gordon, Madden, and Kaelber themselves believed that the new Rochester church was a model for the movement. They thought that the Christian Science church was the latest development in the evolution of religious architecture from the "temple of mystery in ancient Egypt to the temple of learning of our time." Frary argued that the new professionalization of architecture was also positively reflected in the Christian Science church:

The church architecture of this country has been as a whole mediocre during the past century. Much of it has been the work of untrained architects and builders who were incapable, even with the best of intentions, of producing good work. . . . It is gratifying to note at the present time a healthful change in these matters and a general growth in the appreciation of good architecture. The professional training of architects is of a higher order, [building] committees are demanding better things and as a result we have a leaven of well designed church buildings spreading throughout the country, which leaven is bound to work and produce a standard of church architecture which will be a credit and an inspiration to religious organizations.[63]

One criticism Frary leveled at Christian Science architects in general was the lack of color in most of their designs. The Rochester church was an antidote with its stunning and colorful embellishments. Later, these ornaments influenced George Eastman's choice of interior styling for his auditorium at the Eastman School of Music located down the street from the church.

In 1917 a feature article in the *Architect and Engineer of California,* by William Arthur Newman, an Oakland architect known for his local federal government commissions, suggested that the lack of overall cohesion of Christian Science architecture was due to the democratic character of the organization and the independence of each congregation as manifested in building decisions. The church membership was also "cosmopolitan"—derived from those formerly affiliated with other denominations. After lamenting several features of typical Christian Science architecture, including dark Sunday school rooms, Newman wrote, "A religion offering freedom from the mental and physical bondage of the ages is not expressed within the confines of architectural styles founded on such limitations. The very youth of this movement accounts in a measure for many architectural inconsistencies in plan and design, found in costly Christian Science edifices, all of which tend to hamper proper growth and efficiency. Better solutions of these problems, more in harmony with the actual requirements, are being demanded, and through the wise selection of architects will be forthcoming in the future."[64]

Newman's Second Church, Oakland (1916), caught the attention of the editor of the *Architect and Engineer of California,* as an example of a modern Renaissance design, with heavy steel trusses of one-hundred-foot clear spans supporting a slate roof (fig. 73). The interior was noted for its comfort, its excellent acoustics, its advanced ventilation systems, and the indirect lighting, which was becoming popular in Christian Science churches.[65] Newman, a Christian Scientist, was sought after by other congregations following the success of this design and the publicity surrounding it. However, Newman's other Christian Science church in Oakland, Seventh Church (1915, fig. 74), explored a regional approach to design, made famous in the area by Bernard Maybeck, Julia Morgan, and Henry Gutterson. This church resembled a wood-frame bungalow. It was located near the east side of Lake Merritt in a fine residential neighborhood built on reclaimed marshland. The church's small size lent itself to the Arts and Crafts style. The building also resembled Julia Morgan's famous St. John's Presbyterian Church in Berkeley (1908) with its clerestory and nested gables. The popular press sometimes misattributed the building to Morgan due to its mingling of Craftsman and academic styles.[66]

Figure 73. William Arthur Newman, Second Church of Christ, Scientist, Oakland, 1916 (Ivey).

Figure 74. William Arthur Newman, Seventh Church of Christ, Scientist, Oakland, 1915 (Ivey).

By the 1920s, new suggestions for the direction of the architecture of the Christian Science church emerged even though over sixty-five new churches were built in the classical style.[67] The Chicago architect William Gray Purcell, who, like Gill, had worked briefly with Louis Sullivan, was concerned about the new proliferation of Chicago designs. His Third Church, Portland, built in 1926, expressed his strong commitment to modern nonhistorical principles (fig. 75). However, the Christian Science churches built between 1908 and 1925 in Oregon and the Puget Sound area continued the tradition of classicism. For instance, several Seattle branch churches, namely, First, Third, and Fourth Churches, were classical buildings.[68] Some East Coast architects were beginning to favor colonial designs for smaller congregations in suburban areas. Bernhardt E. Müller, a New York architect and Christian Scientist, designed several different styles of churches for Christian Science congregations but mostly utilized the Georgian and colonial styles.[69]

By the mid-1920s the Georgian and colonial styles began to compete with a purer classicism for dominance in Christian Science commissions. In 1924 William Edgar Moran suggested that the academic lecture theater was the most appropriate model for the Christian Science church, particularly if done in those styles.[70] By the late 1920s, planning books for other denominations that were building addressed some of the same arguments that had been prevalent in earlier Christian Science debates. A Methodist publication in 1928 stated that to build a classical church was to emphasize administrative function, whereas the Gothic church emphasized the devotional and mystical aspects of the church. To build a classical edifice was, in the words of one architect, "to place too much paganism in the structure and to come too close to our statehouse and post offices," as the Christian Scientists had done.[71]

By 1930, Georgian and colonial revival buildings became popular as the Chris-

Figure 75. William Gray Purcell, Third Church of Christ, Scientist, Portland, 1926 (Church History, Division of the Church of Christ, Scientist, Boston).

tian Science movement expanded to the suburbs, and smaller, more affordable churches of brick were needed to fit into these environments. This was particularly true following the publication of William Pope Barney's article on the planning of Christian Science churches, which supported his own firm's colonial designs, and a short article on Barney's ideas that appeared in the *Christian Science Monitor*.[72] Eugene Clute noted in 1928 that the Christian Scientists were abandoning their interest in classical architecture in order to build "some charming buildings of a moderate size that have as their prototype the small English country church. This type of church fits into its surroundings especially well in suburban and rural localities." There were important exceptions to this. Third Church, Dallas, Texas, for example, completed a sizable Romanesque-style church in 1931, designed by Mark Lemmon, an important Dallas architect.[73]

When Bernard Maybeck designed two campuses for the Christian Scientists' Principia College at Elsah, Illinois, in the 1920s and 1930s, he chose the colonial style for the campus chapel.[74] The campus (1930–38) itself, though, was a novel simulacrum of a Cotswold village, conceived to create a total organic and harmonious experience of environmental unity for the students. The chapel (1931–32) was a direct reference to Christopher Wren's work and to the New England meetinghouse (fig. 76). The church with high spire was built of poured concrete over steel trusses fronted with 5,800 pieces of rusted Indiana limestone, each of a unique size and shape, symbolizing the uniqueness of every student. Principia students had requested a building in the New England colonial style in recognition of the fact that Christian Science was founded in Massachusetts.[75]

Maybeck held an architectural ideal that many Christian Scientists found consoling. In 1929 he suggested to Frederic Morgan, president of Principia College, that "college buildings should be so spiritual that the students without knowing it get the qualities which we need to make leaders."[76] Such a statement is further evidence of Christian Scientists' belief that the appropriate environments could promote good qualities all by themselves.

In his 1926 history of the Christian Science movement, William Lyman Johnson summed up the earlier architectural debates this way:

> Many were obsessed by the thought that all that was necessary was a *spiritual* church, that an edifice modeled after any of the existing types was a return to old theology. . . . At the time when the information was given out that there was to be a church edifice in Concord, New Hampshire, one Scientist, so well known that I do not care to mention his name, made the statement that he hoped Mrs. Eddy would not have a steeple or a tower on the building, because such ornaments represented old theology. . . . In about 1907 there was considerable literature on the question as to what style of architecture symbolizes the teachings of Christian Science. Many of our buildings had been designed in harmony with the lines of the Greek architecture, the cost of which is lower than that of the Gothic or Renaissance. But when it is looked upon as suitably symbolizing Christian Science, a doubt must enter the mind of the thoughtful. They can but wonder if an architecture developed and perfected for the worship of pagan gods can be fittingly representative of our faith.[77]

Figure 76. Bernard Maybeck, Chapel at Principia College, Elsah, Illinois, 1932 (Ivey).

In 1905, Ralph Adams Cram had condemned all classical forms in church build-ings for denying the rich thousand-year history of Christianity.[78] In 1929, however, he finally asserted that the Christian Scientists had properly chosen the classical style, because it was an honest architecture according to their theological position. He declared that he would support different styles of church architecture as long as they were "treated intelligently, with a real regard for principles rather than accident of detail."

Whether it is Gothic or some other style the return is all along the line to the best types of the pre-Reformation art of Christianity. Nothing else would, of course, have been possible since no contribution was made to Christian art after this period. Such a return is natural and rational in the case of the Roman Catholic and Episcopal Churches, but it is a little startling where Protestantism is concerned, though, of course, inescapable, since this movement was consistently opposed to art in any form, and as a matter of fact did away with as much of it as it could lay hands on. Invariably, however, the Protestant denominations now go back to Gothic of some sort. . . . Christian Scientists very properly eschew all Medieval prototypes, generally adopting some modernized classical form.[79]

Cram's book *American Church Building of Today* included Christian Science designs by Charles Klauder, Elmer Grey, and Charles Faulkner. Faulkner, along with Spencer Beman, became central to the reorientation of Christian Science architecture from the classical to the Georgian and colonial styles in the thirties and forties.

By 1930, the art and architecture critic Sheldon Cheney suggested that Christian Science had continued the basic Protestant mode of church building with architecture that was "unadventurous, uncreative, colorless." He wrote, "Strangely modified classic temples have had a vogue where large structures were raised. . . . For the sort of passive structure that the Christian Scientists apparently want, [a] . . . design by Eliel Saarinen seems to come as clean and as near architectural richness as one could wish. Yet one asked what there is here to suggest spiritual exercise, to remind one even vaguely that religion lives in the region of high serenity and deepest ecstasy."[80] The Saarinen design (fig. 77), created in 1925 for a Christian Science congregation in Minneapolis, was never built, but the planned grandiose interior rivaled those of the Mother Church Extension and several British branch churches of the twenties and thirties.[81] In Britain, Christian Scientists constructed several conspicuous buildings, utilizing the talents of prominent architects such as Sir Herbert Baker, Sir John Burnett, Ramsey Traquair, Edgar Woods, and Lanchester and Rickards.[82]

Regional characteristics, particularly on the west coast of the United States, continued to be asserted over classical models. For example, Henry H. Gutterson, an architect who was a church member, designed the Arts and Crafts–influenced Second Church, Berkeley, in 1926 (fig. 78).[83] In consultation with Maybeck, he also completed the Sunday school building for First Church, Berkeley, in 1928 (fig. 79). Second Church was vaguely Romanesque but, as in Maybeck's First Church, the building materials of unpainted concrete and plaster, rough natural wood, and leaded glass were exposed, producing a rustic effect appropriate to the building's natural bramble-like garden setting.

Gutterson's other designs had an influence in the Bay Area. He designed at least ten churches for Christian Science congregations as well as the French chateauesque building for the Christian Science Benevolent Association of the Pacific Coast in San Francisco (1930) and a building for the Christian Science College Organization (1932) in Berkeley.[84] Most of these churches were done in a mission/Byzantine style, which suited large edifices such as Third Church, Oakland (1930–42, fig. 80), and Ninth Church, San Francisco (1941), as well as smaller residential-sized ones such as those

Figure 77. Eliel Saarinen, "Christian Science Church Project, Minneapolis," 1925–26, section, pencil on paper, 11¾ × 22⅛ in. (Collection of Cranbrook Art Museum, gift of Dorothy M. and Edgar R. Kimball).

at San Vallejo (1927) and San Leandro (1927). Gutterson's Ninth Church, San Francisco, was very similar to his Third Church, Oakland, and also First Church, Santa Barbara (1931). The fact that many Christian Scientists in California chose the mission/Byzantine as their new church style supports the argument that Christian Science churches were designed to fit into broader public architectures, since that style also appeared in many public buildings in the state.[85]

During the Christian Science building boom of 1894–1930, the rational and authoritative connotations of the classical style won out over architectural metaphors derived from nature and architectural evolution. However, a forward-looking regional modernism was manifested in many building projects, particularly in California. Innovative concepts, including those that mixed the metaphoric potentials of natural materials and ideal pure geometries exemplified in Frank Lloyd Wright's unbuilt Bolinas church (1957, fig. 81),[86] were carried out in contemporary buildings, such as Charles Callister's beautiful First Church, Belvedere (1951–52, fig. 82).[87] Callister's redwood church, located in a pleasant residential setting, evoked Maybeck's masterpiece across San Francisco Bay and also blended into its natural setting, making its modern style complicit with the natural and organic.

California was eclipsing the Midwest as the most popular domain for Christian Science. The "Chicago architectural idea," as Grey termed it, could not possibly be

Figure 78. Henry Gutterson, Second Church of Christ, Scientist, Berkeley, 1926 (Ivey).

Figure 79. Henry Gutterson, Sunday school addition for First Church of Christ, Scientist, Berkeley, 1928 (Ivey).

Figure 80. Henry Gutterson, Third Church of Christ, Scientist, Oakland, 1942 (Ivey).

Figure 81. Frank Lloyd Wright, Christian Science Church Project #2, Bolinas, California, 1957, 5527.009 (© 1998 Frank Lloyd Wright Foundation, Scottsdale, Arizona).

successful in the last great American frontier, which was marked generally by a freedom from European examples.[88]

Although individual congregations nationwide chose diverse stylistic solutions to the problems of church design throughout the building boom, the classical style was unquestionably triumphant in urban areas and is still associated with Christian Science today. Clearly, church architectures negotiated the church's complex relationships with the social, cultural, and civic trends of the times and helped define its public image. However, discussions concerning the religious and social values of architec-

Figure 82. Charles Callister, First Church of Christ, Scientist, Belvedere, California, 1952 (Photo by Ernest Braun, Callister Gately Associates).

tural styles in Christian Science began to wane by the 1930s as Christian Science became a more quiet, conservative, and respectable movement and the membership showed signs of a general suburbanization.

NOTES

1. Alfred Farlow, "Christian Science Church Architecture," *New England Magazine* 32 (Mar. 1905): 44.

2. *Craftsman* 7 (Mar. 1905): 691–92.

3. Ibid., 692. For coverage of Christian Science architecture outside of church publications, see Wilder Quint, "The Growth of Christian Science," *New England Magazine* 47 (Sept. 1909–Feb. 1910). Quint wrote that Christian Scientists "build churches of rare attractiveness; seldom do we find one of bizarre design or tawdry decoration, as too many of the religious homes of other denominations are. . . . There is education of the best sort in the noble auditorium of the temple in Boston, or in the exquisite lines of the new church in Los Angeles" (315). Many newspapers also began to carry articles on Christian Science and its architecture in particular. In 1907 many articles appeared in popular magazines, from serialized accounts of Mrs. Eddy's life, such as Sibyl Wilbur's in *Human Life* magazine. Other magazines running stories were *Success, Arena, Cosmopolitan, Broadway Magazine,* and *Fine Arts Journal.* Among the magazines running stories on Christian Science were *New England Magazine, North American Review, World Magazine, The World To-day Magazine, Ladies Home Journal, Twentieth Century Magazine, Metropolitan Magazine, The*

Era, Granite Monthly, The Bystander, Illinois Illustrated, Michigan Illustrated Review, Out West, Pall Mall, The American Queen, The Craftsman, Indoors and Out, National Magazine, Contemporary Review, Saturday Review, National Review, Independent, Blackwood's Magazine, Current Literature, The Outlook, Westminster, Overland, Popular Science, Catholic World, and *The Nation,* as well as architectural periodicals such as *Architectural Record, American Architect and Building News, Architectural Reviewer, Western Architect, Architecture* (New York), *Architect and Engineer of California, Architecture* (London), *Architectural Forum, Brickbuilder, Inland Architect,* and *The Architect.*

4. The magazine was one of the top Chicago periodicals, with a circulation nearing 100,000. See Frank Mott, *A History of American Magazines, 1885–1905* (Cambridge, Mass.: Harvard University Press, 1957), 499–500.

5. Solon Spencer Beman, "The Architecture of the Christian Science Church," *The World To-Day* 12, no. 6 (June 1907): 582–90.

6. Ibid., 583. Beman's Architectural Scrapbook, Burnham and Ryerson Library, Art Institute of Chicago, contains an undated article from the *Boston Transcript* entitled: "St. Marks, The Most Perfect and Consummate Work of Architecture in the World, A Day's Study of the Great Church." The article supports Beman's own ideals, saying:

> A gothic cathedral is simply impressive in effect and exquisite in detail but almost completely invariably *lacking,* it is wholly wanting in concentration and unity. . . . This, then, is the first quality, the chief glory, of St. Marks. Its organic and vital proportion is equal to the purest Greek and displayed in a work of incomparably greater complexity than any that Athens ever looked upon. . . . There is no school of architecture in the world comparable with that founded by Richardson; yet, it is justifiable to presume to criticize the work of this extraordinary man, that which seemed chiefly wanting in his power was precisely the quality of St. Marks—simplicity of proportion and crystalline quality. If we can go to Venice and St. Marks and learn the fundamental importance of these things, then we can create in America an architectural style that will stand in advance of any that has been known in the past four centuries.

7. Beman, "Architecture of the Christian Science Church," 587–88.

8. Ibid., 588.

9. *St. Louis Mirror,* June 13, 1907, quoting from the *New York Sun* (June 2, 1907). Parts of Beman's article were republished in other newspapers, such as the *Madison Democrat* (Aug. 11, 1907), Seattle's *Post-Intelligencer* (June 16, 1907), and Albuquerque's *The Record* (July 16, 1907).

10. *Minneapolis Tribune,* June 14, 1907.

11. Quoted in "Church History, First Church of Christ, Scientist, South Bend," undated ms., CHD, 26.

12. Henry Van Brunt, "Classic Architecture (1895)," in *Selected Essays of Henry Van Brunt, Architecture and Society,* ed. William A. Coles (Cambridge, Mass.: Harvard University Press, 1969), 344.

13. Frank N. Howe, "The Development of Architecture in Kansas City, Missouri," *Architectural Record* 15, no. 2 (Feb. 1904), 151–52.

14. John Wheeler, "The Development of the Christian Science Movement in Missouri," *Illustrated Review* [c. 1911]: 7; see also Alfred Farlow's brief description of First Church and Second Church on page 13 in the same issue. For a more complete account of the Second Church project, see "Historical Record of Second Church of Christ, Scientist, Kansas City, Missouri," undated ms., CHD, 5.

15. *Christian Science Journal* 30 (1912–13): 348.

16. The church building was bought by the Lake Merritt United Methodist Church and was scheduled to be razed in 1987. A citywide controversy over the preservation of historically significant buildings resulted. The building was finally torn down in 1988, but it was replaced with a new church, by Terrill Wade, that at least evoked the classical edifice in its design. See *Oakland Heritage Alliance News* (Spring 1987–Spring 1988); *San Francisco Chronicle,* May 20, 1987.

17. Letter, Carl Werner to Board of Directors, Masonic Cathedral Association, Scottish Rite Cathedral, Oakland, California, Jan. 12, 1924, Historical Collection, Oakland Masonic Temple.

18. Ruth Hendricks Willard, *Sacred Places of San Francisco* (Novato, Calif.: Presidio Press, 1985), 186.

19. The Christian Science churches in the Oakland area added to a stupendous record of building in the Oakland metropolitan area after the First World War. In Alameda County, a building was completed every six minutes during every working day of 1925. E. W. Shaw, "Great Building Record Established by Oakland and Metropolitan District," *Oakland Tribune Yearbook* (Oakland, 1925), 17. Frederick W. Jones writes in "Some Recent Work of Carl Werner, Architect," *The Architect and Engineer* 73, no. 351 (June 1923), that Werner's church commissions conformed with the "style that has been adopted quite generally by the Science church for all its new edifices" (64).

20. See, for example, First Church, Worcester, Massachusetts, *Brickbuilder* 24 (June 1915): plates 89–90; Clifford A. Woodard, "Recent Growth of Christian Science in New England," *New England Magazine* (Apr. 1914): 57–66; Henrietta Williams, "Among the Christian Science Churches," *Granite Monthly* 28, no. 5 (May 1900): 264–78.

21. Omen Washburn, "The Architecture of a Christian Science Church," *Architectural Record* (Feb. 1904): 159.

22. Ibid., 160.

23. See Thomas Hastings, "A Plea for the Renaissance in Ecclesiastical Architecture," *Architectural Review* 12 (1905): 184–86.

24. Elmer Grey, "Indigenous and Inventive Architecture for America," *American Architect and Building News* 68, no. 1278 (June 23, 1900): 91–92.

25. Grey, quoted in "Report on the Convention," *Brickbuilder* 9 (June 1900): 113. Grey's talk is published in the same issue (121–23). Sullivan is also quoted in Narciso G. Menocal, *Architecture as Nature: The Transcendentalist Idea of Louis Sullivan* (Madison: University of Wisconsin, 1981). Menocal believes that Grey's paraphrastic paper, which Sullivan was compelled to comment on, set the tone for the meeting. He writes that Sullivan pointedly "denounced once more the worthlessness of using past architectural styles, which he thought were valid only as historical and social records" (85).

26. Grey, in "Report on the Convention." Sherman Paul, *Louis Sullivan, an Architect in American Thought* (Englewood Cliffs, N.J.: Prentice Hall 1962), has it, "To this and the spirited applause, Sullivan responded by addressing the convention. He spoke extemporaneously for half an hour, extolling Grey's paper, which was close to his own thought, and developing his own ideas of inspiration in nature" (56).

27. Elmer Grey, "Christian Science Church Edifices and What They Stand For," *Fine Arts Journal* (Oct. 1907): 43.

28. B. O. Flower, "Elmer Grey and His Dream of a New-World Architecture," *Arena* 40 (Sept. 1908): 198–204; for more information on Grey's architectural theories, see article with the byline "an architect who writes," *Architectural Record* (Jan. 1905); Elmer Grey, "Architecture in Southern California," *Architectural Record* 17, no. 1 (Jan. 1905): 1–15; "Some Country House Architecture in the Far West," *Architectural Record* (Oct. 1922): 308–9.

29. Elmer Grey, "The Architecture of the Christian Science Church," *Arena* 40 (Aug.–Sept. 1908): 193–94. See also Elmer Grey, "The Style of Christian Science Church Edifices," *Architect and Engineer of California* 49 (Dec. 1916): 61–72.

30. Grey, "The Architecture of the Christian Science Church," 194.

31. Edward Carpenter, "Civilization, Its Cause and Its Cure" (1889), quoted in *Western Architect* (Jan. 1915), note with plate 17.

32. Fragment of a clipping, signed "EAB," from undated issue of *Brickbuilder*, CHD. For a more complete consideration of Grey's oeuvre, see Robert Craik McLean, "The Works of Elmer Grey, Architect, F.A.I.A.," *Western Architect* (Aug. 1916): 112–16.

33. Flower, "Elmer Grey and His Dream," 201.

34. Elmer Grey, *The Planning of Christian Science Church Edifices* (Los Angeles: Kingsley, Ma-

son, and Collins, 1916). Besides the fourteen illustrations, the pamphlet included advertisements for electricians, heating and ventilation specialists, and church furnishings manufacturers.

35. Grey said that he was not a member of the church but that he owed it his "present health and happiness." Flower, "Elmer Grey and His Dream," 203. An account of his healing was published in the *Christian Science Sentinel* (Mar. 2, 1907).

36. Elmer Grey, "Some First Impressions of Christian Science," *Christian Science Journal* 27, no. 4 (1909): 21. Other articles by Grey include, "Student of Christian Science," *Christian Science Sentinel* 10, no. 7 (Oct. 19, 1907): 124; "Investigating Christian Science," *Christian Science Journal* 27 (1909): 87; and "Not with Head Alone," *Christian Science Journal* 29 (1911): 22.

37. Flower, "Elmer Grey and His Dream," 203.

38. *Christian Science Journal* 30 (1911–12): 349.

39. Quoted in George Wharton James, "The Christian Science Architecture of California," *Out West* 4, no. 2 (Aug. 1912): 77. For other accounts of First Church, Los Angeles, see *Architecture and Building* 46 (Dec. 1914); *Brickbuilder* 24 (June 1915); *Western Architect* 24 (Aug. 1916).

40. On First Church, Palo Alto, see *American Architect* 114, no. 2226 (Aug. 21, 1918), plates and plans; *Western Architect* 24 (Aug. 1916), plates and plans. On First Church, Long Beach, see *American Architect* 105, no. 2005 (May 27, 1914), plates and plans.

41. See *Inland Architect* 51 (Jan. 1908); Bayerd Still, *Milwaukee: The History of a City* (Madison: University of Wisconsin Press, 1948), 84. Later this society was renamed Sixth Church of Christ, Scientist.

42. Willard Mattox, "Christian Science Architecture," *Illinois Illustrated Review* (Aug. 1909): 61.

43. James, "The Christian Science Architecture of California," 71.

44. Ibid., 72.

45. See Earl C. Ward, *A Goodly Heritage, a Brief Account of the Establishment and Growth of the Christian Science Movement in Riverside, California, with Particular Reference to First Church of Christ, Scientist, of This City* (Riverside, 1973).

46. Fannie M. McKoon, "History of First Church of Christ, Scientist, San Diego," undated ms., CHD, 16.

47. Esther McCoy suggests that the membership voted to include a dome, to Gill's dismay, but the dome appears in his original sketches and the truss system seems deliberately engineered to support an impressive dome. Perhaps it was when the membership voted down the expensive art glass dome, which Gill originally favored, that he walked out of a membership meeting. See McCoy, *Five California Architects* (New York: Reinhold, 1960), 61. Letters have recently come to light indicating that there were disagreements concerning the size of the dome. The letters are in the possession of First Church of Christ, Scientist, San Diego. The church has now been splendidly restored. For an account of the church restoration, see "Saving Grace," *San Diego Union Tribune*, Nov. 13, 1994.

48. James, "The Christian Science Architecture of California," 79.

49. See Timothy N. Wittman, "Third Church of Christ, Scientist," Staff Report, Commission on Chicago Landmarks, 1988; "A Church Built of Enamel Brick," *Brickbuilder* 10, no. 11 (1901): 241; Bernard C. Greengard, "Hugh M. G. Garden," *Prairie School Review* 3, no. 1 (1966): 5–18; Wesley I. Shank, "Hugh Garden in Iowa," *Prairie School Review* 5, no. 3 (1968): 43–47; Hugh M. G. Garden, "The Chicago School," *Prairie School Review* 3, no. 1 (1966): 19–22; Stephen Longstreet, *Chicago, 1860–1919* (New York: McKay, 1973), 435; Mark L. Peisch, *The Chicago School of Architecture: Early Followers of Sullivan and Wright* (New York: Random House, 1964), 69–72.

50. See "Second Church of Christ, Scientist, Boston," *Architectural Forum* 26 (Feb. 1917): 69.

51. Press release quoted in *Chicago Inter-Ocean* (July 14, 1901). See also *Christian Science Sentinel* 3, no. 47 (July 25, 1901); *Christian Science Journal* 19 (Aug. 1901). See also Garden's ideals expressed in "The Influence of the New Thought in Design on Architecture," *Inland Architect and News Record* 62 (Dec. 1903): 35.

52. Wittman, "Third Church of Christ, Scientist, Chicago," 5.

53. All three disks are illustrated in "A Church Built of Enameled Brick," plates 83 and 86.

54. Wittman, "Third Church of Christ, Scientist, Chicago," 5.

55. This church was razed in 1985. See Shank, "Hugh Garden in Iowa"; Richard Guy Wilson and Sidney K. Robinson, *The Prairie School in Iowa* (Ames: Iowa State University Press, 1977); Roger G. Kennedy, *American Churches* (New York: Stewart, Tabori, and Chang, 1982), 36.

56. Shank, "Hugh Garden in Iowa"; "A New Scientist Church," Marshalltown *Evening Times-Republican,* Nov. 4, 1902.

57. Richard Guy Wilson and Sidney Robinson, *Modern Architecture in America: Visions and Revisions* (Ames: Iowa State University Press, 1991), suggest that Wright designed parts of the Coonley House specifically to address the privacy needs of Mrs. Coonley, a public Christian Science practitioner who had offices at the house and needed to ensure the privacy of her clients.

58. The four were the Presbyterian Church (1879), the Episcopal Church (1888), the Methodist Church (1901), and St. Mary's (1901). Information from the "History of First Church of Christ, Scientist, Riverside," undated ms., CHD.

59. Building Committee Minutes, "Church History of First Church of Christ, Scientist, Riverside," undated ms., CHD.

60. On Cheney see Leonard K. Eaton, *Two Chicago Architects and Their Clients* (Cambridge, Mass.: MIT Press, 1969). Besides this church, Howard Cheney designed the classical First Church, St. Petersburg, Florida (see *The Architect* 10 [Apr. 1928]: 89–97); the classical Fourth Church of Christ, Scientist, Washington, D.C., in 1930 (see *The Architect* 14 [Sept.–Oct. 1930]: 611); and possibly several other Chicago-area churches.

61. "Church History of First Church of Christ, Scientist, Riverside," undated ms., CHD.

62. I. T. Frary, "First Church of Christ, Scientist, Rochester," *Architectural Record* 41, no. 3 (Mar. 1917): 209.

63. Ibid.

64. William Arthur Newman, "The Second Church of Christ, Scientist, Oakland, California," *Architect and Engineer of California* 48, no. 1 (Jan. 1917): 46.

65. Ibid., 41, 45.

66. See *Oakland Tribune,* May 14, 1918.

67. There were noteworthy exceptions, particularly in California. See Meyer and Hollers's 1924 Tudor-style Ninth Church of Christ Scientist, Los Angeles, and Allison and Allison's 1926 Moorish-style Thirteenth Church of Christ, Scientist, Los Angeles. See Bird Stewart Scotland Collection, CHD. This collection is comprised of thirty-two scrapbooks containing items on the history of Christian Science clipped from secular periodicals, and it includes several volumes of announcements of buildings and dedications.

68. Seattle's First Church (Bebb and Mendel, 1914) was in the Capitol Hill district; Third Church (1922) and Fourth Church, Seattle (1922), were both designed by the Christian Scientist architect George Foot Dunham. All of these churches are in a style reminiscent of Beman's. Beman's First Church, Portland, was built in 1908 and set the standard for classical designs in the Northwest.

69. See "Odd Church Being Erected in Maplewood," *Newark Evening News,* Apr. 29, 1923; "Architectural Types of Beautiful Maplewood," *Maplewood News,* May 29, 1931; *The Architect* (May 26, 1926): plates 25–27. Also see Müller's churches for the congregations at several locations in New York: Bay Ridge (see *Architectural Record* 52 [Dec. 1922]: 485–87), Bronxville, Brooklyn (Second Church), Flushing, Hempstead, Patchogue, Port Chester, Schenectady (a classical edifice illustrated in *Architecture* [Dec. 1922]: plate 92), and Staten Island; as well as for those in Elizabeth, New Jersey, and Fitchburg, Massachusetts. A member wrote of the church at Bronxville: "I appreciate your successful efforts at designing beautiful Christian Science churches and thereby helping to do away with the—as you say—'bank buildings' which design is becoming too numerous." Letter, Virginia Gilbert Downer to Bernhardt Müller, Apr. 12, 1925, CHD.

70. William Edgar Moran, "Plan and Design of Christian Science Churches," *Architectural Forum* (Apr. 1924): 145–48. Moran mentioned that by 1924 over two thousand churches had been erected. Moran believed that, stylistically, Christian Science's "religious inheritance" was the "Clas-

sic Roman" and therefore variants such as colonial and Georgian were, with a few exceptions, the preferred types.

71. Mouzon William Brabham, *Planning Modern Church Buildings* (Nashville: Cokesbury Press, 1928), 32–37. For other comments on the relationship of architectural style to theology, see Von Ogden Vogt, *Art and Religion* (New Haven: Yale University Press, 1921); Vogt writes, "In many ways it is, in the nature of the case, easier to express new thoughts by the usage of some one of the classical periods as the inspiration for a modern church building. Yet it is not easy to select any one of these as an adequate mode. To go far back to Greece or to Rome is to place too much paganism in the structure and also to come too close, as the Christian Scientists have done, to the forms characteristic of our state houses and post offices" (201).

72. See William Pope Barney, "The Planning of Christian Science Churches: An Interview with William Pope Barney, Architect," *Architecture* 61 (Apr. 1930): 194–201. His firm designed First Church, Ardmore, Pennsylvania; First Church, Swarthmore, Pennsylvania; First Church, Burlington, New Jersey; and First Church, Atlantic City, New Jersey. See also *Architectural Forum* 64 (Mar. 1936): 175–76; William Gray Purcell, "A Place of Assembly That Can Be Built in Units," *Christian Science Monitor,* June 25, 1925; Charles Draper Faulkner, *Christian Science Church Edifices* (Chicago: Privately printed), 1946.

73. Eugene Clute, *The Practical Requirements of Modern Buildings* (New York: Pencil Points Press, 1928), 61. On Third Church, Dallas, see "Christian Scientists Use Romanesque," *Architectural Record* 126, no. 4 (Apr. 1938): 57–60. The anonymous author states that the beautiful church was "a unique departure from the traditional colonial and classical churches of that creed" (57).

74. See Robert M. Craig, "Bernard Maybeck and the Principia: Architecture as Philosophical Expression" (Ph.D. diss., University of California, Los Angeles, 1972).

75. Mary Kimball Morgan founded The Principia as a grade school for Christian Science children in 1898. A four-year college was started in 1932 and was moved to Elsah, Illinois, in 1935. As early as 1923, Maybeck had been invited to meet with students. By 1925, Frederic Morgan, president of the college, who was much impressed by Maybeck's Berkeley church design, took the architect to the East Coast to look at chapels. They were both particularly impressed by the stone Congregational church at Williams College and many small meetinghouses, as well as by King's Chapel in Boston. Morgan wrote of Maybeck, "He is a fascinating character and for all his seemingly vague and poetic approach, he is one of the most hardheaded people I know, because his ideals and ideas are laid on a concept of beauty that is based on absolute truth and on a spiritual concept of balance. To him nothing can be good that is in any way insincere or superficial or that creates a false front." Letter, Frederic E. Morgan to a Principia trustee, Feb. 27, 1943, Principia College Collection, Elsah, Illinois.

76. Quoted in the *Principia Pilot* 30 (Nov. 19, 1971). For other articles concerning the chapel, see the *Principia Alumni Purpose* (July 1932).

77. William Lyman Johnson, *The History of the Christian Science Movement,* vol. 1 (Brookline, Mass.: Zion Research Foundation, 1920), 106.

78. Ralph Adams Cram, "A Note on Architectural Style," *Architectural Review* 12 (1905): 181–95.

79. Ralph Adams Cram, *American Church Building of Today* (New York: Architectural Book Publishing Co., 1929), vii.

80. Sheldon Cheney, *The New World Architecture* (New York: Longmans, Green, 1930), 343–44.

81. Saarinen's design was illustrated in *Pencil Points* 17 (Sept. 1936): 486; *Architectural Record* (May 1928); see also the museum catalog *Design in America: The Cranbrook Vision, 1925–1950* (Detroit: Detroit Institute of Arts and the Metropolitan Museum of Art, 1983), 56–58.

82. On Herbert Baker's Ninth Church of Christ, Scientist, Westminster, see J. S. Braithwaite, "Christian Science Churches: Their Plan Requirements as Exemplified in the Latest London Building," *Architect's Journal* (Dec. 16, 1931): 806–9. On Oswald Milne's Eleventh Church of Christ, Scientist, London, see Henry Fletcher, "The Latest Christian Science Church," *Architect's Jour-*

nal (Mar. 2, 1927): 309–15, with plans. For other information on the church in England see Frederick Dixon, "The Growth of Christian Science in England," *World To-Day* (Feb. 1908): 178–83.

83. The Second Church, Berkeley, was featured in the *Architect and Engineer* (June 1927): 89–90.

84. See *A Tribute to Marvin Randolph Higgins* (San Francisco: Privately printed by John Henry Nash, 1937). Gutterson studied at the University of California at Berkeley and at the Ecole des Beaux-Arts in Paris. Early in his career he worked for John Galen Howard, served on the design staff for the Panama Pacific Exposition, and also worked on the city of Oakland architectural staff, until he set up his own office in 1916. His architectural practice consisted of building over seventy mainly residential commissions in Berkeley and in San Francisco Woods. See Susan Dinkelspiel Stern's pamphlet *Henry Higby Gutterson* (Berkeley: Berkeley Architectural Association, 1979).

85. The congregation of First Church, San Mateo, for instance, hired Ernest L. and John L. Norberg to remodel a "plain church" according to Byzantine styling; see *Architect and Engineer* 94, no. 3 (Sept. 1928): 335–36. There are many references to California Christian Science churches throughout the run of the *Architect and Engineer*.

86. See Edgar Kaufmann Jr., "Frank Lloyd Wright, Three New Churches," *Art in America* 45 (Fall 1957): 22–25. Kaufmann described the plan for the Christian Science church (25):

> The smallest, most peaceful of the three designs shown here is a hymn to the ideal—two pure forms, circle and square, that guide men through a multiplicity of sensory experiences toward the reliability of structural order. Set squarely on a large circular plinth, raised at the entrance and nestled in at back, the church is largely glass under a wide square slab. Low side walls dip in echo of the plinth and the circles of seats within: deep louvers shield trellis-lit windowpanes. The entrance opens to the fullest: within, a low screen of mural painting protects the auditorium and its raised platform from disturbance. This screening also provides for utilities, stairs, stacks, with imprinting on the strict geometry of the architectural themes. The least apparatus here yields abundant significance.

See also Bruce Brooks Pfeiffer, *Frank Lloyd Wright,* vol. 8, ed. Yukio Futagawa (Tokyo: A.D.A. Edita, 1988): "There is no darkness, no mystery, no cavernous vast interior spaces to force humans to their knees in fear and supplication. On the contrary, this church speaks directly of clear trust and faith in pure thought" (262–63). Wright also designed two schemes for a Christian Science reading room for the congregation in Riverside, Illinois, in 1956.

87. See Albert Christ-Janer and Mary Mix Foley, *Modern Church Architecture: A Guide to the Form and Spirit of Twentieth-Century Religious Buildings* (New York: McGraw-Hill, 1962), which featured Callister's designs. The Belvedere church (1951–52) was built of roughhewn redwood and concrete as a modern indoor-outdoor church. The congregation had met in one of the earliest homes in the area—a log cabin—and wanted a church design that incorporated the rustic, rugged character of that building in their new church home. Christ-Janer and Foley conclude, "Although the Christian Science societies have been somewhat ahead of others in the architectural expression of their faith, today they might draw inspiration from some of the recent Catholic and Protestant churches that have been based upon the Liturgical Revival. The circle, the oval, the spiral, the rhomboid, the triangle, the square, all can express the unity that is fundamental to Christian Science" (262).

88. James, "The Christian Science Architecture of California," 72.

Epilogue

The last truly polemical statement on the architecture of the Christian Science movement appeared in 1946, when Charles Draper Faulkner privately published his *Christian Science Church Edifices*. This volume contained photographs, building dimensions, and discussion of various styles of architecture from the history of the movement. The book's emphasis was on buildings from the 1920s through the 1940s. Faulkner designed a number of churches in the Midwest in the classical, Georgian, and even Byzantine styles through the 1960s.[1] He believed that the church building activity had been "passing through a formulative or 'adolescent' stage. Parts of it are sweet and beautiful, parts are ungainly and awkward. To the end that dignity may be appreciated and attained,—just as economically as ugliness,—we may pause and consider our ways."[2] Even though the classical style presented a majestic or dignified appearance for the church, Faulkner thought the style was simply not homey enough.[3]

Faulkner expressed his ideals at a time of dramatic increase in the growth of suburbs, when religious buildings were needed to fit into them. It was also a period when some larger urban Christian Science churches were being depopulated. His firm subsequently became the leader in Christian Science commissions nationwide, building nearly 140 churches. For example, his 1938 First Church, Mount Lebanon (a Pittsburgh suburb), was designed as a "Georgian structure with Corinthian Columns and a steeple which was to be lighted to serve as a beacon to guide and welcome those in search of truth." Faulkner maintained the conviction that church architecture was important in attracting newcomers, writing that "if some person is drawn into Science even thru first being attracted to the building, then it will have been a complete success from my point of view. I am sure that you realize that the structure will be a desirable influence for the Cause in your community. It commands respect with its simple dignity and obvious attractiveness."[4]

With the passage of time some architects tired of the prevailing Christian Science building designs, which began to look dated. By 1953 a number of architects lamented the lack of originality in the denomination's buildings. According to Paul Thiry, for example, "The Christian Science church . . . could have developed an architecture expressive of its practitioners' own belief. But in Charles Faulkner's *Christian Science Church Edifices* are shown Spanish monasteries, Greek Temples, Gothic Cathedrals, colonial meeting houses, and almost every kind of imitation except perhaps a Mayan Temple. There is not one church in the whole book which shows, through its architecture, Christian Science as a twentieth century religious concept, which of course, meant Modernist churches."[5]

Others hoped that Christian Science could still produce a vital new architecture, since some unusual edifices had been produced from the very start of the building boom. In the United States, Maybeck's First Church, Berkeley, seemed to signal the possibility of a new eclectic religious style as early as 1910–11. But most of the outstanding examples were to be found in Europe. The most noteworthy were First Church, Manchester, England (1903, fig. 83), an Arts and Crafts design by Edgar Woods, and First Church, the Hague, a modernist design by Hendrik Berlage (1925, fig. 84), which was inspired by Louis Sullivan's St. Paul's Church in Cedar Rapids and Wright's Unity Temple in Chicago.[6] Significant church designs reflecting the stripped-down-modernist aesthetic can be found in O. R. Salvisberg's First Church, Basel (1936), and in Hans Hofmann's First Church, Zurich, Switzerland (1938).[7]

As late as 1963, Milton Grigg published in the *AIA Journal* a guide to planning edifices for the church. Summing up the building movement, he suggested that Christian Science could produce a truly modern American religious architecture:

A high quality of construction and conservative restrained taste may be said to characterize Christian Science church edifices. . . . It is considered to be expressive of the worthy intent of the giver to endow a structure of above-average permanence and sacred dignity. Stylistically there is no characteristic idiom. As the [Original Mother Church] reflected the influences of the last years of the Romantic Revival, so edifices built in later times reflect local traditions and the current fashions and tastes. For a time it seemed that the Greek Temple might become the outward symbol of this religion, but a few years later, and, indeed, in some areas even to the present, the "cult of the Colonial" was all-influencing. Edifices in contemporary styling are becoming more common, and less academic styling seems to reflect an awareness on the part of the builders that Christian Science is now of maturity and capable of architectural expression as unique in form as it is in spiritual and intellectual content.[8]

Since the mid-fifties, a number of notable contemporary designs have been commissioned by individual congregations. Edifices such as Maynard Lyndon's Twenty-eighth Church, Westwood Village, Los Angeles (1955), and Harry Weese's Seventeenth

Figure 83. Edgar Woods, First Church of Christ, Scientist, Manchester, England, 1903 (Church History, Division of the Church of Christ, Scientist, Boston).

Figure 84. Hendrik Berlage, First Church of Christ, Scientist, The Hague, 1925 (Church History, Division of the Church of Christ, Scientist, Boston).

Church, Chicago (1968, fig. 85), were Modernist church designs. Weese's church, built of travertine, abstractly echoes the earlier classical models of the Chicago building boom. Araldo Cossutta's Third Church and Christian Science Monitor Building, Washington, D.C. (1967–71); Paul Rudolph's now-razed brutalist Christian Science College Organization Building, Champaign, Illinois (1962); Vernon Swaback's Third Church, Tucson (1994, fig. 86); and Moore, Ruble, and Yudell's First Church, Glendale, California (1988–89), are also exemplary. With the exception of Swaback's edifice, which was inspired by Frank Lloyd Wright's ideas, these buildings are indicative of late modernist and even postmodernist architectural approaches.[9]

Christian Science began with a call for the "revolt of the individual" against the often complacent sanctuaries of traditional Protestantism. Its teachings were a modern religious response to changes in economic, social, and gender roles and expectations at the turn of the century. The organization grew and prospered and began to fix its theological and social ideals as formal traditions. Early in the church's history there were those who tried to position the new denomination in terms of the strength of the Puritan mode of historical Christianity represented through more traditional architectures. Others viewed the new institution as thoroughly modern, separate from and superior to other religious and social institutions—a new church for the advancement of spiritual and material capital.

Architects involved in Christian Science commissions, particularly those who

Figure 85. Harry Weese, Seventeenth Church of Christ, Scientist, Chicago, 1968 (Photo by Orlando R. Cabanban, Harry Weese and Associates).

Figure 86. Vernon Swaback, Third Church of Christ, Scientist, Tucson, Arizona, 1993 (Photo by William Lesch, Vernon Swaback Associates).

practiced Christian Science, believed that their buildings reflected, however faintly, the true spiritual character of both Christian Science and architecture. Interpretations of Christian Science theology in architecture, however, emphasized either the autonomous, fixed, and rational nature of timeless Truth, or the dynamic and even evolutionary progressive unfolding of spirituality that was believed to characterize the onward march of "the people" in historical Christendom.

Christian Science, in its concern for the preservation of individualism, recognized the freedom of individual congregations to choose appropriate architectures. However, the predominance of classical architecture implied a solidification of a Christian Science theology and practice that was aligned with progressive civic movements of the day. The early Chicago-inspired classical revival edifices fit with the institutional representation being supported by the "enlightened" business elite who were often attracted to the new religion at that time. In the scheme of this group, the classical style represented not only culture but a return to the democratic values of the early Republic and footnoted the very cradle of democracy itself. Architecture based on this model would help bring about methodical "progressive" social change. Moreover, the Christian Science image of the world was one of fixed spiritual Truth, which was available through the forceful affirmations voiced in the face of personal, economic, social, and cultural change. Classical architecture consolidated this image of the world as a perfect and unified model.

The dream of the rational self-adjusting city in Christian Science depended on key locales for worship set up rationally within established communities. The dynamism of urban change was not considered in the congregations' theories of social development. And yet this dynamism and change at the turn of the century were precisely what propelled Christian Science into the popular consciousness.

Institutionalization changed the highly individualistic orientation of early Christian Science. The importance of personal vision, inspiration, and interpretation was balanced by the need to establish congregations that conformed to the disciplinary mandates of the larger institution. At first the unification of the movement enhanced the formation of a group identity, via spiritual ideals for successful living, new methods of church work, and even new architecture. However, in time innovation was transformed into a comforting ritual. The standardizing of Christian Science theology and worship paralleled the need to protect the organization and to ensure its orderly propagation in the early twentieth century.

Christian Science architecture emerged from a regional heterogeneity as the organization itself became centralized. It was particularly important to follow or relate architecturally to the larger movement once the domed Mother Church Extension became a model and a visible sign of the authority vested in the Boston headquarters. In Chicago, the architecture of the Columbian Exposition and the beliefs of Daniel Burnham and others that architecture could foster conscientious civic behavior corresponded with the theology of Christian Science. The building boom developed during a crisis in other churches, making the classical facades of the new buildings all the more visible to those denominations that were rapidly losing their social influence.

While classical elements adorned the exteriors of Christian Science churches, they were often eclipsed by the modern innovations inside. Excellent acoustics, thermal and visual comfort, innovative lighting, open "pure" spaces, and new building technologies were utilized behind the facades.

Christian Science was particularly successful among women, but its influence on feminist practice was limited. Many women took advantage of the growing capital of their spouses to build up the nationwide network of Christian Scientists, and they made important contributions as public practitioners, reading room librarians, and Sunday school teachers and superintendents. Their public healing practices tended to insert religion and health concerns back into the female "sphere," where those concerns had been centered earlier in domestic settings, prior to aggressive urbanization.

The urban context for building churches was never fixed, and it continued to change with the growth and shift of population patterns of cities. At the same time there were demographic changes and declines in the Christian Science church membership itself. Today, congregations are still erecting small edifices, sometimes consolidating urban memberships, but many of the grand churches have been closed, sold, remodeled, or destroyed. Current congregations have returned to a regional vernacular heterogeneity in the styles of their buildings.

In the end, it is the stylistically diverse architecture of the Mother Church and its Extension that is important in unifying Christian Scientists around church architecture. Most members of branch churches are also members of the Mother Church, so the Boston buildings continue to be potent symbols of Mrs. Eddy's healing mission. In the absence of traditional religious symbols, one finds that photographs and other depictions of the Mother Church, the Extension, and the new Church Center abound in the branch church clerk's offices, board rooms, and reading rooms.

The church is losing members, and some critics view the historical and contemporary desire for visibility as one of the primary reasons for this. As Robert Peel and Stephen Gottschalk both suggest, Mrs. Eddy's frequent efforts to hold her followers back from religious display and external signs of success have gone unheeded.[10]

During the period of the building boom, the Christian Science movement began evolving from a "movement on the move" into a respectable denomination. The current administration of the Christian Science church not only emphasizes the global networks of information and news, but encourages a public fascinated with "new age" religion to recognize the potency of Christian Science's disciplined spiritual healing. In earlier times, however, Christian Science religious and social values were also forcefully presented through buildings that had a significant impact on the church architecture of their day. These structures stand now as a last legacy of an early twentieth-century religious vision and cultural impulse that conferred upon architectural style a powerful moralizing social role. With a heightened awareness of the social, political, and physical changes in cities in the United States today, it is perhaps desirable to ponder the well-built edifices of the early Christian Science movement and consider possible new uses for them. As even the staunch critic Edward Farnsworth foresaw in 1911:

> The future historian of the rise and fall of fads and cults will find interesting material in the annals of the Eddy movement; and the people of that day, among whom may be under the spell of some new delusion, will point to the costly and enduring Temples originally dedicated to Christian Science worship, and much they will marvel in the allness of "Good," and the nothingness of evil; a belief then extinct. . . . What then, in all fairness, can be said for Christian Science? . . . In these days of crumbling foundations and tottering edifices of outworn dogmas, the pseudo idealism of Mrs. Eddy, Mrs. Stetson, and the rest of the following, is a provisional structure which, if judiciously remodelled, would bear some resemblance to the ethereal and high towering temple of Truth yet reared by mankind amidst these poor, earthly clods of matter.[11]

NOTES

1. See a typical early classical design by Faulkner for the church in Lakewood, Ohio (1924), *American Architect/Architectural Review* (1924): 649–53. See also mainly colonial examples in *American Architect* 133 (Mar. 20, 1926); *Architectural Forum* (Mar. 1929): 339–41; *Architectural Record* 100 (Oct. 1946): 114. There is also a Byzantine example, Eighteenth Church, Chicago, in his book;

see *Christian Science Church Edifices* (Chicago: Privately printed, 1946). Faulkner's son, Charles D. Faulkner Jr., joined the practice in 1949 and continued to build and remodel Christian Science churches in partnership with his father through the 1970s.

2. Faulkner, *Christian Science Church Edifices*, 33. The Christian Science Board of Directors also published a pamphlet, *Branch Church Building* (Christian Science Publishing Society, 1953, 1959), that suggested that "churches constructed along the so-called contemporary lines can sometimes be built more economically and with just as good effect as a building executed in the so-called period or traditional styles which require the expenditure of considerable amounts of money to carry out the steeples, ornamentation, and so on" (9–10).

3. Faulkner, *Christian Science Church Edifices*, 395.

4. Letter, Charles Draper Faulkner to Board of Trustees, First Church of Christ, Scientist, Mount Lebanon, Pennsylvania, Dec. 26, 1939, Church Records, First Church of Christ, Scientist, Mount Lebanon, Pennsylvania. Faulkner also designed First Church, Lakewood, Ohio (1919, while still influenced by Solon Beman); Fourth Church, Milwaukee (1921); First Church, Montclair, New Jersey (1926); Eighteenth Church, Chicago (1927); First Church, Marshall, Michigan (1948); First Church, Dearborn, Michigan (1949); Eighth Church, New York (1950); First Church, Williamsburg, Virginia (1957); First Church, Miami Beach, Florida (1959).

5. Paul Thiry, *Churches and Temples* (New York: Reinhold, 1954), 9. For other examples of church architecture polemics, see John Ragsdale, "We Will Build Modern Churches," *Architectural Record* (Oct. 1946); "The Slow Evolution of Religious Architecture," *Architectural Record* (Dec. 1949); Joseph Hudnot, "The Modern Spirit Enters Contemporary Church Architecture," *American Architecture* (Dec. 1932).

6. On Woods see Nikolaus Pevsner, *The Buildings of England: Lancashire, The Industrial and Commercial South* (Harmondsworth, Eng.: Penguin, 1969), 48, 322. Pevsner writes that this church is the "boldest religious building of the early [twentieth century]." Also on Woods, see "Arts and Crafts in Daisy Bank Road," *Architect's Journal* 165, no. 25 (June 1977); *Journal of the Royal Institute of British Architects* (Dec. 1954); *Manchester Guardian* (Aug. 4, 1972); B. Tatham Woodhear, *An Historical Sketch of the Beginnings of Christian Science in Lancashire and the North of England, and the Early Days of First Church of Christ, Scientist, Manchester* (Manchester, Eng.: John Taylor, 1934); Christopher Stell, *Nonconformist Chapels and Meeting-houses in the North of England* (London: HMSO, 1994). On Berlage see Sergio Polano, *Hendrik Petrus Berlage, Complete Works* (New York: Rizzoli, 1987), 26–29, 240–41. Berlage was "propagandized" by his friend William Gray Purcell in May 1918. Purcell wrote to him: "I think you will be interested to know that in America the new spirit has touched religion and produced a faith expressing itself with the simplicity of primitive Christianity but taking full account of modern intellectual equipment and world machinery" (241). For more on Berlage, see also Leonard K. Eaton, *American Architecture Comes of Age* (Cambridge, Mass.: MIT Press, 1972), 208–32; Don Gifford, ed., *The Literature of Architecture* (New York: Dutton, 1966), 607–16; H. Paul Rovinelli, "H. P. Berlage and the Amsterdam School, 1914–1920," *Journal of the Society of Architectural Historians* 43, no. 3 (Oct. 1984): 256–64; Charles B. Hosmer Jr., "Hendrik P. Berlage, Architect of First Church of Christ, Scientist, The Hague, Netherlands," *Quarterly News, Longyear Historical Society and Museum* 22, no. 1 (Spring 1985): 333–36; *Christian Science Monitor*, Dec. 8, 1925. The *Christian Science Monitor* for Aug. 15, 1927, quoted the Dutch newspaper *Het Haagsche Volk* regarding Berlage's church in the Hague: "The building reminds one hardly in any respect of the traditional church edifice."

7. For Swiss examples, see Dorothy West Pelzer's "The Christian Science Branch Church: An Architectural Type Study" (M.A. thesis, Massachusetts Institute of Technology, 1950). See also John Cutler, "An Architectural Study of the Christian Science Church" (B.A. thesis, Massachusetts Institute of Technology, 1941). Curiously, the important Sacramento architect Clarence C. Cuff designed a modern Christian Science church in 1909–10 that appears to have been inspired by the Viennese Secessionist architect Otto Wagner. See "Recent Work of Mr. Clarence C. Cuff, Architect," *Architect and Engineer* 35, no. 1 (Nov. 1913): 51.

8. Milton L. Grigg, "A Guide for Planning Buildings for Christian Science," *AIA Journal* (Oct. 1963): 95.

9. On Cossutta's building see "Church Building Progress Report, Third Church of Christ, Scientist, Washington, D.C.," undated ms., CHD. On Paul Rudolph's building see "Architecture Strongly Manipulated in Space and Scale: Christian Science Student Center," *Architectural Record* 141 (Feb. 1967): 137–42; "Christian Science Organization Building," *Architecture and Urbanism* 80 (July 1977): 130, 240–41; *Religious Buildings, by the editors of Architectural Record* (New York: McGraw-Hill, 1979), 26–31; Lydia M. Soo and Robert Ousterhout, "On the Destruction of Paul Rudolph's Christian Science Building: The Vicissitudes of Functionalism," *Inland Architect* 31, no. 2 (Mar.–Apr. 1987): 66–73. On Weese's church see John Morris Dixon, "Church in a Grove of Skyscrapers," *Architectural Forum* 130, no. 5 (June 1969): 42–45; *A Guide to 150 Years of Chicago Architecture* (Chicago: Chicago Review Press, 1985). On the Glendale church see Charles Moore, John Ruble, and Buzz Yudell, *Moore Ruble Yudell* (London: Academy Editions, 1993), 206–13.

10. See particularly Robert Peel, "Decision at the Crossroads," in his *Health and Medicine in the Christian Science Tradition: Principle, Practice and Challenge* (New York: Crossroads Press, 1989), and idem, *Mary Baker Eddy: The Years of Authority* (New York: Holt, Rinehart, and Winston, 1977), 162.

11. Edward C. Farnsworth, *The Passing of Mary Baker Eddy* (Portland, Me.: Smith and Sale, 1911), 27–29.

SELECTED BIBLIOGRAPHY

Abell, Aaron Ignatius. *The Urban Impact on American Protestantism 1865–1900*. Cambridge, Mass.: Harvard University Press, 1943.

Ahlstrom, Sydney. *A Religious History of the American People*. New Haven: Yale University Press, 1972.

Albanese, Catherine L. *America, Religions and Religion*. Belmont, Calif.: Wadsworth, 1981.

Andrews, Wayne. *Architecture, Ambition, and Americans*. New York: Free Press, 1978.

"The Architecture of Christian Science Churches, East and West." *The Craftsman* 7 (Mar. 1905): 689–94.

Arkansas Historical Records Survey, Inventory of the Church Archives of Arkansas, Church of Christ, Scientist. Little Rock: Arkansas Historical Records Survey, 1941.

Armstrong, Joseph. *The Mother Church*. Boston: Christian Science Publishing Society, 1897.

Bach, Richard Franz. "Church Planning in the United States." *Architectural Record* (July–Dec. 1916).

Badger, Reid. *The Great American Fair: The World's Columbian Exposition and American Culture*. Chicago: Nelson, Hall, 1979.

Bagenal, Hope. "Church Form and Christian Science." *Architect's Journal* (May 25, 1927): 727–28.

Bancroft, Hubert H. *The Book of the Fair, an Historical and Descriptive Presentation of the World's Science, Art, and Industry, as Viewed Through the Columbian Exposition at Chicago in 1893*. 3 vols. Chicago: Bancroft Co., 1893.

Barker, Eileen, ed. *New Religious Movements: A Perspective for Understanding Society*. New York: Edwin Mellen Press, 1982.

Barney, William Pope. "The Planning of Christian Science Churches: An Interview with William Pope Barney, Architect." *Architecture* 61 (Apr. 1930): 194–201.

Barrows, Rev. John Henry, D.D. *World's Parliament of Religions*. 2 vols. Chicago: Parliament Publishing Society, 1893.

Bartlett, Dana W. *The Better City: A Sociological Study of a Modern City*. Los Angeles: Neuner Co., 1907.

Bates, E. Sutherland, and John V. Dittemore. *Mary Baker Eddy: The Truth and the Tradition*. New York: Knopf, 1932.

Beasley, Norman. *The Continuing Spirit.* New York: Duell, Sloan and Pearce, 1956.

———. *The Cross and the Crown.* New York: Duell, Sloan, and Pearce, 1952.

Bednarowski, Mary Farrell. *New Religions and the Theological Imagination in America.* Bloomington: University of Indiana Press, 1989.

Bellwald, A. M. *Christian Science and the Catholic Faith.* New York: Macmillan, 1922.

Beman, Solon S. "The Architecture of the Christian Science Church." *The World To-day* 12, no. 6 (June 1907): 582–90.

Bennett, Edward H., and Daniel H. Burnham. *Plan of Chicago.* Edited by Charles Moore. Chicago: Commercial Club, 1909.

Blake, Channing. "The Architecture of Carrère and Hastings." Ph.D. diss., Columbia University, 1976.

Bloome, Arnold. *A Voice Is Calling.* New York: Putnam, 1926.

Bluestone, Daniel. *Constructing Chicago.* New Haven: Yale University Press, 1991.

Boyd, John Taylor. "Mary Baker Eddy Memorial." *Architectural Record* 21, no. 5 (May 1917): 449–50.

Boyer, M. Christine. *Dreaming the Rational City: The Myth of American City Planning.* Cambridge, Mass.: MIT Press, 1983.

Boyer, Paul. *Urban Masses and Moral Order in America, 1820–1920.* Cambridge, Mass.: Harvard University Press, 1978.

Brabham, Mouzon William. *Planning Modern Church Buildings.* Nashville: Cokesbury Press, 1928.

Braden, Charles. *Christian Science Today: Power, Policy, Practice.* Dallas: Southern Methodist University Press, 1958.

Braithwaite, J. S. "Christian Science Churches, Their Plan Requirements as Exemplified in the Latest London Building." *Architect's Journal* (Dec. 16, 1931): 806–9.

Brooks, H. Allen. *Prairie School Architecture: Studies from "The Western Architect."* Toronto: University of Toronto Press, 1975.

Buckley, James Monroe. *Faith Healing, Christian Science and Kindred Phenomena.* New York: Century, 1892.

Burchard, John, and Albert Bush-Brown. *The Architecture of America: A Social and Cultural History.* Boston: Little-Brown, 1966.

Burg, David F. *Chicago's White City of 1893.* Lexington: University Press of Kentucky, 1976.

Burgess, Ernest W., and Donald J. Bogue, eds. *Contributions to Urban Sociology.* Chicago: University of Chicago Press, 1964.

Burrell, Joseph Dunn. *A New Appraisal of Christian Science.* New York: Funk and Wagnalls, 1906.

Burton, Edmund F. *Why I Became a Christian Scientist.* Des Moines: The Midwestern, 1908.

Campbell, James. *What Christian Science Means and What We Can Learn From It.* New York: Abingdon Press, 1920.

Cardwell, Kenneth H. *Bernard Maybeck: Artisan, Architect, Artist.* Santa Barbara, Calif.: Peregrine Smith, 1977.

Carrolls, H. K. *Religious Forces of the United States.* New York: Scribner, 1912.

Casson, Herbert N. *The Crime of Credulity.* New York: Peter Eckler, 1901.

Chapel, Gage William. "Christian Science and the Rhetoric of Argumentative Synthesis." Ph.D. diss., University of Southern California, 1972.

Cheney, Sheldon. *The New World Architecture.* New York: Longmans, Green, 1930.

Christiano, Kevin J. *Religious Diversity and Social Change: American Cities, 1890–1906.* New York: Cambridge University Press, 1987.

Christian Science: A Sourcebook of Contemporary Materials. Boston: Christian Science Publishing Society, 1990.

Christian Science Journal. 1883–present.

Christian Science Monitor. 1910–present.

Christian Science Publishing Society. *Church Building in Christian Science.* Boston: Christian Science Publishing Society, 1908, 1966.

Christian Science Sentinel. 1898–present.

Christian Science Wartime Activities. Boston: Christian Science Publishing Society, 1922.

Christ-Janer, Albert, and Mary Mix Foley. *Modern Church Architecture: A Guide to the Form and Spirit of Twentieth-Century Religious Buildings.* New York: McGraw-Hill, 1962.

Ciucci, Giorgio, et al. *The American City: From the Civil War to the New Deal.* Cambridge, Mass.: MIT Press, 1979.

Clark, Gordon. *The Church of St. Bunco: A Drastic Treatment of a Copyrighted Religion—un-Christian Non-science.* New York: Abbey Press, 1901.

Coburn, Frederick W. "The New Christian Science Temple in Boston." *Indoors and Out* 4 (July 1906): 174–79.

Comes, John Theodore. *Catholic Art and Architecture.* Pittsburgh: N.p., 1920.

Commons, John R. *Social Reform and the Church.* New York: Crowell, 1894.

Condit, Carl. *The Chicago School of Architecture: A History of Commercial and Public Buildings in the Chicago Area, 1875–1925.* Chicago: University of Chicago Press, 1964.

Conover, Elbert M. *The Church Building Guide.* New York: Interdenominational Bureau of Architecture, 1946.

Cook, George Shaw. "Christian Science in Chicago." *American Queen* (Apr. 1907): 8–9.

———. "Growth of Christian Science in America: What Christian Science Is Accomplishing." *Fine Arts Journal* (May 1907).

Cooke, G. W. "The Institutional Church." *New England Magazine* 14 (Aug. 1896): 645–60.

Cottrell, Charles H. "Description of the New Building" (First Church, New York). *Architectural Record* (Feb. 1904): 165–71.

Coveney, Charles. "The Designing and Building of the Mother Church Extension, Boston, Massachusetts." Unpublished reminiscence, 1934, CHD.

Cox, Richard H., ed. *Religious Systems and Psychotherapy.* Springfield, Ill.: Charles C. Thomas, 1973.

Cram, Ralph Adams. *American Church Building of Today.* New York. Architectural Book Publishing Co., 1929.

———. *American Churches.* 2 vols. New York: American Architect, 1915.

Cross, Robert D., ed. *The Church and the City, 1865–1910.* Indianapolis: Bobbs Merrill, 1967.

Cunningham, Raymond J. "The Impact of Christian Science on the American Churches, 1880–1910." *American Historical Review* 72 (1967): 885–905.

Cunningham, Sarah Gardner. "A New Order: Augusta Emma Simmons Stetson and the Origins of Christian Science in New York City, 1886–1910." Ph.D. diss., Union Theological Seminary, New York, 1994.

Curtis, Susan. *A Consuming Faith: The Social Gospel and Modern American Culture.* Baltimore: Johns Hopkins University Press, 1991.

Cushman, Herbert Ernest. *The Truth in Christian Science.* Boston: James H. West, 1902.

Dakin, Edwin Franden. *Mrs. Eddy: The Biography of a Virginal Mind.* New York: Scribner, 1929.

DeNood, N. B. "The Diffusion of a System of Belief." Ph.D. diss., Harvard University, 1937.

Dickey, Adam. *Memoirs of Mary Baker Eddy.* Boston: Marymount Press, 1927.

Dixon, A. C. *The Christian Science Delusion.* Chicago, 1903. Reprint. Boston: Ruggles Street Baptist Church, 1904.

———. *Is Christian Science a Humbug?* Boston: James Earl, 1901.

Dixon, Frederick. "Mrs. Eddy and Her Detractors." *American Queen* (July 1907): 8–9.

Douglas, Ann. *The Feminization of American Religion.* New York: Knopf, 1977.

Drummond, Andrew Landale. *The Church Architecture of Protestantism: An Historical and Constructive Study.* Edinburgh: T. and T. Clark, 1934.

Drummond, Henry. *The Greatest Thing in the World and Other Addresses.* London: Hodder and Stoughton, 1904.

Dunbar, Herbert L. *Illustrated Historical Sketches Protraying the Advancement in Christian Science from Its Inception to the Present Time, Including Some of Its Church Edifices.* Boston: Herbert Dunbar, 1898.

Eaton, Leonard K. *Two Chicago Architects and Their Clients.* Cambridge, Mass.: MIT Press, 1969.

Eddy, Mary Baker. *The First Church of Christ Scientist and Miscellany.* Boston: Christian Science Publishing Society, 1913.

———. *Manual of the Mother Church, The First Church of Christ, Scientist, in Boston, Massachusetts.* 89th ed. Boston: Christian Science Publishing Society, 1908.

———. *Message to The First Church of Christ, Scientist, or The Mother Church, Boston, June 15, 1902.* Boston: Christian Science Publishing Society, 1902.

———. *Miscellaneous Writings, 1883–1896.* Boston: Christian Science Publishing Society, 1896.

———. *Pulpit and Press.* Boston: Christian Science Publishing Society, 1895.

———. *Retrospection and Introspection.* Boston: Christian Science Publishing Society, 1892.

———. *Science and Health with Key to the Scriptures.* 1875; final revision, 1906. Boston: Christian Science Publishing Society, 1971.

Edgell, G. H. *American Architecture To-Day.* New York: Scribner, 1928.

Editorial Comments on the Life and Work of Mary Baker Eddy, Discoverer and Founder of Christian Science, and Author of the Christian Science Textbook, "Science and Health with Key to the Scriptures." Boston: Christian Science Publishing Society, 1911.

Ellwood, Robert S. *Alternative Altars: Unconventional and Eastern Spirituality in America.* Chicago: University of Chicago Press, 1979.

Euster, W. T. *The Philosophy of Church Building: How to Build a Beautiful Modern Church or Parsonage at Half Price.* Pendleton, Ore.: Jack Huston, 1908.

Farlow, Alfred. *Christian Science: Historical Facts.* Boston: Puritan Press, 1902.

———. "Christian Science in Business Life." *American Business Man* 11 (May 1908): 155–57.

———. "Christian Science Church Architecture." *New England Magazine* 32 (Mar. 1905): 33–47.

———. *A Critic Answered.* Boston: Christian Science Publishing Society, 1904.

———. "A Glance at the Personnel of the Christian Science Movement: A Statement of Mrs. Eddy's Faith, and the Names of Some Prominent People Who Believe in It." *Human Life* 4 (Jan. 1907): 5, 22.

———. "Mary Baker Eddy and Her Work." *New England Magazine* 47 (Dec. 1909): 420.

———. "The Relation of Government to the Practice of Christian Science." *Government, a Magazine of Economics and Applied Politics* 1, no. 2 (May 1907): 1–20.

Farnsworth, Edward C. *The Passing of Mary Baker Eddy.* Portland, Me.: Smith and Sale, 1911.

———. *The Sophistries of Christian Science.* Portland, Me.: Smith and Sale, 1909.

Faulkner, Charles Draper. *Christian Science Church Edifices.* Chicago: Privately printed, 1946.

Fisher, H. A. L. *Our New Religion.* London: Ernest Benn, 1929.

Flower, B. O. *Civilization's Inferno, or Studies in the Social Cellar.* Boston: Arena, 1893.

———. "Christ, the Sick and Modern Christianity." *Arena* 39 (May 1908): 557–64.

———. "Christian Science and Organic Disease." *Arena* 40 (1908): 442–53.

———. *Christian Science as a Religious Belief and a Therapeutic Agent.* New York, 1909.

———. "Elmer Grey and His Dream of a New-World Architecture." *Arena* 40 (Sept. 1908): 198–203.

————. "The Recent Reckless and Irresponsible Attacks on Christian Science and Its Founder, with a Survey of the Christian-Science Movement." *Arena* 37, no. 206 (Jan. 1907): 47–67.

————. "The Rise and Onward March of Christian Science." *Twentieth Century Magazine* 4, no. 22 (July 1911): 304–15.

Fox, Margery. "Power and Piety: Women in Christian Science." Ph.D. diss., New York University, 1973.

Frankiel, Sandra S. *California's Spiritual Frontiers: Religious Alternatives in Anglo-Protestantism, 1850–1910.* Berkeley: University of California Press, 1988.

Gaustad, Edwin Scott. *Dissent in American Religion.* Chicago: University of Chicago Press, 1973.

Gestefeld, Ursula N. *Statement of Christian Science.* Chicago: Ursula N. Gestefeld, 1889.

Gilbert, James. *Perfect Cities: Chicago's Utopias of 1893.* Chicago: University of Chicago Press, 1991.

Gilbert, Levi. "The Downtown Church Again." *Christian City* 10, no. 2 (Feb. 1898): 380–83.

Gilman, James F. *Reminiscences of James F. Gilman.* Providence, R.I.: Privately printed, 1917.

Ginger, Ray. *Altgeld's America, 1890–1905: The Lincoln Ideal versus Changing Realities.* New York: Funk and Wagnalls, 1958.

Gladden, Washington. *Applied Christianity: Moral Aspects of Social Questions.* Boston: Houghton Mifflin, 1886. Reprint. New York: Arno Press, 1976.

————. *Social Salvation.* Boston: Houghton Mifflin, 1902. Reprint. Hicksville, N.Y.: Regina Press, 1975.

Goodwin, William McAfee. *A Lecture Entitled The Christian Science Church.* Washington, D.C., 1916.

Gottschalk, Stephen. "Christian Science and Harmonialism." In *The Encyclopedia of the American Religious Experience,* edited by Charles H. Lippy and Peter W. Williams, vol. 2, 901–16. New York: Scribner, 1988.

————. *The Emergence of Christian Science in American Religious Life.* Berkeley: University of California Press, 1973.

Gowans, Alan. *Images of American Living: Four Centuries of Architecture and Furniture as Cultural Expression.* New York: Harper and Row, 1976.

Gray, David. *Thomas Hastings, Architect.* Boston: Houghton Mifflin, 1933.

Greengard, Bernard C. "Hugh M. G. Garden." *Prairie School Review* 3, no. 1 (1966): 5–18.

Grey, Elmer. "Architecture in Southern California." *Architectural Record* 17, no. 1 (Jan. 1905): 1–15.

————. "The Architecture of the Christian Science Church." *Arena* 40 (Aug.–Sept. 1908): 191–97.

————. "Christian Science Church Edifices and What They Stand For." *Fine Arts Journal* (Oct. 1907): 40–50.

————. *The Planning of Christian Science Church Edifices.* Los Angeles: Kingsley, Mason, and Collins, 1916.

————. "Southern California's New Architecture." *Architecture* 39, no. 3 (Mar. 1919): 57–61.

————. "The Style of Christian Science Church Edifices." *Architect and Engineer of California* 49 (Dec. 1916): 61–72.

Grigg, Milton L. "A Guide for Planning Buildings for Christian Science." *AIA Journal* (Oct. 1963): 92–96.

Haldeman, I. M. *An Analysis of Christian Science, Based on Its Own Statements.* Philadelphia: Philadelphia School of the Bible, 1909.

————. *Christian Science in the Light of Holy Scripture.* New York: Fleming H. Revell, 1909.

Handy, Moses P. *The Official Directory of the World's Columbian Exposition.* Chicago: W. B. Conkey, 1893.

Handy, Robert T., ed. *Religion in the American Experience: The Pluralistic Style.* Columbia: University of South Carolina Press, 1972.

Hanson, J. W., ed. *World's Congress of Religions—Addresses and Papers Delivered before the Parliament.* Chicago: W. B. Conkey, 1894.

Hanson, Penny. "Woman's Hour: Feminist Implications of Mary Baker Eddy's Christian Science Movement." Ph.D. diss., University of California, Irvine, 1981.

Harwood, Anne. *An English View of Christian Science: An Exposure.* New York: Fleming H. Revell, 1899.

Hasbrouck, Stephen. *Altar Fires Relighted: A Study from a Non-Partisan Standpoint of Movements and Tendencies at Work in the Religious Life of To-Day.* New York: Burnett, 1912.

Hastings, Thomas. "A Plea for the Renaissance in Ecclesiastical Architecture." *Architectural Review* 12 (1905): 184–86.

Hayden, Dolores. *The Grand Domestic Revolution: A History of Feminist Designs for American Homes, Neighborhoods, and Cities.* Cambridge, Mass.: MIT Press, 1981.

Hegeman, J. Winthrop. "Must Protestantism Adopt Christian Science?" *North American Review* 198, no. 6 (Dec. 1913): 823–34.

Higinbotham. "The Growth of Christian Science in Illinois." *Illinois Illustrated Review* (Dec. 1909): 171–73.

Hines, Thomas S. *Burnham of Chicago.* New York: Oxford University Press, 1974.

Holt, L. M. *Christian Science Church Architecture, Giving Exterior and Interior Views.* Los Angeles: Press of Times-Mirror, 1908.

Hopkins, Charles Howard. *The Rise of the Social Gospel in American Protestantism, 1865–1915.* New Haven: Yale University Press, 1967.

Hopkins, Henry Reed. "The Progress of Eddyism." Reprint. *American Medical Quarterly* (1900).

Houghton, Walter R. *Neely's History of the Parliament of Religions and Religious Congresses at the World's Columbian Exposition.* Chicago: F. T. Neeley, 1893.

Howe, Frank N. "The Development of Architecture in Kansas City, Missouri." *Architectural Record* 15, no. 2 (Feb. 1904): 134–57.

Huckel, Oliver. *Christian Science and Common Sense: A Contribution toward a Rational Explanation of the Phenomena of Mental Healing.* Baltimore: Arundel Press, 1899.

Hume, Hugo. *The Superior American Religions.* Los Angeles: Libertarian Publishing Co., 1928.

Isbouts, Jean-Pierre. "Carrère and Hastings, Architects to an Era." Ph.D. diss., Kunsthistorisch Instituut, Rijksuniversiteit, Leiden, 1980.

James, George Wharton. "The Christian Science Architecture of California." *Out West* 4, no. 2 (Aug. 1912): 71–79.

Janet, Pierre. *Psychological Healing.* Translated by Eden and Cedar Paul. New York: Macmillan, 1925.

Jenkins, Charles E. "Solon Spencer Beman." *Architectural Reviewer* 1, no. 1 (Feb. 1897): 47–101.

Johnsen, Thomas. "Christian Science and the Puritan Tradition." Ph.D. diss., Johns Hopkins University, 1983.

———. "Christian Scientists and the Medical Profession: A Historical Perspective." *Medical Heritage* (Jan.–Feb. 1986): 70–78.

Johnson, Joseph Kelly. "Christian Science: A Case Study of a Religion as a Form of Adjustment Behavior." Ph.D. diss., St. Louis University, 1938.

Johnson, William Lyman. *History of the Christian Science Movement.* 2 vols. Brookline, Mass.: Zion Research Foundation, 1920.

Johnston, William A. "Christian Science in New York: History of the New York Organizations." *Broadway Magazine* 18, no. 2 (May 1907): 154–68, 265–66.

Jones, Edgar. "A Criticism of Christian Science Values." Ph.D. diss., University of Denver, 1912.

Jordy, William H. *American Buildings: Progressive and Academic Ideals at the Turn of the Twentieth Century.* Garden City, N.Y.: Doubleday, 1972.

Judah, J. Stillson. *The History and Philosophy of the Metaphysical Movements in America.* Philadelphia: Westminster Press, 1967.

Judson, Edward. "The Institutional Church." *Sunday School Times* 38, no. 48 (Nov. 28, 1896): 766–67.

Kamau, Lucy Jayne. "Systems of Belief and Ritual in Christian Science." Ph.D. diss., University of Chicago, 1971.

Kane, Paula M. *Separatism and Subculture: Boston Catholicism, 1900–1920.* Chapel Hill: University of North Carolina Press, 1994.

Kennedy, Hugh A. Studdert. *Christian Science and Organized Religion.* San Francisco: Farallon Press, 1930.

———. *Mrs. Eddy: Her Life, Her Work, and Her Place in History.* San Francisco: Farallon Press, 1947.

Kennedy, Roger G. *American Churches.* New York: Stewart, Tabori, and Chang, 1982.

Kidder, F. E. *Churches and Chapels.* New York: William T. Comstock, 1900.

Kidney, Walter C. *The Architecture of Choice: Eclecticism in America 1880–1930.* New York: Braziller, 1974.

Kimball, Edward. *Lectures and Articles on Christian Science.* Chesterton, Ind.: Edna K. Wait, 1921.

Knee, Stuart E. *Christian Science in the Age of Mary Baker Eddy.* Westport, Conn.: Greenwood, 1994.

Kohn, Alfred D. *Christian Science from a Physician's Standpoint.* Chicago: Privately printed, 1906.

Kramer, George. *The What and How and Why of Church Building.* New York: N.p., 1897.

Krull, V. H. *A Common-Sense View of Christian Science,* 5th ed. Collegeville, Ind.: St. Joseph's Printing Office, 1914.

Lamme, A. J., III. "From Boston in One Hundred Years: Christian Science in 1970." *Professional Geographer* 23 (1971): 329–32.

Lamme, Ary Johannes. "Spatial and Ecological Characteristics of the Diffusion of Christian Science in the United States 1875–1910." Ph.D. diss., Syracuse University, 1968.

Lane, George. *Chicago Churches and Synagogues.* Chicago: Loyola University Press, 1981.

Lea, Charles Herman. *A Plea for the Thorough and Unbiased Investigation of Christian Science.* London: J. M. Dent, 1915.

Lears, T. J. Jackson. *No Place of Grace: Antimodernism and the Transformation of American Culture, 1880–1920.* New York: Pantheon, 1981.

Lees, Andrew. *Cities Perceived, Urban Society in European and American Thought, 1820–1940.* New York: Columbia University Press, 1985.

Leete, Frederick deLand. *The Church in the City.* New York: Abingdon Press, 1915.

Legal Aspects of Christian Science. Boston: Christian Science Publishing Society, 1899.

Leiffer, Murray H. *The Effective City Church.* Nashville: Abingdon-Cokesbury Press, 1949.

Levine, Lawrence. *Highbrow/Lowbrow: The Emergence of Cultural Hierarchy in America.* Cambridge, Mass.: Harvard University Press, 1988.

Longstreet, Stephen. *Chicago, 1860–1919.* New York: McKay, 1973.

Longstreth, Richard. *On the Edge of the World: Four Architects in San Francisco at the Turn of the Century.* Cambridge, Mass.: MIT Press, 1983.

Loomis, Samuel Lane. *Modern Cities and Their Religious Problems.* New York: Baker and Taylor, 1887. Reprint. New York: Arno Press, 1970.

Lord, Myra. *Mary Baker Eddy: A Concise Story of Her Life and Work.* Boston: Davis and Bond, 1918.

MacFarland, Charles S. *Lyman Pierson Powell, Pathfinder in Education and Religion.* New York: Philosophical Library, 1945.

Mangasarian, M. M. *What Is Christian Science?* Chicago: Independent Religious Society, 1921.

Mars, Gerhardt C. *The Interpretation of Life.* New York: Appleton, 1908.

Marsten, Francis Edward, D.D. *The Mask of Christian Science.* New York: American Tract Society, 1909.

Marty, Martin. *Modern American Religion. Vol. 1: The Irony of It All, 1893–1919.* Chicago: University of Chicago Press, 1986.

———. *Righteous Empire: The Protestant Experience in America.* New York: Dial Press, 1970.

———, ed. *Protestantism and Social Christianity.* New York: K. G. Saur, 1992.

Mattox, Willard S. "Christian Science Architecture." *Illinois Illustrated Review* (Aug. 1909): 61–64.

McCoy, Esther. *Five California Architects.* New York: Reinhold, 1960.

McCracken, W. D. "The Meaning of Christian Science." *Arena* 37 (May 1907): 464–77.

McDannell, Colleen. *Material Christianity.* New Haven: Yale University Press, 1995.

McDonald, Jean Angela. "Rhetorical Movements Based on Metaphor, with a Case Study of Christian Science and Its Rhetorical Vision, 1898–1910." Ph.D. diss., University of Minnesota, Minneapolis, 1978.

Mead, George Whitefield. *Modern Methods in Church Work: The Gospel Renaissance.* New York: Dodd, Mead, 1897, 1909.

Meehan, Michael. *Mrs. Eddy and the Late Suit in Equity.* Concord, N.H., 1908.

Menocal, Narciso G. *Architecture as Nature: The Transcendentalist Idea of Louis Sullivan.* Madison: University of Wisconsin Press, 1981.

Meyer, Donald. *The Positive Thinkers: A Study of the American Quest for Health, Wealth and Personal Power from Mary Baker Eddy to Norman Vincent Peale.* Garden City, N.J.: Doubleday, 1965.

Miller, Joseph Dana. "The Growth of Christian Science." *Era, a Philadelphia Magazine* 10 (1902): 14–33.

Mills, Edward. *The Modern Church.* New York: Praeger, 1956.

Milmine, Georgine. *The Life of Mary Baker G. Eddy and the History of Christian Science.* New York: Doubleday, Page, 1909.

Moran, William Edgar. "Plan and Design of Christian Science Churches." *Architectural Forum* (Apr. 1924): 145–48.

Mott, Frank Luther. *A History of American Magazines, 1885–1905.* Cambridge, Mass.: Harvard University Press, 1957.

Moulton, Robert H. "Eleventh Church of Christ, Scientist." *Architectural Record* 51 (May 1918): 426–33.

Muccigrosso, Robert. *American Gothic: The Mind and Art of Ralph Adams Cram.* Washington, D.C.: University Press of America, 1980.

Newton, R. Heber. *Christian Science: The Truths of Spiritual Healing and Their Contribution to the Growth of Orthodoxy.* New York: Putnam, 1899.

Norton, Carol. *The Christian Science Church, Its Organization and Polity: The History of the Apostolic Church and the Formation of the Christian Science Church Compared.* Boston: Christian Science Publishing Society, 1904.

———. *The Christian Science Movement.* Boston: Christian Science Publishing Society, 1899.

———. *Legal Aspects of Christian Science.* Boston: Christian Science Publishing Society, 1899.

Onians, John. *Bearers of Meaning: The Classical Orders in Antiquity, the Middle Ages, and the Renaissance.* Princeton: Princeton University Press, 1988.

Oughton, Charles M. *Crazes, Credulities, and Christian Science.* Chicago: E. H. Colegrove, 1901.

Paget, Stephen. *The Faith and Works of Christian Science.* New York: Macmillan, 1909.

Park, Robert. "The City: Suggestions for the Study of Human Behavior in the City Environment." *American Journal of Sociology* 20 (Mar. 1915): 577–612. Reprinted in *Cities and Churches, Readings on the Urban Church,* edited by Robert Lett. Philadelphia: Westminster Press, 1962.

Parker, Gail Thain. *Mind Cure in New England: From the Civil War to World War One.* Hanover: University of New Hampshire Press, 1973.

Paul, Sherman. *Louis Sullivan, an Architect in American Thought.* Englewood Cliffs, N.J.: Prentice-Hall, 1962.

Peabody, Frederick W. *The Religio-Medical Masquerade: A Complete Exposure of Christian Science.* New York: Fleming H. Revell, 1910.

Pease, Charles. *Exposé of Christian Science Methods and Teaching Prevailing in the First Church, C.S., New York City.* New York: Restoration Publishing Co., 1905.

Peel, Robert. *Christian Science: Its Encounter with American Culture.* New York, 1958.

——. *Health and Medicine in the Christian Science Tradition: Principle, Practice and Challenge.* New York: Crossroads Press, 1989.

——. *Mary Baker Eddy: The Years of Authority.* New York: Holt, Rinehart, and Winston, 1977.

——. *Mary Baker Eddy: The Years of Discovery.* New York: Holt, Rinehart, and Winston, 1966.

——. *Mary Baker Eddy: The Years of Trial.* New York: Holt, Rinehart, and Winston, 1971.

——. *Spiritual Healing in a Scientific Age.* San Francisco: Harper and Row, 1987.

Permanency of the Mother Church. Boston: Christian Science Publishing Society, 1954.

Pfautz, Harold W. "A Case Study of an Urban Religious Movement: Christian Science." In *Contributions to Urban Sociology,* edited by Ernest W. Burgess and Donald J. Bogue, 284–303. Chicago: University of Chicago Press, 1964.

——. "Christian Science: A Case Study of the Social Psychological Aspect of Secularization." *Social Forces* 34 (Mar. 1956): 246–51.

——. "Christian Science: The Sociology of a Social Movement and a Religious Group." Ph.d. diss., University of Chicago, 1954.

Phelps, James. "A History of Christian Science in Wisconsin." *Illinois Illustrated Review* 3, no. 5 (Nov. 1910): 3–8.

Podmore, Frank. *Mesmerism and Christian Science: A Short History of Mental Healing.* Philadelphia: G. W. Jacobs, 1909.

Powell, Lyman. *Christian Science: The Faith and Its Founder.* New York: Putnam, 1907.

——. *Mary Baker Eddy: A Life-Size Portrait.* Boston: Christian Science Publishing Society, 1930.

Purrington, William A. *Christian Science: An Exposition of Mrs. Eddy's Wonderful Discovery, Including Its Legal Status, A Plea for Children and Other Helpless Sick.* New York: E. B. Treat, 1900.

Quint, Wilder D. "The Growth of Christian Science." *New England Magazine* 47 (Sept. 1909–Feb. 1910): 311–20.

Reed, Charles A. L. *Christian Science: A Sociological Study.* Cincinnati: McClelland, 1898.

Reimers, David. "Protestantism's Response to Social Change: 1890–1930." In *The Age of In-*

dustrialism in America: Essays in Social Structure and Cultural Values, edited by Frederic Cople Jaher, 364–83. New York: Free Press, 1968.

Riley, I. Woodbridge. *American Thought from Puritanism to Pragmatism and Beyond.* New York, 1923.

Riley, I. Woodbridge, Frederick Peabody, and Charles Humiston. *The Faith, the Falsity, and the Failure of Christian Science.* New York: Fleming H. Revell, 1925.

Riseley, H. M. "A New Million Dollar Church." *National Magazine* 19, no. 6 (Mar. 1904): 707–9.

Robinson, Charles Mulford. *Modern Civic Art; or The City Made Beautiful.* New York: Putnam, 1903.

Rubenstein, Isadore Harold. *A Treatise on the Legal Aspects of Christian Science.* Chicago: Crandon Press, 1935.

Sandt, Rev. George W., D.D. *A Brief Study of Christian Science.* Philadelphia: General Council Publication House, 1918.

Schlack, Lawrence. "Solon Spencer Beman." *Quarterly News, Mary Baker Eddy Museum* 16, no. 1 (Spring 1979): 241–43.

Schlereth, Thomas J. "A High-Victorian Gothicist as Beaux-Arts Classicist: The Architectural Odyssey of Solon Spencer Beman." *Studies in Medievalism* 3, no. 2 (Fall 1990): 128–52.

———. "Solon Spencer Beman, 1853–1914: The Social History of a Midwest Architect." *Chicago Architectural Journal* 5 (Dec. 1985): 8–31.

Schuyler, Montgomery. *American Architecture and Other Writings.* 2 vols. Edited by William Jordy and Ralph Coe. Cambridge, Mass.: Harvard University Press, 1961.

———. "Recent Church Building in New York." *Architectural Record* 13 (June 1903): 508–34.

Schwenke, John. "An Analysis of the Contributions of Christian Science to the Basic Human Needs of People Living in Modern Urban Society, with Special Emphasis on Evidence Collected in the Chicago Metropolitan Area." B.D. thesis, Chicago Theological Seminary, 1948.

Scotford, John R. *The Church Beautiful: A Practical Discussion of Church Architecture.* Chicago: Pilgrim Press, 1945.

Searchlights on Christian Science. Chicago: Fleming H. Revell, 1899.

Sellers, Charles. *The Private Life of Mary Baker Eddy.* Detroit: Privately printed, 1935.

Shand-Tucci, Douglass. *Built in Boston: City and Suburb, 1800–1950.* Amherst: University of Massachusetts Press, 1988.

———. *Church Building in Boston: With an Introduction to the Work of Ralph Adams Cram and the Boston Gothicists.* Concord, N.H.: Rumford Press, 1975.

———. *Ralph Adams Cram: American Medievalist.* Boston: Boston Public Library, 1975.

Sherman, Bradford. *Historical Sketch of the Introduction of Christian Science in Chicago and the West.* Chicago: F. M. Leyda, 1915.

Singleton, G. H. *Religion in the City of Angels: American Protestant Culture and Urbanization, Los Angeles, 1850–1930.* Ann Arbor: UMI Research Press, 1979.

Siry, Joseph M. *Unity Temple: Frank Lloyd Wright and Architecture for Liberal Religion.* New York: Cambridge University Press, 1996.

Skinner, Charles K. "Christian Science and Its Church Homes in Michigan." *Michigan Illustrated Review* 1, no. 2 (Aug. 1910): 18–22.

Smith, Clifford P. *Christian Science: Its Legal Status, A Defense of Human Rights.* Boston: Christian Science Publishing Society, 1914.

———. *Christian Science and Legislation.* Boston: Christian Science Publishing Society, 1905–1909.

————. *Historical and Biographical Papers: Sketches from the Life of Mary Baker Eddy and the History of Christian Science.* Boston: Christian Science Publishing Society, 1936, 1941.

Smith, Hanover. *Writings and Genius of the Founder of Christian Science.* Boston: Hanover Smith, 1886.

Smith, James Ward, and A. Leland Jamison, eds. *Religious Perspectives in American Culture.* Princeton: Princeton University Press, 1961.

Smith-Rosenberg, Carroll. *Religion and the Rise of the American City.* Ithaca: Cornell University Press, 1971.

Snowden, James H. *The Truth About Christian Science.* Philadelphia: Westminster Press, 1921.

"Some Christian Science Churches throughout the Country." *American Queen* (Mar. 1907): 9.

Stephens, Percy W. *Christian Science, Its Pedigree, Principle and Posterity.* Chicago, 1917.

Stern, Robert, Gregory Gilmartin, and John Massengale. *New York 1900: Metropolitan Architecture and Urbanism, 1890–1915.* New York: Rizzoli, 1983.

Stern, Robert, Gregory Gilmartin, Thomas Mellins. *New York 1930: Architecture and Urbanism between Two World Wars.* New York: Rizzoli, 1987.

Stetson, Augusta E. *Augusta E. Stetson Refutes the Statement of Mr. Clifford P. Smith, That She Is Not a Christian Scientist.* New York: Augusta Stetson, 1927.

————. *Reminiscences, Sermons and Correspondence Proving Adherence to the Principle of Christian Science as Taught by Mary Baker Eddy, 1894–1913.* New York: Putnam, 1913.

————. *Vital Issues in Christian Science: A Record.* New York: Putnam, 1914.

Stieger, Henry W. *Christian Science and Philosophy.* New York: Philosophical Library, 1948.

Stokes, Anson Phelps, and Leo Pfeffer. *Church and State in the United States.* New York: Harper and Row, 1964.

Strong, Josiah. *The New Era, or The Coming Kingdom.* New York: Baker and Taylor, 1893. Reprint. Hicksville, N.Y.: Regina Press, 1975.

————. *Our Country: Its Possible Future and Its Present Crisis.* New York: Baker and Taylor, 1891. Rev. ed. Edited by Jürgen Herbst. Cambridge, Mass.: Harvard University, 1963.

————. *The Twentieth-Century City.* New York: Baker and Taylor, 1898.

Sturge, M. Carta. *The Truth and Error of Christian Science.* London, 1903; New York, 1909.

Sturgis, Russell. "Modern Style Founded on Ancient Greek Architecture." In *Journal of the Proceedings of the Twenty-eighth Annual Convention of the American Institute of Architects,* 84–92. Providence, R.I.: E. A. Johnson, 1895.

Sullivan, Louis H. *The Autobiography of an Idea.* New York: Norton, 1926.

————. *Kindergarten Chats and Other Writings.* New York: Wittenborn and Schultz, 1947.

Sweet, William Warren. *Story of Religion in America.* New York: Harper, 1939.

Swihart, Altman K. *Since Mrs. Eddy.* New York: Henry Holt, 1931.

Thiry, Paul. *Churches and Temples.* New York: Reinhold, 1954.

Thorner, Isidor. "Christian Science and Ascetic Protestantism." Ph.D. diss., Harvard University, 1951.

Thurston, Herbert. *Christian Science.* New York: Paulist Press, 1925.

Tucker, Cynthia Grant. *A Woman's Ministry.* Philadelphia: Temple University Press, 1984.

Twain, Mark (Samuel Clemens). *Christian Science.* New York: Harper, 1899, 1907.

Twitchell, Remington Edwards. "An Analysis of the Published Writings of Mary Baker Eddy to Determine Metaphysical Concepts That Christian Scientists Might Apply to Selected Business and Personal Financial Problems." Ph.D. diss., New York University, 1977.

Underhill, Rev. Andrew F. *Valid Objections to So-Called Christian Science.* Yonkers, N.Y.: Arlington Chemical Co., 1902.

Upjohn, Everard M. *Richard Upjohn: Architect and Churchman.* New York: Columbia University Press, 1939.

Van Brunt, Henry. *Architecture and Society: Selected Essays of Henry Van Brunt.* Edited by William A. Coles. Cambridge, Mass.: Harvard University Press, 1969.

Van Horne, E. S. *Some Christian Science Churches.* Columbus, Ohio: Privately printed, 1911.

Varley, Henry. *Christian Science Examined.* New York: Fleming Revell, 1898.

Vogt, Von Ogden. *Art and Religion.* New Haven: Yale University Press, 1921.

Vosburgh, George Bedell. *Christian Science Examined.* Denver: N.p., 1906.

Walsh, Mary Roth. *"Doctors Wanted, No Women Need Apply": Sexual Barriers in the Medical Profession, 1835–1975.* New Haven: Yale University Press, 1979.

Washburn, Omen R. "The Architecture of a Christian Science Church." *Architectural Record* (Feb. 1904): 159–65.

A Week at the Fair. Chicago: Rand McNally, 1893.

Wheeler, John H. "The Development of the Christian Science Movement in Missouri." *Illustrated Review* (Chicago) [c. 1911]: 4–11.

White, James F. *Protestant Worship and Church Architecture.* New York: Oxford University Press, 1964.

White, Ronald C., and C. Howard Hopkins. *The Social Gospel: Religion and Reform in Changing America.* Philadelphia: Temple University Press, 1976.

Whitehill, Walter Muir. *Boston: A Topographical History.* Cambridge, Mass.: Belknap Press of Harvard University Press, 1968.

Whitney, Mrs. A. D. T. *The Integrity of Christian Science.* Boston: Houghton Mifflin, 1900.

Wilbur, Sibyl. *The Life of Mary Baker Eddy.* New York: Human Life Publishing Co., 1907.

Wilby, Thomas W. *What Is Christian Science?* New York: John Lane, 1915.

Williams, Henrietta. "Among the Christian Science Churches." *Granite Monthly* 28, no. 5 (May 1900): 264–78.

———. "The Founder of Christian Science." *New England Magazine* 21 (Nov. 1899): 291–305.

Williams, Peter W. *Houses of God: Region, Religion, and Architecture in the United States.* Urbana: University of Illinois Press, 1997.

———. *Popular Religion in America: Symbolic Change and the Modernization Process in Historical Perspective.* Englewood Cliffs, N.J.: Prentice Hall, 1980.

———. "Religious Architecture and Landscape." In *The Encyclopedia of the American Religious Experience,* edited by Charles H. Lippy and Peter W. Williams, 1325–39. New York: Scribner, 1988.

Williamson, Margaret. *The Mother Church Extension.* Boston: Christian Science Publishing Society, 1939.

Wilson, Bryan. *Sects and Society: A Sociological Study of the Elim Tabernacle, Christian Science, and Christadelphians.* Berkeley: University of California Press, 1961.

Wilson, Richard Guy, and Sidney K. Robinson. *Modern Architecture in America: Visions and Revisions.* Ames: Iowa State University Press, 1991.

Wilson, William H. *The City Beautiful Movement.* Baltimore: Johns Hopkins University Press, 1989.

Wiltsee, Herbert L. "Religious Developments in Chicago, 1893–1915." Master's thesis, University of Chicago, 1953.

Wirth, William G. *Christian Science X-Rayed.* Mountain View, Calif.: Pacific Press, 1921.

Wolcott, P. C. *What Is Christian Science?* New York: Fleming H. Revell, 1896.

Woodard, Clifford A. "Recent Growth of Christian Science in New England." *New England Magazine* (Apr. 1914): 57–66.

Woodrow, Mrs. Wilson. "Christian Science and What It Means: A Plain Exposition of the

Newest Religious Cult, Which Numbers among Its Enrolled Adherents One Million Intelligent Persons." *Metropolitan Magazine* 14, no. 1 (July 1901): 76–83.

Wright, Gwendolyn. *Building the Dream.* Cambridge, Mass.: MIT Press, 1983.

———. *Moralism and the Modern Home: Domestic Architecture and Cultural Conflict in Chicago, 1873–1913.* Chicago: University of Chicago Press, 1980.

Zueblin, Charles. *American Municipal Progress: Chapters in Municipal Sociology.* New York: Macmillan, 1902.

———. *The Religion of a Democrat.* New York: B. W. Huebsch, 1908.

Zukowsky, John, ed. *Chicago Architecture, 1872–1922: Birth of a Metropolis.* Munich: Prestel, 1987.

INDEX

Paul Eli Ivey is an associate professor of art history

at the University of Arizona, Tucson.

Typeset in 11/14 Adobe Garamond
with Centaur display
Designed by Copenhaver Cumpston
Composed at the University of Illinois Press
Manufactured by Cushing-Malloy, Inc.